The Future of Workplace Fear

How Human Reflex Stands in the Way of Digital Transformation

Steve Prentice

Apress®

The Future of Workplace Fear: How Human Reflex Stands in the Way of Digital Transformation

Steve Prentice
Toronto, ON, Canada

ISBN-13 (pbk): 978-1-4842-8100-0 ISBN-13 (electronic): 978-1-4842-8101-7
https://doi.org/10.1007/978-1-4842-8101-7

Copyright © 2022 by Steve Prentice

This work is subject to copyright. All rights are reserved by the Publisher, whether the whole or part of the material is concerned, specifically the rights of translation, reprinting, reuse of illustrations, recitation, broadcasting, reproduction on microfilms or in any other physical way, and transmission or information storage and retrieval, electronic adaptation, computer software, or by similar or dissimilar methodology now known or hereafter developed.

Trademarked names, logos, and images may appear in this book. Rather than use a trademark symbol with every occurrence of a trademarked name, logo, or image we use the names, logos, and images only in an editorial fashion and to the benefit of the trademark owner, with no intention of infringement of the trademark.

The use in this publication of trade names, trademarks, service marks, and similar terms, even if they are not identified as such, is not to be taken as an expression of opinion as to whether or not they are subject to proprietary rights.

While the advice and information in this book are believed to be true and accurate at the date of publication, neither the authors nor the editors nor the publisher can accept any legal responsibility for any errors or omissions that may be made. The publisher makes no warranty, express or implied, with respect to the material contained herein.

    Managing Director, Apress Media LLC: Welmoed Spahr
    Acquisitions Editor: Susan McDermott
    Development Editor: Laura Berendson
    Coordinating Editor: Jessica Vakili

Distributed to the book trade worldwide by Springer Science+Business Media New York, 1 New York Plaza, New York, NY 100043. Phone 1-800-SPRINGER, fax (201) 348-4505, e-mail orders-ny@springer-sbm.com, or visit www.springeronline.com. Apress Media, LLC is a California LLC and the sole member (owner) is Springer Science + Business Media Finance Inc (SSBM Finance Inc). SSBM Finance Inc is a **Delaware** corporation.

For information on translations, please e-mail booktranslations@springernature.com; for reprint, paperback, or audio rights, please e-mail bookpermissions@springernature.com.

Apress titles may be purchased in bulk for academic, corporate, or promotional use. eBook versions and licenses are also available for most titles. For more information, reference our Print and eBook Bulk Sales web page at http://www.apress.com/bulk-sales.

Printed on acid-free paper

To Henry and Bryana

Table of Contents

About the Author xi

Foreword xiii

Chapter 1: The Fear Lies Deep 1
    From a Big Fish to a Big Phish 4
    From a Big Phish to a Big Fear 6
    Emotion Always Wins 10

Chapter 2: Digital Transformation Is Here 11
    Digital Transformation and Fear 12
    Fear Is Not Always Terror 13
    What Is Digital Transformation Anyway? 14
    Digital Transformation and Video Chat Fatigue 18
    Digital Transformation and Zoom Gloom 22
    The Personalization of Fear 26

Chapter 3: Fear As a Life Force 31
    Fear Is Contagious 34
    Why Does Fear Seem Larger at Night? 36
    Maslow's Hierarchy of Needs 37
    The Kubler-Ross Grief/Change Model 41
    Forming, Storming, Norming, and Performing 42
    Managing the Fear of Change 43

TABLE OF CONTENTS

Closing the Gate 43
Bring the Facts Up to Meet the Fear 44

Chapter 4: The Fear of Change 47
Why Do I Have to Learn This? 47
Dealing with the Fear of Change 48
The Curse of Passwords 49
The Comfort of Passwords 52
The Fear of Effort 53
The Fear of the Password Manager 54
Managing the Fear of the Password Manager 56
The Fear of the Hot Desk 57
The Fear of Losing Identity 61

Chapter 5: The Fear of the Unknown 65
The Fear of Gym Class 65
The Fear of Messages 68
The Fear of Silence 74

Chapter 6: The Fear of Losing Your Job 81
The J-O-B Syndrome 83
Blame Steve 84
The Zoom Call Gaffe 86
Fear of Face Time Bias 87
Taking Your Keys Away 90
The Distributed Team vs. the Remote Team 92
The Great Resignation: When Work Is Not Worth It 94
What Can Employees Do to Handle This? 96
What Can Companies Do to Handle This? 96

TABLE OF CONTENTS

Chapter 7: The Fear of Looking Stupid 99
The Fear of Making Mistakes 100
The Act of Learning 100
The Fear of Not Being Able to Keep Up 106
The Internal Spotlight Effect 109
The Fear of Failure 111

Chapter 8: The Fear of Losing Control 115
The Pressing Problem of Bicycle Face 115
From Bicycle Face to Face Time Bias 117
Study of Microsoft Employees Shows Bicycle Face Still Possible 118
You Can't Manage What You Can't See 120
A Matter of Trust 122
Fear of Delegation 126

Chapter 9: The Fear of the Known 131
Willful Blindness and Overload 131
Willful Blindness and MFA 135
Willful Blindness: The Watering Hole Concept 136
The Fear of Delay, and the Power of Defiance 137
I Am Not in Denial 140
Problems with Prioritization and Procrastination 143
The Password Manager Example Revisited 147

Chapter 10: The Fear of Communicating 149
Message in a Bubble 151
Leadership Needs Communication 153
Why Not Just Pick Up the Phone? 155
The Fear of Appearing Outside the Bubble 157

TABLE OF CONTENTS

The Fear of Saying No 158
The Power of the Restaurant Menu 160
The Fear of Not Knowing Where You Stand 162
The Fear of Breaking Linear Thought 163

Chapter 11: The Fear of Losing the Business 167

Trying to Grasp the Infinite 170
The Fear of Ransomware 171
The Fear of the Cost of Prevention 172
Pay the Ransom Already! 174
When You Were Ten 177
The Challenge of Agility 179

Chapter 12: The Fear of Missing Out 183

Gap It 186
The Fear of Not Fitting In 188
The Fear of Being a Nerd 189
How Loss of Critical Thinking Leads to Hate and to the Madness
of Crowds 190
How Hate Leads to Bullying 194
I Know What You Did 195

Chapter 13: The Fear of Keeping Your Job 199

What Is the Cost of Your Money? 200
Let's Play Around with Closure 204
The Artisan's Curse 205
Let's Not Bring Scurvy into This 206
Boosting the Quality of Work Life 208
Jellyvision's Graceful Goodbye 210

Chapter 14: Turning Things Around 213
   Fear Fatigue 213
   Imposter Syndrome and FUD 214
   Can Anything Be Done? 216
   Listen and Talk 217
   The Five-Why Analysis 217
   Make It Tangible 222
   Mountains Have More Than One Face 223
   The Job Insecurity Paradox 224

Chapter 15: Is This the Day I Get Fired? 229
   Fear Fatigue 229
   The 80/20 Rule and Firing Your Weakest Customer 230
   You As-A-Service 232
   Networking: The Little Black Book 233
   Networking on Twitter 235
   Lifelong Learning 236
   Career Fear As the Ultimate Trap 237
   Don't Forget Your Humanness 237

Chapter 16: The Digital Transformation of People 239
   Digital Transformation Is Not Just Digital 242
   Suggestions 243
   Yes, But 246
   The Fear of Being Wrong 247

Postscript: Two Apologies 251
Index 253

About the Author

Steve Prentice is a specialist in organizational psychology, with additional background in project management and journalism. By working as a speaker, author, consultant, and writer, he helps people understand the technologies they face in the workplace and the changes that these present, and has been doing so since Windows and Y2K were top of mind. His clients include major names in IT, industry, government, healthcare, and media. He is regularly called upon to explain issues such as cybersecurity, AI, blockchain, and the future of work.

Steve has written three business books and has worked as a ghostwriter for other tech sector executives worldwide. He is a visiting lecturer at Ontario Tech University, and regularly delivers keynotes, interviews, papers, and podcasts. He also lives a second life as a singer and guitarist, performing locally in the Toronto area.

Foreword

Of the many technological advances in business I have been privileged to witness over the years, the most personally satisfying are the ones that bring people closer to equality. Every step taken down the long road of collaboration technology has provided some measure of improvement in our lives.

Yet, as much as new technologies succeeded in bringing many of us together, their success also highlights the plight of those who still can't fully participate. Reasons vary – from economic circumstances or geographical location to linguistic ability to physical ability. These have remained as barriers, both to individuals' own personal aspirations and to the companies who could truly benefit from their talents. Modern collaboration technology will not have fully succeeded until everyone gets a chance to engage and participate fully. People must not only be accessible; they must be access-able.

Steve Prentice is someone who has always been fully conscious of this human element. He knows that technology by itself can do little unless the people who work with it feel part of something special and valued. Change and innovation will always be greeted with fear or mistrust simply because it is different, and confidence and competence take a long time to establish themselves in the mind and body.

FOREWORD

Humans have a strange way of reacting to innovations that digital transformation experts are 100% confident in, and these reactions can derail progress entirely. Being aware of the power and the sheer variety of human fear is an essential component of modern management, and Steve's book sheds some light on some deep and dark corners that can no longer be overlooked.

Aruna Ravichandran
Vice President & Chief Marketing Officer
Cisco Webex Collaboration

CHAPTER 1

The Fear Lies Deep

The movie *Jaws* came out in the summer of 1975 and, to this day, it remains an unmatched case study of fear in its deepest, simplest, and most sublime form. There have been scary movies for as long as there have been movies, but in most of these, the monster, or the bad guy with the knife, comes into view very quickly, and the enjoyability factor of the film is the suspense the viewers feel while they wait for the inevitable confrontation. But few films can make something scary out of nothing. *Jaws* was one of those.

"Hold on," you might say, "a 25-foot great white shark is hardly nothing." And you would be right. Except that the shark, whose name was Bruce, by the way, named after Steven Spielberg's lawyer,[1] did not actually appear until one hour and twenty-one minutes into the film. Considering that the movie's running time is two hours and four minutes, that's a heck of a long time to wait to make an entrance.

The secret to the success of *Jaws* was that the fear had no true shape until long after it had radiated its contagious energy to every character in the movie. It was the fear of what we couldn't see that grabbed theatergoers and held them in a truly primordial trance.

---

[1] Watts, Marina. "Bruce, the Last 'Jaws' Shark, Got His Name From Spielberg's Lawyer." Newsweek. November 23, 2020. Retrieved from www.newsweek.com/bruce-last-jaws-shark-got-his-name-spielbergs-lawyer-1549616.
This Newsweek article also has a great story about how one of the original shark models was found, restored, and moved to its new home at the Academy Museum of Motion Pictures in Los Angeles.

CHAPTER 1   THE FEAR LIES DEEP

Then there was the two-note signature theme music that penetrated our senses, sounding like the growling of something big, something predatory and stealthy.[2] The rhythm of those two notes, played back and forth and with increasing tempo, was meant to represent the velocity of a chase, as well as symbolizing the self-assured, determined rhythm of a shark tugging its prey from side to side. In the words of its composer, John Williams, the theme was designed to be "instinctual, relentless, and unstoppable."[3]

Master storyteller and director Steven Spielberg built up the movie's suspense factor consistently as the story unfolded, layer by layer. He employed perfect wordless imagery: a child playing innocently in the sand, telltale ripples passing by in the water, and the bobbing yellow buoys.

One of the film's most iconic representations of this invisible yet tangible fear was undoubtedly the silent expressions of mutual alarm between the people in the know – eye contact held just a little too long, transmitting and compounding a shared and mounting panic that no one dared openly admit to.

Spielberg staged the vacationers' swimming scenes by placing the camera at "treading water" level – where the swimmers' faces were barely above the surface, their peripheral vision limited, and where any errant wave would have been able to quickly engulf mouth, nose, and eyes. This is a place of extreme vulnerability for humans.

Anyone who has ever swum in the ocean knows the special fear that comes with it. Deep inside the recesses of your brain and nervous system lies an awareness that from the chin on down, you are exposed to a world you cannot control – one that is no longer ours – containing unseen creatures that possess millions of years' worth of steadily evolving survival

---

[2] Check out YouTube for copies of the theme. Here's one: https://youtu.be/1V8i-pSVMaQ

[3] John Williams. Jaws Theme. Retrieved from www.classicfm.com/composers/williams/music/jaws-theme/

CHAPTER 1   THE FEAR LIES DEEP

skills, and who might right now be all-too-close. It is a world made up of waves and water that can quickly envelop and eliminate any air-breathing creature of the land.

Then there is Robert Shaw's pivotal scene. Some call it the Indianapolis scene, and it is one of his finest moments as an actor. It is getting late. The *Orca*, the small fishing boat that the three characters played by Shaw, Roy Scheider, and Richard Dreyfus, now call home, is sitting motionless on the water, far from land. The deck and rigging creak slightly as it rests there, vulnerable and tiny, atop a universe filled with life. There is no breeze. The boat seems passive, as if it, too, is trying not to be noticed.

Inside the cabin, Shaw's character, Quint, the grizzled sea-dog, recounts a story of the only time he felt truly afraid. The scene is shot in medium close-up, Quint's eyes focused on a spot far beyond the boat's walls, and far back in time. He is recounting a nightmare that he survived and then relived ten thousand times. Hooper, played by Richard Dreyfus, and Brody, played by Roy Scheider, slowly lose the jocularity of their dinnertime banter and macho one-upmanship as Quint takes them back into the terror of his past. Hooper is seen fixing his gaze on Quint's expression, and his own face drops into a mask of serious dread.

Quint recounts how, as a navy sailor in World War II, after his ship, the USS Indianapolis, had been sunk by a Japanese torpedo, he and hundreds of his fellow crew members clung to life rafts and debris in shark-infested water, waiting for rescue. It took days for the Navy to take note of the sinking, and when rescue finally came, the number of crew still alive had dwindled from 1,200 to 300, through injury, exposure, dehydration, and shark attacks. Quint describes the paralyzing fear he felt, still being in the water, while others around him were being pulled to safety – the fear of wondering if his time would run out, even with rescue in sight. The fear of not knowing.

The intimacy of the scene, taking place within the boat's small cabin, with Quint's eyes glinting as he relives the terror once again, speaks to every one of us. It speaks to our primordial dread at the thought of being devoured by something larger and uncontrollable. Spielberg doesn't use a shark in this scene. He doesn't have to. The isolation of the boat, and the placid sea, the silence, all speak to a sense of helplessness and aloneness out there on that boat, knowing that something is not right and that this is all inescapably bad.

The three characters on board the *Orca* know the shark is near and that it is in control. Their voices are tinged with the distraction of dread. They speak haltingly, with one ear tuned to the sounds of the sea, silently praying that the yellow marker buoys, attached to the shark's back with long rope harpoons, do not suddenly burst above the surface and signal the return of the giant.

From a Big Fish to a Big Phish

In December 2020, the security team at a well-known Internet domain registrar and web hosting company sent out an email to its 500 employees, offering each a $650 holiday season bonus if they clicked on a link within the email and supplied information about themselves and their location, before a fixed deadline date. Two days later, those same employees received a follow-up email that stated, essentially, "you failed our phishing test." Instead of receiving money, the employees would be receiving additional security training.

It would be an understatement to say this exercise did not go well. Social media lit up with customers and commentators who labeled it "tone deaf," especially in light of the financial hardships and layoffs that had happened as a result of the Covid-19 pandemic, which was still in full swing at that time. Some customers threatened to move their accounts elsewhere. There were calls, including many from within the IT community itself, for its employees to quit *en masse* in protest.

CHAPTER 1 THE FEAR LIES DEEP

This internal phishing test was not unique. Many companies routinely perform them. But this one, perhaps because of the time of year, and because of the type of year it had been, struck a particularly sour note. The company's officials apologized and promised to refine their testing processes in the future. They stated that they had done a bad thing, and many in the business community and even the cybersecurity community agreed, saying this type of stunt would not fix the phishing problem.

But others disagreed. They suggested that as cruel as the exercise was, the fact remained, the bad guys – those threat actors out there who make billions by stealing data to sell or to hold for ransom – aren't going to stop sending phishing emails just because it's the holiday season. A hacking group that is willing to bring a hospital to its knees with ransomware is not going to stop using deceit to spare anyone's feelings.

This is an interesting test case for a discussion about the impact of fear on digital transformation. It brushes up against the unmistakable and oft-confirmed fact that human beings are always going to be the weak point in any cybersecurity defense. Cybersecurity is the guardian of all things digital and, consequently, is the guardian of all things that *digital* touches. Because of that, a company's success and safety depend heavily on it and on all the people who interact with it.

The phishing failure also suggests that reflexes cannot be trained out of people, and that periodic training is not enough. Stuart Madnick, professor of information technology and engineering systems at MIT Sloan Executive Education, told *ZDNet Security Update* recently, "The 30-minute video you're obligated to watch once a year doesn't do the job." Madnick, who has been at MIT since 1972 and has served as the head of MIT's Information Technologies Group for more than 20 years, reiterates that organizations need to build a culture of cybersecurity that actively involves everyone.[4] Even cybersecurity specialists themselves fall for phishing and social engineering hacks, for many of the same reasons. They may know much about cybersecurity, but they are still human.

My interest in the reaction to this particular phishing fiasco does not make me side with either the defenders of the staff members who were duped, nor with the IT team who devised and delivered the phish. My interest was in the source of the reaction. There's something lurking deeper in this one story than just the mechanics of a phishing test; something that goes even beyond a company's own cybersecurity concerns. These people didn't seem to be just ashamed of getting caught – and the ones who objected weren't simply protesting a cybersecurity test. There was a deeper fear at play.

This dark shadow of fear, circling lazily in the depths of our subconscious, has fascinated me for my whole career. From the very moment I met my first client – thirty-five years ago – a person who was afraid of sending an email, I have been fascinated with the fear people live with, especially when it comes to technology. Even the most trivial of technology-related fears hint at its presence.

From a Big Phish to a Big Fear

Humans are complicated creatures and, from an evolutionary perspective, our assembly is far from complete. In fact, we are only half-baked. We have developed substantial knowledge of our surroundings and we have mastered the capacity to manipulate objects into tools. We record

---

[4] Palmer, Danny. "Cybersecurity training isn't working. And hacking attacks are only getting worse." *ZDNet*. January 6, 2022. Retrieved from www.zdnet.com/article/your-cybersecurity-training-needs-improvement-because-hacking-attacks-are-only-getting-worse/ Accessed January 2022.

CHAPTER 1   THE FEAR LIES DEEP

and remember our past and we actively contemplate our future. Yet we collectively have not yet moved to a point where we can permanently shed instinctive and irrational fear, like some sort of prehensile tail.

We struggle with fear inwardly and outwardly, and it is our constant companion through life. Every minute of our lives, we host an internal battle, as our intellect and our emotions tussle with each other. It's a yin and yang interdependence that roils like a street fight.

On one side of the fight, we have our conscious thinking brain, the cerebral cortex, that bumpy outermost part of the brain's structure that everyone sees when they look at a picture of one. The cerebral cortex shares its cramped cranial apartment with a number of other areas and parts. At the far end, poking out the back and connecting to the spinal cord, is the historically oldest part of the brain structure. It's the brain stem, a piece that is common to every living creature that has a central nervous system. Colloquially, it is known as the lizard brain, but it also goes by the formal moniker of *medulla oblongata.*

Whereas the thinking brain – the cerebral cortex – is a product of humanity's most recent chapter of evolution, with its nooks, crannies, and fissures there to maximize surface area without needing our heads to grow literally larger and heavier, the *medulla oblongata* looks to manage the basic, instinctive forces of life itself. It controls regulatory systems such as hormones, body temperature, and blood pressure.

Situated between these two extremes is the limbic system which focuses on behavioral and emotional responses, especially those needed for survival, such as feeding oneself, reproduction, and fight-or-flight responses. It watches for danger and takes no chances. One of the key areas within the limbic system is a pair of almond-shaped components called the *amygdala*. That's where fear lives.

To be more specific, the left and right amygdalae "play a central role in our emotional responses, including feelings like pleasure, fear, anxiety and anger. The amygdala also attaches emotional content to our memories, and so plays an important role in determining how robustly

CHAPTER 1 THE FEAR LIES DEEP

those memories are stored. Memories that have strong emotional meaning tend to stick. The amygdala doesn't just modify the strength and emotional content of memories; it also plays a key role in forming new memories specifically related to fear." [5]

The brain is enormously complex, and many books and lifetimes have been dedicated to its study. My simplified description does not do justice to the brain itself or to the scientists who study it, but, for the purposes of this book, I am hopeful that we can accept that we basically do all of our higher-level thinking in the cerebral cortex, while the interior of the brain dedicates itself to sensory processing such as vision, hearing, taste, touch, and smell, while other areas coordinate balance and memory, and oversee all the other functions of the body.

This, together, is our operating system and firmware – sometimes called *wetware* by IT people who wish to blame a failure of a system or device on user error. Our brain constantly wrestles with its dual payloads of logic and emotion. It is an organ of flesh and chemical electricity that has allowed us, over the centuries, to achieve greatness on behalf of our species, learning, for example, how to defy gravity and fly, and how to develop science to a point where we can stave off death through medicines and agriculture.

Yet at the same time, ours is a brain that is prone to following primitive superstitions and denial as ways to counter the fear that drives it. At one time, before there were scientific and provable explanations for events such as solar eclipses and earthquakes, superstitious and religious faith delivered the needed reassurance: it provided answers that were craved as a means to rationally understand the phenomena of the world, while delivering emotional comfort to soothe the overpowering emotions of terror and grief.

> *Thinking is difficult. That's why most people judge.*
>
> —Carl Jung

---

[5] Queensland Brain Institute: The Limbic System, retrieved from https://qbi.uq.edu.au/brain/brain-anatomy/limbic-system

CHAPTER 1   THE FEAR LIES DEEP

Retaining thoughts and processing facts take a great deal of energy. Literally, it takes calories to think. For example, chess masters playing in the world's great tournaments are known to lose ten to fifteen pounds over the course of a multi-day tournament, burning up to 6,000 calories a day, according to Robert Sapolsky, professor of neurology and neurosurgery at Stanford University.[6] This is due in part to the intense mental processing that the game demands, added to additional stress responses that occur as a result of the pressure of the tournament. But it still shows how much work goes into thinking.

Because thinking is hard, it presents a challenge to the human brain. While the outermost layer seeks to understand what it doesn't know, the more basic areas need only to conserve calories, avoid danger, and stay alive. It is this instinctive aversion to thinking – from an energy conservation perspective – that may have led to an overall cultural distaste for intellectual pursuits such as science, computers, or math in schools. Cultures the world over tend to glorify athletes whose physical strength and attractiveness remain the ideal procreative model for furthering the species. Those whose talents are more intellectual are forever perceived as nerds – less attractive, and whose skills take more energy to understand. This can be seen to this day in the struggle to attract people to study the sciences.

There is always a socio-cultural schism in any society or country between thinkers and feelers – those who think through problems to seek a scientific understanding, and those who rely on their gut feeling and belief to make their decisions. The schism has also been exposed in sharp relief during the stages of the Covid-19 pandemic, specifically between maskers and anti-maskers and pro-vaxx and anti-vaxx groups.

It is also the essence of politics at every level, and has been amplified in recent years to worrisome levels of extreme polarization. For the bulk of

---

[6] www.cnbc.com/2019/09/22/chess-grandmasters-lose-weight-burn-calories-during-games.html

CHAPTER 1   THE FEAR LIES DEEP

the world's human population through the many centuries of its organized existence, it has always been easier and safer to turn to a leader who will interpret the mysteries of the world through faith and charisma, than one who uses facts and reason.

So we inhabit a body that must live according to the whims of a system in perpetual conflict, with emotion and logic constantly struggling to establish dominance in every situation. But here's the spoiler: emotion always wins.

Emotion Always Wins

When a person makes a decision, it is emotion that carries it over the line. Whether it involves something small like buying a pair of shoes or something large like buying a house, something new like choosing to accept a new job, or something familiar like staying with the existing one, these are all actions that involve some amount of logical analysis. But in the end, humans will go with the gut feeling. They will go with what "feels right."

Emotion rules the human roost, and though there is a wide variety of emotions that people can go through in a day or even within a minute, there can only be one strongest emotion. It's not love. It's not happiness. It's fear.

Fear is what seeks to keep death away by being wary of threats and of the unknown. Because fear is what keeps us alive, a great many of the things we fear, and a great many of the reactions we experience toward uncertainty and change are rooted in fears that are located much further below the surface. A fear of a new type of technology or of a new process is seldom just a literal fear of that specific thing. It's primordial and extraordinarily powerful. It's a fear that, like a great predatory shark, circles unseen, down there in the dark.

CHAPTER 2

Digital Transformation Is Here

In general, every new change that individuals encounter will be experienced through the filter of "what do I stand to lose?" as opposed to "what do I stand to gain?" while every old thing that they have grown used to will serve as a frame of reference, often more preferable to the new *status quo*. So, no matter how great and innovative a transformation appears to be, it has monumental obstacles to overcome within the minds, hearts, and instincts of the humans for whom it is being designed.

Fear is a constant within the workplace. It shouldn't be that way, but it is. Life, after all, involves friction. Every action we undertake involves interaction with people and objects around us. We strive to get ahead, and in so doing we encounter and interact with forces that seek to slow us down. Many of these forces originate from other people, both as their own *selves*, as well as in the things they place in our way: tasks, deadlines, conflicts, and change. They may not *intend* to slow us down, but their mere presence means we must interact with them, grind against them metaphorically, like tectonic plates, or a glacier over rock, and this cannot help but create friction.

But at the same time, nothing can be done without it. Friction is what we must use to gain purchase and move ahead. It is up to each person's mind and personality to determine how to handle it and thrive both with it and in spite of it.

But let's face it – work is called *work* because it is often difficult, and because it is based on friction. From CEOs to first-day new hires and everyone in between, we spend each day struggling with the forces that define our work, and at each level, beneath the friction, there is fear. Fear doesn't belong to the work; it belongs to us, but because of this, it seems to be attached to the work as well.

We are living in an age of ever-accelerating change. Frankly, a person could have said this one hundred years ago as they watched Charles Lindbergh's Spirit of St. Louis fly overhead. They could have said it two hundred years ago at the dawn of the first Industrial Revolution. The fact is, change continues to accelerate and broaden at an exponential pace, while we humans, physiologically speaking, have not advanced quite as quickly. We are the same beings that walked the earth 10,000 years ago, with the same instincts, and the same internal mechanics.

Digital Transformation and Fear

If only digital transformation had been named more completely. If only it had been branded the *digital transformation of people.* In talking about digital transformation, attention is paid to the technology and tools that are developing around us, yet it is people who are expected to use them correctly.

Technological innovation has an annoying habit of moving faster than most people can handle. It is driven largely by our relentless and innate desire to conquer challenges and improve our situation. But that motivation gets funneled through a very small number of people – the visionaries, the modern-day Thomas Edisons who possess the brilliance and the magnetism to pull together a group of other brilliant people to build that better mousetrap and change the world.

But these innovators represent a tiny minority of the human population. They are the bright sparks, the leading-edge thinkers, and the technical visionaries, feverishly riding their own wave of progress and streaming the results back to other companies and organizations across the world. But for every Elon Musk and Steve Jobs, for every Grace Hopper (developer of one of the world's first computers and the code to run it) and Hedy Lamarr (famous as a film actress, but also a gifted mathematician and engineer who laid the groundwork for GPS, Bluetooth, and WiFi), there are millions more average people who must face the results of these innovators' efforts.

Overall, most innovations end up being helpful to the rest of us, and maybe we should be more grateful. But the speed at which they come about, and the fact that such changes were seldom actually asked for, means that their reception and integration into society is sometimes a little rough.

Digital transformation is a real thing, but it is still a blend of fact and marketing lore. It offers some amazing new ways of doing things and, like so many of the transformations that have come before it, many of these innovations will simply soon become part of our normality, making way for other, even more transformative innovations to come.

It all becomes normal eventually, but before it does, we humans have to learn whether we can run the gauntlet of emotion-based doubts and fears, along with the desire to reject the changes outright, because that's how we're built.

Fear Is Not Always Terror

The condition we call *fear* does not have to always mean being in a state of abject terror. Most of the fears described in these forthcoming chapters do not lead to wide-eyed screaming, but some could indeed cause nightmares and heart palpitations. Fear can also present as reluctance, procrastination, sadness, anger, or outright refusal, but it always emanates from the same dark, deep place, far below the surface, and it always has enormous influence over our individual *selves* and over the potential for the success or failure of a company's digital transformation undertakings.

CHAPTER 2   DIGITAL TRANSFORMATION IS HERE

What Is Digital Transformation Anyway?

Digital transformation is one of those terms that is vague enough to encompass an enormous collection of concepts, tools, technologies, procedures, and dreams, and it also has a nice ring to it. Of the many definitions available, customer service company Zendesk puts it like this:

> *Digital transformation is an ongoing journey of using digital technology and digital strategy to fundamentally change an organization's customer experience, business and operating processes, or culture.*[1]

Kinda neat, eh? In other words, digital transformation is about doing things better and seeking better outcomes using digital tools and a mindset to match. But what actually comes to mind when someone mentions the term digital transformation? Perhaps cloud computing, artificial intelligence, machine learning, collaborative technology, communication technology, e-commerce, social media, and maybe even blockchain. These are all fascinating and real technologies that are already changing the world.

Digital transformation exists in smaller actions, too. Sandra Wenzel, a cybersecurity transformation engineer for VMware, puts it like this:

> *I think it's a misnomer for people when we talk about digital transformation. Just because you go from a data center to the public cloud doesn't necessarily mean you're going through a digital transformation. I feel that companies out there that actually don't do digital transformation accurately are going to crumble and fall.*

---

[1] Retrieved from www.zendesk.com/blog/digital-transformation/ Accessed December 2021.

CHAPTER 2　DIGITAL TRANSFORMATION IS HERE

OK, that was a good tech-speak description, but here's the piece I like better. She continues:

> *I was not typically a Starbucks person. But the moment Starbucks let me use an app to order, pick up and leave without talking to anyone or touching anything, was probably the biggest reason I became a Starbucks user. That's what we talk about when we talk about digital transformation.*[2]

Sandy became a regular Starbucks customer because of digital technology that transformed her coffee-buying experience, and made her feel better about it, especially during the Covid pandemic. The technique was digital, but it was *she* who was transformed.

The technologies of digital transformation have already changed the way we do things. That's the amazing thing about digital transformation. It's not something *out there* in the future. We're already soaking in it. It's just that the tech stuff that we've become used to doesn't seem to be that transformative anymore, because it has become parts of our new normal. These items are now travelling at the same speed as us.

Taking a selfie and posting it to Instagram is so simple it could easily slip under the radar of digital transformation. But think about it more deeply. A high quality camera mounted inside a portable cellular phone takes a photo or video that is then effortlessly edited, perfected, and then transported to a personal billboard like Instagram by way of reliable and fast WiFi or cellular connectivity, where it can be immediately seen and reacted to by people anywhere on the planet. That's a long way from snapping a roll of 35mm film in the family camera and then waiting a week for the photo center at Walgreens to process it.

A Roomba is a world famous robot vacuum cleaner and a source of entertainment for many a house cat. But it's only a robot until you get used to it, and then it becomes an appliance. Its robotic novelty dissolves itself

---

[2] Interview held with Sandra Wenzel in August 2021. Used with permission.

into everyday home life. The same goes for intelligent assistants like Alexa, or the device that automatically helps you parallel park your car. One moment they're new and weird, the next, they're just a thing.

The process of becoming just a thing is easy for some technologies and more difficult for others. The Instagram selfie, the Roomba, Alexa, and the parallel parking feature are all consumer products. People purchase them enthusiastically because each promises some form of immediate improvement in their lives. Digital transformation on the consumer front can indeed be rife with positivity. A smartphone with a camera is a tool with a thousand benefits, and is one that few people can go without ever again. A Roomba promises a life free from vacuuming, and Alexa seems to offer convenience by simply talking to it. The fear barrier with these innovations is low because the threat barrier is low.

David Spark, Executive Producer of the *CISO Series* podcasts, points out that Facebook was the application with the lowest threat barrier of all. In its early days, everyone, it seemed, flocked to it without any fear, just sheer curiosity and passion for human connection. He mentions that every time Facebook made a change to its interface or features, there was initial pushback, but that its users eventually adapted to the changes to the point that they forgot that a change had even been made.[3]

But when it comes to changing the way work is done in the office, the story can be quite different. Employees might express curiosity around the opportunities that digital transformation might bring, such as being able to work from home some or all of the time, and using new tools and apps to help make their jobs more efficient. Yet they also may fear how these same tools will affect their livelihood, how these tools might reveal their inadequacies, how younger, more tech-savvy rivals might poach their job, or possibly how the technology might eliminate their job entirely, and with it, their home and their very identity. In these circumstances, digital

---

[3] Interview with David Spark held January 2022. Used with permission.

transformation can be seen as something that stands *between* a person and their future and that, quite naturally, will be seen as a threat.

People in management positions may also anguish over whether these new transformative technologies will actually help their department thrive in the next few years, and they might shrink back a little from them in fear. For a start, there's the fear of losing control over employees, and a recognition that they have never been able to entirely trust them. There is also the fear of losing a comfortable *status quo* in terms of an office where it is easy to walk the halls and be visible as a manager. These concerns can pair easily with the fear of what problems these technologies might bring, and how this might affect their own career prospects as a manager.

Senior leaders might be shown, by consultants and experts, a bright future for their company – one that includes engaged employees and smart tools that will help move their company into a digitally connected and quickly evolving global ecosystem. But they, too, may fear the implications of technologies they do not fully understand, including choosing which path to follow, which tools to embrace, and how to manage the ever-expanding threat of cybercrime. A company's board of directors expects solid leadership from their senior executives, meaning there will be despair and fear in the corner office when the decision between holding the course and pivoting in the name of digital transformation rises from the floor like a serpent.

Perhaps that's why the people who coined the term digital transformation chose the word *transformation* and not *change*. It sounds less severe, and more magical – not so much a change as a smooth makeover. Maybe they knew just how difficult the change was going to be.

CHAPTER 2   DIGITAL TRANSFORMATION IS HERE

Digital Transformation and Video Chat Fatigue

Digital transformation was already well underway before the pandemic descended upon the world. Companies were already looking to move to the cloud, for example, to benefit from its many promises of scalability, reliability, and cost efficiency. They were starting to discover the proactive efficacy of the *as-a-service* model, in which suppliers that used to simply sell products found there was more to be made by providing subscription-based services to support those very products. Some would even give the products away in order to capitalize on the ongoing service contracts, in much the same way printer companies underprice printers and make the money back on toner.

Strides were also being made in distance collaboration, and ecommerce. Early digital transformation was starting to usher in virtual and augmented reality to meetings, training sessions, and direct applications in hospitals and factories. Driving apps like Waze were already using crowd-sourcing to collect real-time input from other drivers to intelligently calculate the best route for any driver to use at that very moment, while avoiding roadkill and speed traps.

So, digital transformation was certainly well on its way when, in early 2020, the whole world experienced the jarring horror called Covid-19, and we were all sent home to learn how to work remotely. At least the lucky ones were. Those who lost their livelihoods or whose jobs demanded that they go back onsite to perform them had much bigger problems. Meanwhile, millions of knowledge workers who never had any intention of working from home suddenly found out they had to master it quickly.

Much like the phishing test example mentioned in Chapter 1, lockdown was another interesting test case for digital transformation. Almost overnight, companies and organizations of all sizes had to pivot, adopting and expanding their use of video chat technology and turning it into a lifeline for the business. As a result, the providers of video chat apps rode an enormous wave. Zoom, for example, saw sales soar 326 percent to $2.6 billion in 2020. Profits jumped from $21.7 million in 2019 to $671.5 million a year later.[4] Other manufacturers of collaboration technology saw similar jumps in demand and revenue. Daily participants in Zoom calls surged from 10 million a day at the end of 2019 to 300 million in April 2020.

Because video chat technology was available, we used it. But just because we *used it* more doesn't mean we used it correctly, and that's what makes it a good test case. For example, many meeting attendees preferred to turn their cameras off. Some said this was to conserve bandwidth, since not everyone has access to prime Internet connectivity. But for many more, the reason was because they just didn't want to appear on screen. They didn't like it. Some even feared it, and many probably didn't fully know why.

With so many people choosing to mute their camera, the adoption of the video-less video chat essentially turned Zoom, the poster child of lockdown-based digital transformation, back into a simple conference call. In fact, for many of these meetings, a traditional telephone-based conference call might have been easier and better. The audio quality would certainly have been better, and the supporting images and documents could have been sent around in advance by email for everyone to look at on their own computer screens. As the saying goes, "maybe the entire thing could have been an email."

To be fair, this reluctance to use video chat technology was not universal. There were many instances where more experienced presenters took full advantage of what this new medium offered: collaborative whiteboards, animations and multimedia, breakout rooms, polls, and chat. This is a technology that is in truth far superior to the telephone conference call and, therefore, truly is a poster child for positive digital

---

[4] BBC News, March 1, 2020. "Zoom sees more growth after 'unprecedented' 2020." Retrieved from www.bbc.com/news/business-56247489 Accessed August 2021.

transformation. But its learning curve was too steep for a change that happened so fast.

For those who did use the cameras in video chat, many meeting attendees spent most of the meeting looking downward at their own laptop screens, which was where the other participants' faces appeared, rather than into the cameras that were supposed to act as the tool of direct eye contact. It's important to not dismiss this simple act too quickly. When video chat participants look down at the people they see on their laptop screens rather than looking into their camera to simulate direct eye contact, it becomes a perfect metaphor for the challenges of digital transformation.

We are a species that instinctively looks to the past – to the known – for comfort, rather than looking to the future, loaded up, as it is, with myriad unknowns. We tend to go with what we *know* rather than what *can be*. The people we see on the laptop screen represent a known. They represent faces that we would see in a conversation, and we are naturally drawn to looking at them. The habit of making pretend eye contact by looking into an unblinking camera, especially when it is in a different location than the faces of the people themselves, is a new and unfamiliar technique. It's an act of performance that must be consciously practiced despite instinct telling us to go with what feels right.

Video chat calls were simultaneously overused and underused during this period. They were overused in terms of the fact there were way too many of them. It seemed that every meeting held during the work-from-home pandemic period had to be conducted by video, even when they really didn't need to be.

And they were underused in two other significant ways.

The first underuse method delves further into the symptom of meeting attendees turning their video cameras off, and is symptomatic of what happens when change happens too fast. Humans can only deal with new things in the context of what they know, and at a pace that they are willing to handle. Not only were they now forced to contemplate the idea of seeing themselves on screen while others were also seeing them, they also realized that they were bringing their *work life* into their homes in a whole new and uncomfortable way.

Letting work colleagues appear in your living room where they can look around at your décor and see into your private home is not something that most employees had ever signed up for. It crossed that sacred line between work life and home life. In earlier years, an occasional phone call from the office on a day you were home sick was OK. They couldn't see you, so the appropriate work-home barrier was maintained. But strangers in the house is something to be feared.

And then there's the notion of video call fatigue.

In a peer-reviewed academic paper published in the journal *Technology, Mind and Behavior* in February 2021, Professor Jeremy Bailenson, founding director of the Stanford Virtual Human Interaction Lab (VHIL), identified four causes of video call fatigue.[5] In brief, they are:

(1) Excessive amounts of close-up eye contact – it is highly intense. The act of staring at people's faces on the screen, or of staring into the camera eye involves much more and longer-held "eye contact" than we are used to in face-to-face conversations.

(2) Seeing yourself during video chats constantly in real-time is fatiguing. Bailenson compares this to someone constantly holding up a mirror so that you have to keep seeing yourself. This, he says, is unnatural and distracting.

(3) Video chats dramatically reduce our usual mobility. People feel they must stay rooted to the spot and are not able to move around as we would in a live conversation.

---

[5] Bailenson, Jeremy. "Nonverbal Overload: A Theoretical Argument for the Causes of Zoom Fatigue" *Technology, Mind and Behavior*. Volume 2, Issue 1. American Psychological Association. Published February 23, 2021. Retrieved from https://tmb.apaopen.org/pub/nonverbal-overload/release/2. Accessed August 2021.

(4) The cognitive load is much higher in video chats. The lack of gestures and nonverbal cues make it harder to send and receive signals. We must work harder to understand the meaning of what is being said.

There is also the notion of focus and engagement. Conversations over the phone allow for a particular type of engagement that is encouraged precisely because you do not have to be looking at someone. You can look at documents or at your computer screen, out into the middle distance, or even out the window, but there is something in the passive visual distractions of a phone call that allows greater focus and engagement.

Back in the days when all phones were landlines, a great many conversations involved seemingly absent-minded actions like twirling the phone cord, doodling, or playing with a pile of magnetized paper clips. These, too, are actions whose significance should not be overlooked. Actions like these allow humans, who are by nature, active and kinesthetic, to redirect energy that is otherwise being held hostage by the phone conversation, and even more so by a video meeting. This is currently a gaping hole in digital transformation for employees and school-age children alike. Fidgeting is part of learning. Movement is part of life.

This is not to say that video chat technology is useless – quite the opposite – it will be the future of interpersonal communication. But it's not quite there yet, at least in the hearts, minds, and bodies of its users.

Digital Transformation and Zoom Gloom

The second significant underuse pattern of video chat meetings is that they were mostly used for formalized activities, which means meetings. Meetings are an inevitable part of most peoples' jobs, but they are not the sum total of the job. In fact, much of the workday is spent "not in meetings." It is spent doing self-directed work, managing emails, and physically moving around. This vital *non-meeting* component of office life, the act of just being in the office amid the presence of other humans, is a reflection of life itself. It is about existing with general purpose, whereas meetings are specially designed for interacting with a specific purpose.

Working in a common space gives comfort. It's very human to want to be part of a tribe, and workplace colleagues are just that. Even when office life is distracting or annoying, and even when you don't like all of your colleagues, it is still a tribe – a place to coexist with others. This is an indispensable element of work life, but during the forced work-from-home period, the whole casual "non-meeting" part was forgotten about.

Consequently, because video chat technology was used just for meetings, which are formalized events, it tended to magnify the sense of isolation felt by almost everyone, but especially by those who are unused to working from home. Once a video chat meeting comes to an end, and everyone waves goodbye and awkwardly searches their screen for the "leave meeting" button, and once the app closes, each home-bound employee becomes alone once again.

This sensation of amplified solitude was even given a name in honor of the industry leader of the time. It was called *Zoom Gloom*.

In our rush to reproduce the dynamics of the in-person meeting on video, no attention was given to reproducing the non-meeting time, that candid space where a person could see other people walking past, have casual conversations in the kitchenette, or simply wave and say "hi" to colleagues. Maybe no one realized how important this was because we had spent so much time hating it. Most employees did not realize just how much they would miss that atmosphere, and frankly did not have the time to even prepare for it. They were at the office one day, and locked down the next.

There are in fact many apps and virtual online environments that reproduce the casual yet immersive nature of people existing in a shared workplace. They were already in existence before the pandemic, and were on the leading edge, bringing virtual or augmented reality into the "real" reality of day-to-day work. But they were not embraced in any widespread fashion before the lockdowns, and especially not during, even though they would have been perfect. For most people, the idea of working in a virtual space, appearing as a cartoonish avatar in a cartoon representation of an office was seen as too silly or just too alien to be taken seriously. It was too much like video gaming and not enough like work. It was once again, too much of a change, too quick – one digital transformation step too far.

My favorite virtual spaces combine the preferred reality of people's real faces and voices, delivered by their own computer's camera and microphone, within a virtualized floor space, either an office layout, including designated areas like breakout rooms, cubicles, and a kitchenette, or something more vague, but where all the avatars of all the colleagues "at work" today can be seen milling around in some way, even when they are not interacting with each other. They are together in a finite space.[6]

The idea here is that while you work from your home office space, you can place your avatar at a cubicle, or in any of the rooms they offer. The key value is that others in your team can also place themselves in the space. If you see someone you want to talk to, you simply guide your avatar across to the zone they occupy, at which point the mic becomes live and the conversation can start.

Of course, these apps also offer other collaboration tools like whiteboards, messaging, and document sharing, but overall, they add a sense of presence that is real enough to feel comfortable without being surreal enough to feel like you are in a video game.

These technologies are not Zoom meetings – they simply are places to "be' and to be visible to your team between meetings, while your team remains visible to you.

Some of the resistance that I have heard regarding these platforms comes from the notion that it is difficult to have a conversation with an avatar. It feels strange to people who have grown up interacting with other

---

[6] My favorite virtual meeting spaces currently are toucan.events and KosyOffice. This is not a paid endorsement. I just think they work well.

CHAPTER 2   DIGITAL TRANSFORMATION IS HERE

humans face-to-face. Yet everyone seems perfectly comfortable talking to a disembodied voice on the phone, and relating to others by way of bubbles of text on a chat app.

The difference is that we are attuned to focusing in on voices during a phone conversation and by and large have learned to interpret emotion through voice tonality in the absence of visual cues. It's not perfect, but our brains are really good at detecting emotion and meaning from the slightest change in tone or even a delayed response in the communication flow. Texting on a chat app is convenient, but comes with a raft of challenges that are covered in more depth in Chapter 10.

But faces? Faces hold a special place in the mind. Think about how you can scan a wall of hundreds or thousands of faces in a crowded arena, and immediately pick out a friend, or simply someone who seems to be looking directly at you. Even with peripheral vision, most of us can detect when someone seems to be looking at us.

Our minds, and the physical receptors in the brain dedicated to facial comprehension are highly attuned to the messages broadcast by the human face – the slightest arch of an eyebrow, a subtle tensing of the lower eyelid, a momentary flaring of the nostrils. These fall under the umbrella term *non-verbal communication*, but they are innately strong and can be made even stronger through practice. This is one reason why VR avatars – computer generated representations of a person are just not there yet.

Compare the characters from the movie *Polar Express* to those that now exist in every recent Disney Pixar movie. The Polar Express kids were highly realistic for the time, but something about their eyes made them seem lifeless. Modern animated movies, however, have made huge leaps in animating eyes and facial tics in ways that seem much more human, even when the characters themselves are not.

Ultimately, it's all about what each person accepts as a valid representation of the person or people they are talking to. When it comes to the face and to the eyes, there are only two acceptable situations – fully realistic, (Pixar-style or real on-camera video) or none at all (telephone style).

Overall, I believe that a great many people will grow comfortable in the virtual office, logging on and sitting their avatar down at their desk and looking around to see who else is in today. If a spontaneous meeting needs to be held, it will be just as easy to tap on the virtual shoulders of colleagues and march on down to the virtual meeting space.

Video chat – better phrased as video collaboration – has a great future. It still remains a lasting ambassador of digital transformation, since it is slowly nudging people toward an entirely new realm of work, where physical commuting is no longer a barrier, and where physical proximity is delivered through informal digital presence. But this medium needs time to grow into its current puppy ears and paws.

To transform means to change, but it also means to evolve. User sophistication comes through practice and shared experiences. One day we will look back on the stilted, awkward video chats of the early 2020s the same way we currently look at movies from the 1920s, or fashions from the 1980s, or music videos from the early 1990s, and see something in its nascent form, brimming with potential, but not having found itself yet.

The Personalization of Fear

As people turn to face a future filled with digital transformation, that same future must also turn to face us, and it might be surprised as to what we have become. We are not so much "we" anymore. Increasingly, employees and consumers are perceiving themselves more as individuals. We are no longer part of a *customer base* or an *employee base*. Our self-awareness has become highly individualized, and this has much to do with the impact of personalized social media.

Based on the type of algorithm-based services we receive from Amazon, and social media like Facebook, Tik Tok, and Instagram, as well as every website that deposits cookies as we browse, we have come to expect personalized service everywhere and we expect it immediately. We are all sole members of our own audience-of-one.

CHAPTER 2   DIGITAL TRANSFORMATION IS HERE

This is now transforming all aspects of work life, everything, including the way companies must attract, hire, and retain employees, how they manage and lead, and how productivity and culture are encouraged and maintained. It is also transforming public-facing policies in the marketplace. The Internet is now the primary interaction conduit between each individual consumer and the companies they buy from.

So when did this all start? I'm going to suggest it started in 1975, the same year that Jaws was released. That was the year the VCR – the videocassette recorder – started to sell in the electronics stores and department stores of the world. It started to personalize the activity of television watching. Prior to this, families sat around their single television set and watched what the networks and later, cable TV channels, decided they should watch. Some households might have had two or more TVs in operation, but they were still only showing what the TV networks chose to show.

VCRs started us down the path of individualization, into a land where we were able to record and watch shows when we wanted, and later, go out and rent whatever movies we wanted, from the local video store. We had broken free of the bonds of network television, and had entered an age where entertainment had become a matter of personal choice.

Netflix rode this wave extremely successfully, delivering videodiscs by mail before hitting high gear as a personalized online streaming service, and later as a producer of bingeworthy entertainment. YouTube did the same with other, mostly homemade types of videos, and later, Instagram and TikTok allowed any person to become stars in their own media world. Amazon of course became the giant of personalized shopping, and Google became our personal index of everything.

The smartphone, the world's most versatile appliance, was built expressly for an audience-of-one culture. For billions of people, it is now the main source of contextual awareness, the place for personalized entertainment, the home of custom-designed socialization, and the launching point for self-idolatry. There are currently more active smartphone accounts than there are people on planet Earth.

CHAPTER 2   DIGITAL TRANSFORMATION IS HERE

This individualization of the experience of being alive has also emboldened people with a newfound ability to express their anger and magnify their biases. Fear grows in the darkness of our own solitude, and connecting with others who share the same biases creates strength and a reassurance that our fears are well-founded, mutual, and justifiable.

As the science-driven innovations of our digital age push us forward, the emotional fears of change and of the unknown try to pull us back. For example, science develops and distributes a coronavirus vaccine in record time, yet huge numbers of people all over the world resist it, citing fears and conspiracy theories that they themselves cannot prove.

The same resistance did not happen to this degree for polio shots, water fluoridization, tattoos, or car seat belts. Twice a year, almost all the people of the world change their clocks by an hour without rioting in the streets. They have been voluntarily giving up more personal data than they know to Facebook as the price of connecting with others, and many thousands of consumers also happily supply DNA samples to genealogy and ancestry tracing companies. And credit cards and password breaches? They simply shrug.

Humans are strange that way. The behaviors of individualized resistance, passionate followership, and self-absorbed belief are not new to human history. Zealots have been following charismatic visionaries for all of our history, and as already mentioned, superstitious and religious faith have always been there to deliver much needed reassurance. But what happens when this same self-focused mentality chooses to reject the benefits of digital transformation?

If people decide they do not trust biometric security devices such as retinal scanners out of fear that they are somehow implanting tracking technology or reading DNA, then this will thwart a vital component of the practice of multifactor authentication, which is a key layer of protection in the war against breaches and ransomware. What if people refuse to continue updating their Windows software, or refuse to stop using legacy apps that are still functional but are no longer being patched? What would

CHAPTER 2   DIGITAL TRANSFORMATION IS HERE

that do to a company's vulnerability and attack surface? What if just one employee decided to record a video chat conversation without informing the other participants, and parts of that recording found itself stored in a cloud located in a GDPR-bound nation? What if they started using a USB stick that they received in the mail?[7]

The goal of digital transformation is marketed as a transformation of a company's technological workings, but it seems the true transformation must occur within each and every individual with whom the technology comes into contact.

---

[7] Ropek, Lucas. "Hackers Have Been Sending Malware-Filled USB Sticks to U.S. Companies Disguised as Presents." *Gizmodo*. January 7, 2022. Retrieved from https://gizmodo.com/hackers-have-been-sending-malware-filled-usb-sticks-to-1848323578 Accessed January 2022.

CHAPTER 3

Fear As a Life Force

From infancy to full adulthood, there is always something to be scared of. Fear can be uncomfortable, distracting, even downright paralyzing. It can come as brief, temporary experiences, or in waves, or it can be chronic.

To picture an individual existing without any fear at all – calm, dispassionate and unfeeling – would be unnatural, because fear, above all other sensations, emotions, or knowledge, is what makes us human. From fear springs some of our greatest achievements.

> *I learned that courage was not the absence of fear, but the triumph over it.*
>
> —Nelson Mandela

Whether by conquering it, acting through it, or by thoroughly analyzing its source, humans can overcome fear, or at least meet it and match it. But they will discover that even in the simplest of cases, the source of fear lies much deeper than we ever suspected.

In terms of human physiology, fear of any sort is processed primarily in a section of the brain called the *amygdala*. This is a relatively small cluster of cells forming part of the limbic system, and is located about as deep inside the brain as it is possible to go.

When humans perceive a threat, such as a dangerous creature, a car speeding toward them, an expression of horror on another person's face, or a fear-inducing sound, smell, or sensation, the amygdala releases a

CHAPTER 3   FEAR AS A LIFE FORCE

stress signal to the hypothalamus, which is the "command center" for activity. This pushes the body into the well-known concept called fight-or-flight.[1]

This fight-or-flight response is quite fascinating in terms of the number of things it does. It raises the heart rate and blood pressure, stimulating the release of adrenaline, an acid that gives muscle cells temporary added power – the power that gives people super strength, well beyond their normal abilities. It makes the pupils in the eyes and the bronchi in the lungs dilate, to take in additional light and oxygen, respectively. It rapidly changes blood chemistry to add more glucose, a sugar that functions as a source of quick energy. At the same time, non-essential activities, including digestion, are shut down to divert energy to handle the pressing matter of survival.[2]

Fear represents a complex interplay between instinct, emotion, and logic, and it uses other parts of the brain, specifically the hippocampus and the prefrontal cortex for further processing and interpretation. For example, in a typical workplace situation, the sound of a fire alarm might not trigger an immediate fight-or-flight response in many people. Experience has conditioned us to interpret the noise as likely a false alarm and just an inconvenience. We make the conscious decision to expect that very soon an announcement will come over the public address system that the incident is under investigation or that it has been cleared. But if we hear the alarm *and then smell smoke,* that added sensory input makes all the difference. Now things are getting real, and it will likely trigger the fight-or-flight response.

---

[1] No author. "Understanding the Stress Response" *Staying Healthy*. Harvard University Medical School. June 6, 2020. Retrieved from www.health.harvard.edu/staying-healthy/understanding-the-stress-response Accessed September 2021.

[2] Javanbakht, Arash, and Saab, Linda. "What Happens in the Brain When We Feel Fear." *Smithsonian Magazine*. October 27, 2017. Paraphrased from www.smithsonianmag.com/science-nature/what-happens-brain-feel-fear-180966992/ Accessed September 2021.

CHAPTER 3   FEAR AS A LIFE FORCE

At this point, urgency takes over. Dilated pupils and increased blood flow create a form of tunnel vision for a person in crisis, one that focuses solely on survival. This narrowed perspective can be a lifesaver in terms of helping us escape danger, finding strength and drive that we did not know we had, and being oblivious to pain or wounds as we run for safety.

Fight-or-flight need not be solely a selfish instinct – it can also be useful in giving aid to others. Picture, for example, the numerous scenes captured on video of people performing heroic acts without pausing to consider their own mortality, to rescue a person or an animal from a dangerous situation. Tunnel vision lets people exist solely in the moment, without thinking about the possible danger.

But that same non-thinking reaction can turn into a fatal shortcoming when high-stress situations make people forget the right sequence of instructions or actions needed to survive. During a hard landing in a plane, for example, the type where the undercarriage has failed or a sudden wind shear causes the plane to hit the tarmac, once the aircraft comes to a stop and the slides deploy, people will be in shock.

In these moments, it is not uncommon for some of them to forget how to unbuckle their lap belt for a few precious seconds. Habit, formed from years of riding in cars, makes them reach down to the side of their hip as they would when releasing a car seatbelt – an action they have performed thousands of times, and which has been burned into muscle memory. The airplane seat belt buckle is located in the center of their lap, not the side, and also, it opens with a hinge. Some passengers will fumble with this since there are very few other belts or attachments in most peoples' lives that use such a mechanism.[3]

---

[3] Based on an interview conducted by the author with an inflight crew on a Canadian airline, 1990.

This sounds improbable, but until you have experienced the enormous stress and shock of a near-crash in a plane, it is hard to picture anyone having difficulty with their seat belt. But this is an example where the expression of "not being able to think straight" applies. The mind is overcome with the urgency, the disbelief, the horror, and the enormity of the moment, and reverts to instinct rather than memory.

This is in part why flight attendants perform their safety demonstrations with gestures, using an actual seatbelt and breathing mask, and miming the actions along with the announcement. It's why they also implore people to watch and pay attention, which we seldom do. They can't rely on people merely hearing the words to remember the lesson. The flight crews must physically demonstrate how to perform the actions, in an effort to visually transfer muscle memory.

This is also why cruise lines hold lifeboat drills on day one of every voyage, and why workplaces practice safety drills – to ensure everyone experiences the physical actions of leaving potential danger safely and arriving at their muster point – without having to think too much about it.

The same shock-based fight-or-flight responses occur in situations that aren't physical so much as emotional and intellectual, such as receiving sudden news of impending layoffs, or news of the death of a colleague, or of a celebrity. These are situations where normalcy has been shaken, breeding temporary disorientation, confusion, anger, and fear.

Fear Is Contagious

Imagine yourself standing in an elevator in a tall building with ten other people, and you're traveling downward, heading to the ground floor. The elevator lurches to a stop between floors. Much like the smoke alarm example of earlier, you are most likely not going to panic, because somewhere in the back of your mind is the awareness of the safety features built into elevator technology. You also know you can talk to someone at the Security desk by way of the help button. These are things you *know* as logical facts. This factual knowledge helps you to stay calm as you patiently wait for the car to start moving again.

That is, until someone in the elevator shouts out, "Oh my god, we're all going to die!" At that moment, waves of fear instantly radiate through the small space of the elevator, quickly tipping the collective mood from calm to discomfort, pushing the needle slowly toward panic. It's no longer the facts of the situation that are in charge, it's the feeling.

During the early months of the Covid-19 pandemic, before masks and vaccinations became the primary focal points of disagreement, there was a rash of hoarding activities in grocery stores. People started purchasing excessive amounts of cleaning supplies and sanitizers. These activities were often initiated by individuals who already possessed a permanent bunker mentality, but then other people joined the mania – people who originally had no intention of doing anything more than buying regular groceries in regular amounts. But the sight of seeing others load up on these products triggered their own instinctive fears and pushed them into actions they had never previously considered.

The contagion of fear carries itself quickly across and through groups, carrying an unspoken yet extremely clear warning: there is danger ahead. We observe or hear someone expressing fear, and we immediately fall back to it as our default setting.

When an individual feels fear and then expresses it through words, actions, or even subtle facial expressions, it automatically becomes a shared fear. When a shared fear becomes broadcast through an ever-growing number of people, it can become a movement, and when something becomes a movement, it has the ability to stop progress in its tracks and sometimes even reverse it.

CHAPTER 3   FEAR AS A LIFE FORCE

Why Does Fear Seem Larger at Night?

Fear can strike at any time of day, of course, but for many, it seems even larger and worse at night, especially around 3:00 a.m. or so. This is traditionally, and appropriately, called the "dead of night." People who wake up at this time – due to a noise, or simply the conclusion of a sleep cycle – will often find themselves wracked in restless thought, with the concerns of life – family, career, money – seeming larger and even more scary than before.

The reason every thought and worry seems bigger at this time of night is because we humans are, by comparison, a little bit weaker, colder, and more vulnerable at that time, compared to the rest of the day. The body has an internal clock of sorts, called the circadian rhythm, (Latin for *circa* – around, and *dian* – the day) which is regulated by the presence of the sun, both in terms of sunrise, which stimulates body chemistry for action, and sunset, which starts the process of releasing melatonin, the hormone chiefly responsible for sleep.

The dead of night is intended for rest and repair. It is a time when the body directs energy toward fixing up the wear and tear of the day before, and it is also the time when children do most of their growing. Basically it's our all-night body shop.

If you have ever worked a night shift, and you are not a night-owl by nature, you might notice that you will feel a little chilly at 3:00 a.m., even in a normally-heated room. This is because your body is seeking to lower your internal temperature by a degree or so, as part of the temporary "shut-down" and energy redirection process.

This is also the time when many mistakes are made, including highway and industrial accidents, and in the world of cyber sabotage, the dead of night is a great time to release a damaging payload, since most people just will not be at their best at that time.

Consequently, we are a little weaker, if only in terms of being more physically vulnerable while our body focuses more on itself, and therefore it tends to magnify the perceptions of danger, fear, and worry, due to this vulnerable state. As difficult as it may be, one of the best ways to defeat the fears of the middle of the night is to simply recognize that self-same fact; that you are, indeed currently in a physiologically more vulnerable state, and that 3:00 a.m. fear is appearing disproportionately large and out of context. These fears will be better dealt with in the morning in the light of day. Just knowing this is helpful for some people to put them aside for a few more hours.

Maslow's Hierarchy of Needs

In 1943, the psychologist Abraham Maslow published a paper entitled *A Theory of Human Motivation* in the journal *Psychological Review*. The paper included an image that has lasted and stayed mostly relevant for eighty years thus far. Called the Hierarchy of Needs, it is a pyramid that lists the various types of needs that each human experiences. They are prioritized from the most elemental physiological ones like food, water, warmth, and rest, up through safety, then belongingness and love, then esteem, and finally self-fulfillment.

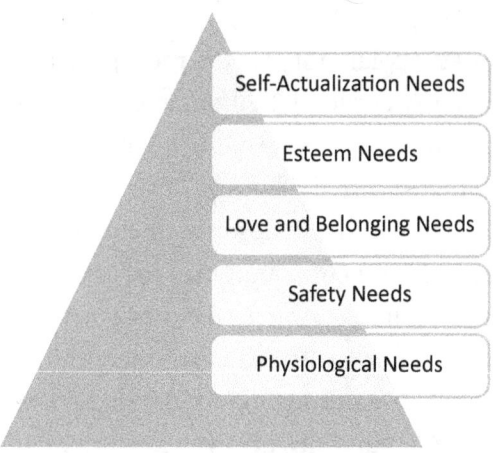

Figure 3-1. Maslow's Hierarchy of Needs. Retrieved from www.agileleantransformation.com/articles.html *Creative Commons license – used with permission*

CHAPTER 3 FEAR AS A LIFE FORCE

The hierarchy is beautiful in its simplicity, and though it does not discuss fear directly, basically, all of the fears we experience tie back to it. Basic mortal concern tends to out-prioritize every other type of need, which is why it connects most directly to the bottom-most layer of this chart. But to be human means that we must take the whole package.

As we look at the immediate impact that digital transformation has on fear and *vice versa*, it will be easy to see how individual fears connect with the levels on this pyramid, sometimes with more than one level at a time.

This is important to keep in mind, especially if these fears are already making themselves evident within your at-work community. Sometimes, even the most lugubrious and negative individual, the person who is steadfastly standing in the way of your organization's progress, might be doing so not because they are a technology-hating Luddite, but because, deep inside, they are terrified of being found out as a fraud, or as incompetent in some way, and the fear they feel stretches up through the entire pyramid, from the realization of not being able to achieve self-affirmation right down to the most profound fear of all: that this change will somehow lead to the death of their livelihood, and with it, the life they have grown used to.

The bands are self-explanatory for the most part, but they are worth a brief description here in order to fit them into the context of this book: How human reflex stands in the way of digital transformation.

Physiological needs form the bottom layer. These are primarily food, air, water, warmth, and rest, since these are the forces that keep us alive. For example, every time you enter a room, a part of you automatically scans the space and smells the air to make sure this is a place that you can enter. If you find yourself outside in extremely cold sub-zero weather without proper protective clothing, as might happen when dashing across the street between office buildings on a windy winter day, you might hear an inner voice saying, "get inside." It's not an actual voice, but it is your instinct telling you that this outdoor situation does not satisfy even the basic level of Maslow's Hierarchy and must be dealt with.

If you are dining with a colleague at a restaurant in which the wait staff bring you your food – as compared to a buffet where you serve yourself – you might notice, if you pay attention, that your colleague's face will freeze for a millisecond, even in mid-conversation, as instinct takes over and assesses the food placed before them, to decide if it is safe for consumption. I call this *food face* and it is great fun to watch this happen.

Both the inner voice and food face are examples of automatic responses to the environment around us. We need to determine that things are not life-threatening before we can move forward into any situation.

The next level of Maslow's Hierarchy is **Safety**, and this questions whether an environment is safe, and that there is no danger of harm. Stepping into an elevator will trigger this type of automatic safety assessment, especially with regard to the physical condition of the elevator car, and the number of people already in it. Walking down a street and mistakenly turning into a darkened alleyway will make most people turn around and walk back out again without a second thought.

Once the basic priorities of life and safety have been satisfactorily addressed, we turn to the middle band which speaks to the desire for **belonging and love**. There is the intimate love of a life partner and the love of family, of course, but this band also addresses the sense of acceptance in a tribe, which includes workplace teams.

Humans for the most part want to feel part of something, and a great deal of office life seeks to support this need through formalized and informal activities, including meetings, birthday celebrations, team-building events, casual days, and even simply hallway conversation. Much of this has, up until recent times, been based on people being in the same physical space at the same time. How we will be able to replicate this in a virtual or hybrid working world is a profound digital transformation-related workplace fear for managers and employees, not just from a productivity standpoint, but from that of being able to keep hold of this *belonging and love* level.

CHAPTER 3   FEAR AS A LIFE FORCE

The **Esteem** level represents a need for self-comfort, which comes from generally feeling OK or even good about oneself in terms of work skills, being able to socialize with colleagues, being able to relate to managers and being comfortable in one's own skin.

Finally, the top layer of the pyramid looks to **self-actualization** – the pursuit and achievement of goals, which would include career goals, life goals, and personal achievements, such as further education, promotion, better work–life balance, or all of these.

It is easy to see how the changes put forward by the prospect of digital transformation must pass through the filter of Maslow's Hierarchy, and it is also possible to see how such changes might snag on quite a few corners as they do so. Everything that we question and assess about change and transformation is voiced in defense of our own selves, from the most basic to the most ambitious, from the most welcome change, to the least.

Those who are in charge of leading people through a digital transformation must be careful to establish a process of comfort, using awareness, exposure, and reinforcement. They must take care to anticipate pushback and fear, and proactively place small interim wins on par with the grand end goal of change. They must prepare and share the emotional nutrients that are vitally needed to keep going. They must communicate and listen with equal amounts of energy, and they must understand that very often, the fear behind resistance to change lies much deeper than we think.

There are exceedingly few areas in life – if any – in which change is welcomed with open arms. Even those life events that are traditionally described as the best of all – for some, this might mean getting married or having a child, rescuing a pet, getting a promotion, or winning the lottery – come with their own share of reservations and doubt. How could they not? The very urges that demand that we stay safe will always have a voice at every significant juncture along life's path.

Managers and leaders who are in charge of introducing change must seek to do so carefully, thawing the ice of complacency with visions of a better future state. They must keep in mind the reality that emotion dominates the human self, and the emotions of fear, doubt, and negativity are the default state. In your back pocket, you must carry the facts that can be presented at the right time – the descriptions and demonstration of the new techniques. But this should not happen first. First must come the thawing period, in which comfort with the norm starts to be awakened or guided toward a vision of a better state. A vision is a concept, an idea, a representation of betterment. Only after this thawing has begun can the facts of the change be introduced.

Once the facts have been introduced, you can still expect pushback and rejection, as the humans confronting the change pass through their phases of grief, in a pattern you might already know as the Kubler-Ross model.

The Kubler-Ross Grief/Change Model

One of the most profound responses to known fears is denial. The social psychologist Elisabeth Kubler-Ross is among the most famous illustrators of the power of denial, especially in her 1969 work, *On Death and Dying*, in which she introduced the world to the *five stages of grief*, also known as the Kubler-Ross model.

She describes the five stages as happening in the following order: denial, anger, bargaining, depression, and acceptance, and this pattern is applicable not only to the trauma of death, but to many other changes that can occur in a person's life.

Like many popular psychologists, including Abraham Maslow, her work has also been critiqued and refuted over the years, some suggesting it lacks scientific rigor, does not take into account cultural diversities, and that the sequence of the five steps is artificial, and may even influence peoples' behavior or the judgement of those who care for them. Some of this may be correct now, given the half-century we have had to both analyze her work and evolve socially, but there are still many components in her process that ring true.

CHAPTER 3   FEAR AS A LIFE FORCE

To me, the five phases and their predictability remains a useful guide, even if the relative severity and duration of each changes from person to person, and even, too, if some people (like myself) seem to pass through this cycle more than once during a protracted grieving and recovery process.

Forming, Storming, Norming, and Performing

This is a sequence that is similar to the Kubler-Ross model in that it is expectable and predictable. As coined by Bruce Tuckman in his 1965 paper, *Developmental Sequence in Small Groups*, it describes the phases that people go through when coming together as a team, which is a type of change unto itself. A group of strangers will behave politely and superficially when they first get together. The formality and novelty of the situation generates a type of curious energy. But this quickly gives way to storms, as peoples' true personalities start to emerge, the Type-As, the alphas, the peacemakers, extroverts, introverts, creative, and analytical types, all struggle to find their place within the pressure of an evolving working group. This is the *storming* phase, and it often leads to dysfunction, confusion, and disillusionment.

This is until the players all find their place, start to work together, and normalize their relationships, which ultimately leads to performing or even outperforming expectations as the capacity of the whole team surpasses the sum of its parts.

Despite the fact that the four terms, forming, storming, norming, and performing, rhyme so conveniently, there is a predictable line of group behavior within this principle that is similar to the path outlined in the Kubler-Ross grief/change model and Maslow's Hierarchy. This gives leaders comfort in knowing that even when things look desperately bad, there is an expectable path that humans will follow.

This has a double benefit for those leading others into digital transformation. First, there is the comfort of knowing that humans will most likely respond in the manner described by Kubler-Ross, Maslow, and Tuckman. This makes the arrival of pushback and rejection at least a little easier to take, given that it's not a total shock.

Secondly, it becomes a useful roadmap for extending that same comfort and guidance to those who will be facing the change.

Managing the Fear of Change

Most successful change management strategies involve some sort of acclimatization process, in which people get used to an idea emotionally before accepting the facts and following a transition plan. As mentioned already, emotion always dominates the human psyche, and to overcome the fear of change, facts must be brought in to meet the fear. But this must be done at the right time and in the right way.

Closing the Gate

Experiencing change is like passing through a gate. As such, it is vital to take the time to close the gate behind you as you pass through. Many departments or organizations that are embracing digital transformation tend to focus exclusively on the newer, greener pasture that lies ahead, the one with the new technology, the better processes, and the faster everything.

But humans need to grieve a loss, and a loss of normalcy is a loss. It's not as severe as the loss of a loved one, but it is made out of the same energy.

CHAPTER 3   FEAR AS A LIFE FORCE

> *The single biggest reason changes fail is that no one has thought about endings or planned to manage their impact on people.*
>
> —William Bridges, Managing Transitions

The gate is a physical place that stands between the past and the future, between normalcy and novelty. It is not a pencil-drawn line on the ground; it is instead a structure, with some width and presence through which people must pass.

As you help people look toward the future, it is vital to help each individual identify what they are losing, exactly, and to acknowledge the loss as part of the grief process. Expect that their work performance might alter somewhat during this time. Treat the past with respect, but at the same time, make sure to identify what is not changing.

For example, if the change being experienced is a shift from a traditional office layout to a hoteling or hot-desking zone in which employees' cubicles have been replaced by desks that are to be reserved by the day, you can be very sure that there will be some resistance. But although the office layout might have been replaced by a hot desking zone, other life constants, perhaps like the boardroom and the downstairs coffee shop are still there.

People will often say "the only constant is change," but you can also say, "in change, there are still constants: some things change, but others remain the same."

Bring the Facts Up to Meet the Fear

Most fear can be allayed by facts. When you give someone some knowledge about the situation or object that is causing fear, that knowledge has the potential to not just *cover up* but actually eliminate the fear. Whatever causes the fear, there is usually a way to fix it, understand it, or handle it. But to do this, we need to manually introduce facts and bring them up to the level where fear already exists.

Fear exists by default. It already has a substantial presence in the mind of the individual. It is driven by emotion and instinct, and will thus dominate. That is at least until we are able to bring facts into the picture to level things out.

When a child fears the monster under the bed, a flashlight, paired with a parent/caregiver's calming reassurance, can do wonders to demonstrate that there is no monster under there. When a person lies awake at 3:00 a.m., as discussed above, the knowledge of why this seems so large may help in getting back to sleep. When a person agonizes over having to learn a new software application, some clear hands-on training will give them the experience they need to see how easy it is. When a manager procrastinates over a meeting with an employee which involves bad news, that manager will need to discover how they can actually help with the next steps and become part of a more positive outcome. If a person fears going to the dentist, they need to be shown that there are still activities in that day that will happen after the dental appointment is done. Things will continue. Life goes on. In all of these cases and so many more, the monster of fear is a figment of instinct and emotion. Facts will help to slay it.

CHAPTER 4

The Fear of Change

Why Do I Have to Learn This?

I started my company in 1990, during the early days of another significant digital revolution, when the personal computer was being introduced to the workforce. My company helped people manage their fear of failing. Our customers were not software developers – they were not creators of code, but rather the end users, employees who had been confronted with a new set of technologies they had never asked for. Having encountered problems with using them, they had been sent by their employers to overcome their emotional and practical logjams.

Anyone who was in the workforce at this time will probably remember that office software applications were not very friendly or consistent back in the early 1990s. They were clunky, not at all intuitive, and by today's standards, extremely slow. Few people enjoyed having to learn how to use them. They were driven by keystroke commands, such as Shift, F7, 1 for printing a document, and they introduced not only a new set of learning challenges, but also new physical demands on the body, especially the back and neck, the eyes, and the wrists.

In addition, new iterations of the applications came out regularly, often with significant changes. The designers and marketers of the apps quite appropriately saw these as improvements and upgrades, but for end users, it was yet more change – new things to learn in the middle of an already busy week. Forty years later, most users of modern office applications like Microsoft Word still do not use it beyond ten percent of its capabilities.

Dealing with the Fear of Change

My company was not about the software *per se*. It was about helping people understand how to deal with their fear of change. Our clients were employees, managers, even executives, working at banks, head offices, government departments, and more. Many of them were well along in their career track, and were suddenly feeling that a whole new world had opened up, one that had been expressly designed for people other than them, people who innately understood the computer ethos – people that society now called *computer savvy*. Their fear was palpable. They were saying, "If I screw up on this, I'll lose my job."

Back then, the primary question was "why?" as in, "why do I have to press all these keys to print a document? Why isn't there simply a key on my keyboard marked *print*?" That was a fair question. Another fair question was, "why do I have to save this document, and what happens if I forget?"

Today's generation of fearful employees ask similarly valid questions, like "why do I have to change my password so often?" and "what is Artificial Intelligence going to do to my job?" These may sound like tech support questions, but they're not. They're people-support questions. They are not asking "how do I do this?" They are asking "why do I have to do this?" That switches up the dynamic from a learning situation to a change management one.

Change is not welcome in the dark recesses of the brain, and as such there will always be resistance to it. Effective management of change requires that we follow a careful pattern that allows habits to transform in league with emotional acceptance. The speed by which that first digital transformation happened back in the 1990s showed that time is not a commodity willingly shared in large amounts, and since then, the pace has only accelerated.

Even today, the fear doesn't always manifest itself as a fear of the technology. Sometimes it's just about the time it takes to learn it, as in: "I have been keeping track of my tasks in a way that works for me and now you want me to join a team-based, cloud-based collaboration tool? Why should I do that when what I have works perfectly well?" The answer doesn't even need words – just that kind of eye contact held just one second too long that says, "you're not part of this team."

The Curse of Passwords

People have never been good with passwords. Ever. There was once an expression that said, "your password history is an accidental diary of your life," since so many people created passwords out of names and phrases that were important to them at a particular moment in their life. Over the years, these tended to evolve along with life's priorities, but they left behind two legacies: a trail of memories for the owner, and a cornucopia of riches for cyberthieves.

These days, people still choose passwords that are easy to remember, such as family names, superheroes, sports teams, celebrities, or simple words and number combinations. These, naturally, are far easier to remember. Forgetting a password is a cause of fear unto itself, even if it is simply due to the anticipation of having to go and find the password from wherever it is written down, or to do one of those tedious "forgot your password?" exercises. And, of course, because they are easy to remember, the temptation is to use these same passwords on many different sites.

So when the request comes around from the IT department for employees to change their passwords, many will simply do one of the following:

(a) Choose another frequently-used and easy-to-remember password.

(b) Add a digit to the existing password, so that *maryjane* now becomes *maryjane1*.

(c) Change their password in accordance with IT's request and then change it back as soon as no one is looking.

According to research conducted by cybersecurity firm My1Login in 2021, two thirds (62 percent) of employees share passwords between business and personal accounts. Apparently, the problem is particularly bad in the healthcare and education sectors, where the survey found especially high rates of password reuse, at 94 percent and 91 percent of employees, respectively.

The My1Login report goes on to show that 85 percent of employees who have received security training in the workplace continue to reuse their passwords. Even 78 percent of those employees who said they had received "a lot" of cybersecurity training were found to still reuse their passwords.[1]

Any one of a thousand research reports written before or since could have been inserted here in place of the My1Login report, and they will all say the same thing: people in general are really bad at password management. They might know what a strong password should look like, and they also might know that they shouldn't reuse their passwords, but that doesn't mean that they are actually obeying the rules. Something is stopping them.

This is so bad. Weak passwords make for easy pickings among cybercriminals. Words that are easy to guess, like *sunshine* or *password* are prime targets for dictionary attacks, in which hundreds of thousands of words are sprayed at millions of password login screens, in a perpetual, and sufficiently successful play at beating the odds.

---

[1] No author. "Why do leaders need to take the responsibility of corporate passwords away from employees?" Posted at My1Login. August 27, 2021. Retrieved from https://blog.my1login.com/why-do-leaders-need-to-take-the-responsibility-of-corporate-passwords-away-from-employees Accessed September 2021.

CHAPTER 4   THE FEAR OF CHANGE

Cybercriminals also know the old trick of replacing certain letters with digits, like replacing the letter *i* in *sunshine* with a number 1 – *sunsh1ne*, or the *e* with a number 3 – *sunshin3* or both – *sunsh1n3*. These, too, are easy for cybercriminals to anticipate, because they spring from the same source: human beings – people who don't want to work hard at creating difficult passwords.

Because of the penchant for creating and then re-using easy passwords, every data breach becomes a goldmine of potentially still-valid passwords for bad actors to use to get in elsewhere. Out there in the cyber-underworld, there are algorithms, bots, and humans who spend all-day, every day, working to apply stolen passwords to any and every login they can find, and often, they succeed. There are others that troll social media sites looking for names of pets, kids, and famous people in order to guess password combinations and spray them everywhere.

When a breach happens, it is common for large companies seeking to avoid a class action lawsuit to offer token compensation in the form of two years of free credit monitoring, or two years of free ID theft protection from a well-known security software brand. But as Will Gregorian, Head of Security and Technical Operations at Rhino suggests, the smart cybercrime organizations simply hold these stolen passwords until the two-year free service expires. The number of victims who choose to renew the credit or security monitoring will be significantly lower than the overall number of stolen passwords that remain active.[2] Time makes for great dividends for the criminals.

Poor password hygiene is a significant speed bump on the road to successful digital transformation. It alone has been and will continue to be responsible for billions of dollars in stolen funds, ransomware payments,

---

[2] Cyber Security Headlines Week in Review, August 20, 2021. Used with permission. Retrieved from https://cisoseries.com/cyber-security-headlines-week-in-review-august-16-20-2021/ Accessed December 2021.

shutdowns, litigation, time wasted, lives altered, and even death, and will be until the day the activity of logging into a protected space becomes human-proof.

Death? Yes. Here's just one example: According to papers filed in June 2020, the mother of a child who was born and later died in a Mobile, Alabama hospital, accused the hospital and its owners of failing to mitigate the effects of a cyber-attack which prevented fetal heart rate monitors from operating and hence led to the child's death. According to the *Wall Street Journal*, medical staff could not access the child's vital information, since the displays had been locked by ransomware. The hospital denied any wrongdoing.[3]

Why are people so bad with passwords? There are two reasons, both equally important, and both based to a great degree in fear.

The Comfort of Passwords

The first is that for the average user there is comfort in using familiar passwords. There's solace in the notion that we will not forget a password, even if it is in reality quite weak. It still *feels* better than creating more complex, unpredictable ones. Feeling better is more emotionally appealing than doing something that we *know* is safer but that is still uncomfortable to undertake.

Using familiar passwords is the digital equivalent of leaving the house key under the doormat, or the car keys in the car. Some might say it's on par with leaving the car running while you duck into a convenience store. Being able to remember an easy password seems to be one less thing to worry about, even though, in reality it should give you one million more things to worry about.

---

[3] Muncaster, Phil. "Infant Fatality Could Be First Recorded Ransomware Death" *Infosecurity Magazine*, October 1, 2021. Retrieved from www.infosecurity-magazine.com/news/infant-first-ransomware-death/ Accessed October 2021.

The Fear of Effort

The second reason people are bad with passwords is the fear of effort. It takes effort to think up new passwords and write them somewhere, especially if they are unusual. If they are not easy turns of phrase, then they're not easy at all. Maryhadalittlelamb is an easy-to-remember password, but that's what makes it easy to guess because it's a well-known nursery rhyme that has been heard or spoken by millions of people. These types of phrases can be sprayed at login pages, paired with hundreds of millions of stolen passwords.

The odds of a match may be slim, but they are not zero. Even a one ten-thousandth of one percent return can generate revenue that far exceeds the cost of running the criminal operation. The overall effort is minimal, making the rewards disproportionately worthwhile.

Some security experts suggest using unusual combinations of words that cannot be easily guessed, and that also incorporate unusual spellings. So a better password to replace Maryhadalittlelamb would be marymotorcyclepurplejam, since it has no logical structure as a sentence.

An even better variation would be marymortoxyclepplejm since this now uses wildly misspelled words. An even better version would be mary$ortoXycl4pplj& since it adds caps, numbers, and other characters.

But who is going to be able to remember any of these variations? Even if you were to write this complex password down on paper, who has the time or patience to retrieve it and key it in correctly? That, too, requires effort, and the human limbic system does not like to spend energy on extraneous activities.

The actions of either looking up a password, or trying to remember it, or of keying it in and potentially getting the password wrong and having to start over – these all cause delay, and create frustration and generally hinder people's momentum, even if just for a few minutes. Even just thinking about it is off-putting. Let's face it, it's a hassle, and no one likes a hassle. It's enough to scare people away, back to the comfort of simpler words, like *111111* or *qwerty*, or *1234567*, or *password*, all of which occupied the list of 2021's top ten most common passwords.[4]

Not only is it a hassle, it's also a consumer turn-off. Steve Zurier, quoting a study on password resets conducted by the security firm Beyond Identity, shows that "48 percent of consumers say it's 'very likely' they would abandon a website when told a new password cannot be the same as their old password." Another 25 percent would 'likely' abandon a shopping cart, if prompted to update their password on checkout.

The article and study quotes Jing Gu, who summarizes the problem succinctly: "The password is a revenue problem. When customers drop off, you can lose them forever."[5]

The Fear of the Password Manager

Enter the password management software app – a linchpin of the digital transformation universe. It delivers the cyberhygiene vaccine – a carefully constructed defense against a virulent enemy.

Password managers replace those too-easy word combinations like youandme123 with virtually impossible-to-crack, randomly generated strings of characters, numbers, and symbols to create passwords like ajR6@5Y^. These generated passwords look like gibberish because they are – to humans at least.

---

[4] Top 200 most common passwords, published by Nordpass. Available at https://nordpass.com/most-common-passwords-list/ Accessed November 2021.

[5] Zurier, Steve. "Nearly 50percent of People Will Abandon Sites Prohibiting Password Reuse" *Dark Reading*. December 22, 2021. Retrieved from www.darkreading.com/risk/nearly-50-of-people-will-abandon-sites-prohibiting-password-reuse. Accessed December 2021. Original report available BeyondIdentity: www.beyondidentity.com/blog/password-resets-and-the-consumer-journey

CHAPTER 4   THE FEAR OF CHANGE

There is no word hashed or hidden inside this string. With a total of 80 possible characters (from a-z, 0-9, punctuation and uppercase) available to select for each position, even an eight-character password – the smallest number of characters generally considered worthwhile for password security, results in a number of potential combinations that exceeds a quadrillion. When a 16 character password based on 80 characters is used, that becomes $(80)^{16}$ or 2.814749767106560e+30 which exceeds a nonillion. Yes, that's what the number $(80)^{16}$ is called, or so people on reddit tell me.

Yes, on occasion, the media does report on a person who is able to hack 16-character passwords, but these are often proof-of-concept demonstrations that involve chaining supercomputers together and using dictionary-only words and tricks like the Markov technique that incorporates predictable variables. These exercises also involve focusing on passwords with digits and lower case characters only – no punctuation or mixed case, which makes the field of variables much smaller.

The truth is that any password can be broken given enough time and resources, and this will be an even more significant problem when quantum computing becomes more widespread. This is a fast-approaching reality that cybersecurity specialists are calling Y2Q. The goal of creating strong passwords is not to make them infinitely, eternally invincible, but to make them too much of a hassle for hackers to want to confront.

So why aren't password managers more enthusiastically embraced by the general public? It's not the effort of having to learn another new software app that's the problem generally; it's that a user must relinquish *control* over their passwords. Very few people have the ability to memorize eight or sixteen random characters. Only the app can do that. And the app doesn't memorize it as a single string. It breaks it up, and inserts additional characters, called hashing, to effectively hide the password inside more randomness, until the moment the password owner logs into the password manager app and effectively "unscrambles the scrambled eggs."

CHAPTER 4   THE FEAR OF CHANGE

This makes complete logical sense. It makes passwords harder to crack. But for most average computer users, it makes no *practical* sense. This type of logic gets easily overruled by fear: the fear of giving up control over their passwords and letting a machine take them over. It's about letting go of actual memorable words and allowing an app to generate passwords that their owners could not possibly hope to memorize. That is a huge leap of faith.

Managing the Fear of the Password Manager

One of the most efficient ways to deliver facts about password manager software would be to let people try it out, in person, safely, on a computer that is not connected to anything important – a sandbox type situation. Give them a physical hands-on experience in a place where they feel safe and where any mistakes they make are harmless.

Giving people a place to try out the password management software is an example of letting the facts meet the fear. They can press the buttons, read the menus, learn how to add passwords, update passwords, and they can ask those *what if* questions: "What if I break something? What if I forget how to set a password? What if the password manager loses my password?"

They can open the password manager vault and see where and how passwords are stored, and reassure themselves that the passwords are indeed real and can be accessed at any time. That is what actual training is supposed to do – transfer skills from one person to another. The practical facts paired with hands-on experience deliver a tangible familiarity which translates to logical knowledge and emotional comfort which together can defeat the fear of this particular unknown.

Put the change into context: Focus on the fact that we have been using passwords for years now and that the password manager is just one more step along the way, keeping pace with advancing threats to password safety. Bring in examples of where invisible password managers are

CHAPTER 4   THE FEAR OF CHANGE

already being used inside tap debit cards, coded car ignition key fobs, and the ability to unlock your phone through facial ID. These are all examples of computers doing the secret processing for us.

Add a little perspective: Show what's really going on out there. Demonstrate how many active cybercrime-related activities are happening every second, using visual real-time maps of DDoS attacks. Pull up a list of well-known companies that have suffered data breaches, and lists of commonly guessed passwords. Use a website such as HaveIBeenPwned.com to perform a real-time search of a person's email or phone number to show whether they have already been unwittingly involved in a data breach.[6] Graphics, visuals, and lists of recognizable names and passwords go a long way in making the threat of cybercrime real and bringing it home. This last point is quite important, because one of the key weaknesses of cyber defense is that the threats never seem tangible enough to end users or even to companies that consider themselves too small and insignificant to matter.

The Fear of the Hot Desk

As organizations start to assess their post-pandemic digital futures, they are having to contemplate a new normal that includes an entirely new working dynamic: the hybrid workspace, in which employees work some of the time in the office and some of the time at home. This in turn is forcing companies to reassess their office layouts, since a great many desks, workstations, and cubicles will go largely unused, creating a lot of expensive empty space.

---

[6] Have I Been Pwned? – yes, that's the correct spelling – was created by security expert Troy Hunt in 2013, and is recognized in the cybersecurity industry as a go-to location for information about data breaches and leaked accounts. It is located at https://haveibeenpwned.com/ The word *pwned* is pronounced "poned" (rhymes with "owned"), and is part of Internet "Leet" speak used primarily by online gamers to mean being dominated in a game or battle.

57

CHAPTER 4 THE FEAR OF CHANGE

One solution to this is the idea of hot desking, also called hoteling. This refers to a simple desk-by-the-day or desk-on-demand concept, in which hybrid work employees can reserve a workspace for the day or days that they come into the office. Sounds simple enough.

But if there is one item in a workplace that presents an image of consistency and grounding for an employee of any rank, it is their own desk, whether in an office, cubicle, or open space layout. It's a personal space, a unique location that answers the instinctive need for safety and shelter and for an unchanging, consistent environment in which to survive the workday. It becomes a person's private territory, which they will demarcate with a photo or two and some other personal memorabilia. These items not only declare that the space as theirs, more importantly, they also declare that it is *not anybody else's.*

As such, there will be a great many people who will naturally resist the idea of hoteling. For them, it removes one more layer of comfort. It presents them with a sense of not knowing where their workplace home base will be from day to day. It is easy to observe, for example, how people like to choose the same non-reserved parking space each day, the same seat in a food court or cafeteria, and when attending two-day or multi-day courses or workshops, how they will return to that same seat on day two, and how finding another person occupying that space can result in annoyance or discomfort.

The comfort that comes from consistency and knowing where your safe space will be, sits on those fundamental foundation layers of Maslow's Hierarchy. The introduction of a new variable is bound to cause discomfort among a significant proportion of any workforce.

But let's look at other areas where progress has been made in the hoteling concept. First, there's the hotel itself, which has been a part of human culture for centuries. No matter what price range you look at, from the most opulent to the most humble, a cardinal rule of hoteliery is that a guest's room should appear as if no one else has ever stayed in it previously.

CHAPTER 4   THE FEAR OF CHANGE

This is an impossibility of course, but a fundamental element of the sense of comfort that every hotel, inn, B&B, and AirBnB is supposed to deliver is that in those first few moments, as the guest enters the room for the first time, no one else's presence remains: no belongings left behind and no impressions on the bed. Everything must deliver a clear message – this room belongs to the guest and no one else. It's not just about the furnishings – it's about privacy, territory, and safety.

More recently, there is the car sharing model, which continues to expand year over year, both in user bases and revenue, surpassing USD 2 billion in value in 2020 and is anticipated to grow at over 20 percent year over year.[7]

The key success factors of the car-by-the-hour model are varied, and represent a more natural transformation than does hot desking. It has proven most popular in cities, where the cost of operating and storing a car have become prohibitive and unnecessary. The ease of reserving, paying for, and unlocking the car have been made far easier through phone-based app technology, and additionally, there has been a significant cultural shift over the past decade with younger consumers not purchasing cars outright at the rate that their parents did.

Significantly, car sharing was not imposed upon people as a forced change; it emerged as an innovation, an improvement over a dated and cumbersome car rental industry, a digital transformation solution whose benefit statement was clear, and which consequently had a very low fear barrier.

It is easy to envision, however, how easily the fear and resistance indicators would climb if any regional or national government mandated car sharing as compulsory. This type of pushback is visible in current policy initiatives such as the phasing out of gas powered vehicles, as many countries and some U.S. states are indeed doing, or attempting to do.

---

[7] Global Market Insights, Car Sharing Market Industry Trends. Retrieved from www.gminsights.com/industry-analysis/carsharing-market

CHAPTER 4   THE FEAR OF CHANGE

But at the end of the day, a major part of the success of car sharing will be that the cars appeared pristine and "unused" for each customer.

Office workers who are facing the concept of hoteling or hot desking for the first time will have similar territorial concerns. These include a sense of a loss of privacy for themselves as well as for their possessions as well as the distaste for occupying a space that has clearly been used by someone else. There will need to be a significant deployment of hotel management skills factored into an office hoteling workspace, including cleanup and hygiene skills assigned either to individual users of the desks or specialist cleaning staff, as the case may be.

Beyond the territoriality and cleanliness issues, there may also be technical challenges around connecting to the office network from a temporary desk, which might be more of a challenge than simply obtaining the office Wi-Fi code or physically connecting to the network. There will be emotional issues as well, as people deal with genuine sentimental attachments to specific desks or locations.

There will also be a sense among employees who have worked at a specific desk for many years that a hot desking floor is not a "real working environment," and who will therefore not take it seriously, at least at first.

There are those who point out that communal desks and work areas help eliminate silos and foster creativity and the exchange of ideas. This is something that has been experimented with for decades – the open concept office environment, paired with a culture that allows and encourages impromptu discussions and the sharing of ideas. This is an ideal working scenario but one that has faced significant resistance, both consciously and unconsciously from the workforce itself.

But there are also people who believe that splitting up groups or zones of workers will do more damage to productivity and morale, since the proximity of people involved in the same department or on the same project allows for focus and collective momentum.

But these are all attitudes carved from a different era, the pre-pandemic era, in which mobile collaboration simply wasn't a thing yet. Hoteling will likely grow to be commonplace. In the same way that commuters seldom get the same seat on the train or bus each day, or do not get to choose which elevator takes them to their floor, or which boardroom is available for a meeting, the idea of a reserved desk-for-the-day has a good chance of becoming a reality, especially for workers who use it just once or twice a week. Like the Roomba and the Alexa, it will eventually become just "a thing."

But in the meantime, the challenge for those who manage the booking for desks in this way will be to either ensure the booking system is equitable, effectively banning someone from placing a year-long reservation on a specific desk, or to factor that very same feature in as a benefit.

Some people may not care which desk they get. They will bring their possessions in with them, lay them out on the desk, and collect them back up at the end of the day, and give it no more thought than they would to which meeting room they are able to book for a meeting.

The challenge will simply be one of managing this new approach to work. It is not a simple lift-and-shift, but will require some degree of expertise and guidance, perhaps pulled from those who have been doing it successfully: airlines, hotels, and car share companies.

The Fear of Losing Identity

Although the idea of working from home is a welcome development for certain employees, for others, not performing their job in a formalized place of work diminishes its legitimacy, and consequently they may feel, the legitimacy of themselves as professionals.

CHAPTER 4   THE FEAR OF CHANGE

Managers, for example, define themselves and their role largely in terms of face-to-face interactions with their team. Many managers believe it is not possible to do this when some or all of the team are working from home, out of sight for much of the time, and seemingly unavailable for a spontaneous chat. This is starting to create crises of trust and of self-confidence among managers. Studies, such as one conducted by Anita Keller, Assistant Professor of Organizational Psychology, University of Groningen (Netherlands), Sharon K. Parker, and Caroline Knight, both of Curtin University (Perth, Australia), published in the *Harvard Business Review* in June 2020, shows that some managers have trouble trusting employees who work from home, and that they also do not believe they have the ability to manage them properly. This is resulting in, in some cases, the use of close monitoring techniques, including spycams and keystroke monitors, along with the reinforcement of an "always on" culture, in which it is expected that employees be visible at their home desks, and be willing to answer messages and texts at pretty much any time of day or evening.[8]

For managers and non-managers alike, identity is defined by presence amongst others. Hairstyle, clothing, cubicle décor, even the food choices people make all serve to define a person, simultaneously distinguishing them as an individual, while reinforcing their connection to a group.

Individual identity is also reinforced through the act of commuting. For years, people have complained about the effort and cost involved in traveling to and from the workplace, but it has also stood as a space within the day that is - or at least can be - a moment of solitude - a patch of *me time* that stands comfortably between work life and home life. Despite the inconveniences of heavy traffic and crowded trains, it forms part of a

---

[8] Keller, Anita, Parker, Sharon, and Knight, Caroline. "Remote Managers Are Having Trust Issues" *Harvard Business Review* July 30, 2020. Retrieved from https://hbr.org/2020/07/remote-managers-are-having-trust-issues Accessed September 2021.

CHAPTER 4   THE FEAR OF CHANGE

self-defining ritual, an opportunity for decompression, ideally out of reach of managers, customers, and the kids. It is much easier to decompress in a train surrounded by strangers than it is at home surrounded by family.

This chapter, then, essentially contains vignettes – encapsulations of fears around software, passwords, workplace, and professional identity. They all share the common root of threatening to dislodge a person from the perceived security of their work, even if on the surface, it simply looks like they are just reacting to a new process. The antidote to this particular toxin will always be facts, knowledge, hands-on experience. In other words, bringing facts up to meet the fear. Because at the root of fear itself is the unknown.

CHAPTER 5

The Fear of the Unknown

The Fear of Gym Class

"Let's go back to high school gym class for a moment." That statement alone should be a trigger of abundant fear for those of us who did not quite grasp the educational or social value of dodgeball.

Imagine you are back in high-school – first-period gym class, out there on the soccer field on a frosty November morning. The gym teacher comes over. You hear one of the two following commands: either "Go out there and give me twelve laps around the field," or "go out there and start running until I blow this whistle." The question is, which of these instructions would you rather follow?[1]

Most people say they would prefer the "twelve laps" command. Why? Because it is finite – it is a known commodity. The reason this is preferable is because it aligns with your instinctive need to know when it will be over. This in turn means your limbic system can work out how much energy it must make available for the run, and how much it can still keep in reserve. That's a big deal for your internal self-preservation system, because its

---

[1] This story was originally published in my time management book, *Cool-Time: A Hands-On Plan for Managing Work and Balancing Time* (Wiley, 2005).

CHAPTER 5   THE FEAR OF THE UNKNOWN

secondary responsibility, after avoiding immediate danger, is to ensure longer-term survival by conserving energy at every opportunity.

You can't do that when you don't know how much you'll need. The fear of the unknown is one of the most powerful fears we have, as it is always hard-coded to avoid danger at every turn.

This means that a 12-lap jogging assignment around the soccer pitch will be treated differently by your body than will an unknown running assignment that just happens to last 12 laps. Stress responses deploy different sets of hormones based on different levels of threat, and this further affects numerous activities in the body ranging from mental concentration to digesting breakfast. A 12-lap assignment is a manageable challenge. An unknown assignment never is.

Now, imagine we change the wording of the "high school gym class" paragraph to a meeting scenario, as follows.

Imagine you are in a meeting, back in the office, at 2:00, in a stuffy boardroom on a dreary November afternoon. The chairperson opens the meeting. You hear one of the two following statements: either "Let's start this meeting so that we can end promptly at 3:00," or "Let's just soldier on with this until we get it all done." The question still is, which of these instructions would you rather follow?

Meetings, whether in boardrooms or online, are still one of the worst time wasters of the entire workday, and much of this has to do with poor or insufficient planning. When a meeting does not take into account the needs of the participants, it becomes a waste. These needs include

- The relevance of the topics
- Physical comforts: room temperature, natural light, comfortable seating
- Engagement and communication
- Timely start, end, and adherence to the agenda
- Strong leadership from the meeting chairperson

Whether the meeting is in-person or online, it is vital that these elements be taken into consideration. When a meeting does not meet these requirements, the fear of the meeting's overall metabolic burden cascades down through the levels of each individual's limbic system, immediately impacting peoples' capacity to concentrate, engage, or even arrive on time.

But here's the thing: when a meeting fails, or is insufficiently productive, the participants tend to receive the blame. In fact, in most cases, the fault lies with the meeting chair – the person who planned and then ran it.

Therefore, when an employee receives an invite to a meeting, it is interpreted by that individual's limbic system as something approaching a threatening event, in terms of its potential for discomfort and boredom, an uncertain duration (even when an end time is posted), paired with the inconvenience of the other work that must be put aside in order to go and attend. This is a particular variant of the fear of the unknown that speaks to the instinctive distaste for anything that is not normal, not stable, and not knowable.

Whereas the fear of change described in the previous chapter focuses largely on moving from a known commodity to a new and unknown one, an activity such as a meeting of uncertain duration is simply an unknown. It is important to remember that the fears described here do not need to be wide-eyed, horror-movie-type fears. They can be instead more subtle but equally disruptive reactions to an unknown situation that trigger the fight-or-flight response. These can still stand in the way of the effective and successful deployment of new digital transformation technologies or techniques.

CHAPTER 5   THE FEAR OF THE UNKNOWN

The Fear of Messages

"You've got mail!" That can't be fear-inducing, can it? Yes, it can. Email is scary on an instinctive level. The arrival of a new message in an inbox of any kind – whether email, SMS on your phone, or new messages in Slack or Teams – becomes a new unknown, and that's bothersome.

New things and newly noticed things are unknown things, and these are quickly pounced on by receptors in the brain. Every time you receive an email or a new message on SMS or a messaging app, regardless of who the sender is and how well you know them, there is an irresistible compulsion to check it out. Whether it's the bold font of a new message in your inbox, or that little red dot on the corner of your phone's messaging app, it's new, and it's urgent in a *must know now* sort of fashion.

This generates fear. Not fear in the "being scared" type of fear, but instead, the instinctive "I need to know what this unknown is. It's in my inbox and I must know what it is" type.

If you have ever walked down a street that you have not visited for a while, you will likely notice if something new has appeared – a new building, a front door that has been painted a new color, maybe some new lawn decorations. They weren't there the last time you were here, but now they are. Similarly, if a friend has changed their hairstyle, you might notice the specific change or you might simply notice something different about them, even if you can't pinpoint what it is.

So that's where the limbic squabble starts. (The Limbic Squabble. Wouldn't that be a great name for a band?) An email arrives. Your cerebral cortex (thinking brain) recognizes it as a message. No big deal. But your instinctive brain says, "Danger! There is an unknown in our midst! I must know what it is!" and this results in the compulsion to want to read it immediately. It can also lead to unthinking, inadvertent clicking on phishing links as the staffers at the website company found out as they teetered on the brink of descending into the dark world of malware, ransomware, and social engineering, as described in Chapter 1.

CHAPTER 5 THE FEAR OF THE UNKNOWN

As innocuous as an email might seem, its presence triggers a smaller version of the fight-or-flight response in the body, just a little less obvious. People generally don't jump up and run away from their computer when an email comes in, but the body still activates many of the same responses internally.

For starters, the sudden awareness of a newly-arrived email (an unknown) elicits a form of tunnel vision and redistribution of blood away from the cerebral cortex that, occurring together, make it difficult to concentrate on the work in front of you. This is followed by an exodus of nutrients from the extremities (including the thinking brain) which happens instantaneously. It's still possible to read and respond to the message, but recovering from this urgency – regaining your train of thought, can take many minutes. This sounds incredibly overdramatic, but it's what happens, and it has been this way since the beginning of the email era.

Every email, text message or other alert that you receive not only costs you the minutes that it takes to read and respond to it, it also costs you the next five to ten minutes which are spent slowly redistributing those nutrients and blood back to the extremities. Due to the unidirectional emergency-only focus of the fight-or-flight reflex, it takes the body much longer to return the nutrients back to the extremities than it did to call them away for action elsewhere.

This means that for the past thirty years, people have been spending most of every working day at a sub-optimal level of mental performance. We are impaired, basically, by an instinct-driven trance and partial mental shutdown caused by an unknown that arrives in the form of an email message.

An analogy of this sub-par mental performance is that of trying to run while waist-deep in a swimming pool. The mental friction of interruption by an unknown is just as palpable as swimming pool water, and recovering from fight-or-flight every single time a message comes in, is just as challenging.

CHAPTER 5   THE FEAR OF THE UNKNOWN

Some might find such a statement rather overdramatic when it comes to email, because few people actually *feel* fear at the thought of receiving an email message, in fact, they are more likely to feel curiosity or a certain Pavlovian happiness – a form of mild excitement, but again, that's because not all fear is "fear" fear. Much of it is purely an instinctive self-preservation response.

The reality is that most people will admit that when an email arrives, they will stop what they're doing in order to read it. Think about that – they stop what they're doing in order to read something that may or may not be worth the interruption. A train of thought, derailed. Five minutes or more mentally running in waist-deep water until they get back to the level of concentration they were at before the email signaled its arrival. Then they wonder where the day went.

Messages hyper-prioritize themselves in peoples' minds, assigning themselves top-level importance without any input from the conscious self. This happens all day, every day, and relatively few people have been able to corral email into a place of control and balance.

From a digital transformation perspective, email is kind of yesterday's news, but with new messaging options, there is now an even greater amount of messaging, leading to an even greater threat to people's concentration.

Without a clear understanding of just how much time and energy are wasted when people fall for candid reactionism there will always be a profound and unavoidable danger that these distractions will continue to slow people down and continue to overtake their day. The answer is to become an expert in managing expectations.

Behind every message, regardless of the channel it travels, there's a human being. This person has been conditioned to expect an instant response to each of their messages and will react when this doesn't occur. We have all been this person and we also have all had to deal with this person. It's completely natural. The speed of expectation matches the speed of the media now being used.

CHAPTER 5   THE FEAR OF THE UNKNOWN

Two centuries ago, this speed of media might have been measured in days, in line with the speed of postal delivery. A person would sit down, pen a letter, hand it to the postal delivery person and wait for it to be delivered and for a reply to come back along the same route. For correspondence between, say, Europe and North America or the Far East in the Middle Ages, this would have been a months-long undertaking.

A century ago, telegraphs, telegrams, and telephones ushered us into the era of instantaneous conversation, and with it came a reprioritization of instant communication. Nothing, it seemed, was more important than getting through to someone. It has been suggested that part of the reason for the tragedy of the Titanic's sinking was that the radio room was so preoccupied with receiving and sending radio messages for their First Class passengers that they actually ignored radio traffic from other ships in the area – messages that contained warnings about the iceberg field.

It has become an obsession and an expectation. If a sender's message is not replied to within the time frame defined by the sender as appropriate, the sender might send a second message to the effect of "did you get my first message?" Or they might also try another channel.

Is this fear? Yes. There's fear on both ends. The recipient must deal with a new unknown and the instinctive urgency that it brings. The sender feels a fear – it could be argued that this is simply impatience, just part of a busy personality, but beneath this impatience is still a fear of the unknown. When will I get a reply?

As soon as a message is sent, we, as senders, immediately crave a response. This particular fear is not just about the individual message. It's a special blend. There's the fear of losing control of specific projects or of the day itself. There's the fear of not being suitably recognized as a colleague or customer. And then there is simply the fear of just not knowing. It's a hole in the fabric of the mental construct of the day – an unresolved transaction that demands reciprocity. It is an incomplete event that distracts the mind and causes instinctive mental stress.

CHAPTER 5 THE FEAR OF THE UNKNOWN

So the fear literally hits us coming and going, sometimes as the sender of a message and sometimes as the recipient. In the pre-pandemic office space era, one of the most common complaints people had about how hard it was to get things done, was all about constant interruptions, mostly from email, as well as from teams-based platforms like Slack. Then, when everyone was sent home due to the pandemic, the dream of being able to work undisturbed from a home office was quickly crushed, as messages continued to arrive at all hours.

In fact, many work-from-home employees discovered that the amount of messaging actually increased and spread across a much longer day, from early morning to late at night.

The solution to the problem of out-of-control messaging lies in proactive expectation management. This means letting people know when they can expect a reply. No one should be expected to be available every minute of the day, but if senders do not know what the parameters are, they can only operate from their current frame of reference, which is usually one of immediacy.

Proactive expectation management can take many forms, but ideally, it should give senders a genuine understanding and sense of comfort that they will hear back from you within an acceptable time frame, such as within two hours or by the end of the day, depending on the nature of your job. By giving senders an anticipated "time until response," you deliver a *known*, which is much more comforting to them than is an unknown.

"Wait!" people will say. Isn't it rude to tell email senders – your colleagues, customers, or managers – that you will get back to them in a couple of hours? The truth is, everything depends on you, your job, and what you hope to get out of each day. But the truth also is that every time you stop to accommodate an inbound message, the cost is much more than just the two minutes or so that the response will take.

First, there's the recovery time described earlier in this chapter. There is also your reputation. What we mistakenly identify as "great customer service" by constantly replying to messages within seconds has the unfortunate side effect of steadily conditioning these senders to always expect instant responses at any time of day or night. This becomes a millstone around your neck and permanently robs you of your control over your time.

Not only this, but it sets up an impossible scenario for you to maintain. As I describe in more detail in Chapter 10, negative memories last longer and more intensely than do positive ones. This means that even if you always respond to messages within seconds of receipt, the one time that you cannot, you effectively break your implicit promise to your senders, and because of its negative impact – disappointment or frustration – this is what will be remembered and will become a ding on your personal relationship credit rating.

The fear of messaging should be balanced by facts: this includes choosing times to review the messages – a time of your choosing, and ideally after a suitable amount of focused work has been completed. It also includes informing the senders and managing their expectations with facts – giving them an approximate timeline by which they can expect satisfaction.

Expectation management might appear as a form of bad news and therefore something to be feared in its own right. "I'm sorry, I can't respond to you now, but I can reply in two hours." This always seems to be such a harsh thing to say. But as I have already described, humans are much better at dealing with knowns than unknowns, and this is why bad news is better than no news. Knowing that your gym class running assignment is exactly twelve laps is much better than facing an unknown number of laps around a soccer field. Being asked to wait ten minutes is better than being simply made to wait with no timeline given. A tangible amount of expectation management is not bad news at all. It's just news. Expectation management is a skill. It is a critical soft skill that, when maintained consistently, will empower individuals to finally gain control of their time, while proactively managing the pace and increasing amount of communications that digital transformation will continue to deliver.

CHAPTER 5   THE FEAR OF THE UNKNOWN

The Fear of Silence

There was a time, just a couple of decades ago, when an elevator was a place where people stood without speaking, evenly spaced throughout the car, all facing forward. They stood, as if frozen in time, each alone with their thoughts, enjoying a temporary respite from the busy-ness of the office they just left. After a minute or two of this Zen-like presence, they completed their descent to the ground, the doors opened, and each person rushed out to join the momentum of the other people on the ground floor. They even had music to make the experience even more comfortable. It became a genre unto itself: elevator music.

Then one day, someone thought, "why not digitally transform the elevator experience? Why not put a video screen in that elevator car? In fact, why not put one in *every* elevator car?" This changed the dynamic of the elevator completely. Now, everyone felt compelled to stare at the screen. It had news and entertainment headlines in there, a stock ticker, the weather report – it was difficult not to pay attention, because that's what eyes and ears do naturally and without prompting.

One of the most successful companies in the elevator media business is a company named Captivate, and I have to say that is one of the best company names I have ever heard of, quite simply because it says everything that needs to be said, in one word.

In the time since digital media took over the elevators of the world, it has become almost impossible to find a public place that does not have a screen – a visual siren that pulls your attention toward it and extinguishes yet another moment of private thinking time. If you go to a restaurant or bar, there will be TVs showing sports. If you go to a gym, there will be TVs on every wall and on every machine. They are in taxis, on buses, and on walls. It's a *Blade Runner*-type world where visual stimulation is everywhere, and there is nowhere neutral to look, or for the mind to rest.

In fact, it seems people don't actually want somewhere neutral to look. There is a palpable fear of silence, of stopping, because it, too, reveals several unknowns, including not knowing what to do, not knowing what to say, and not knowing how to fill the time. When people find themselves paused for a moment, the first reaction is often to pull out the phone and check for new messages. If there aren't any messages, then we start doomscrolling Twitter or Instagram. For most people, their phone is the last thing they look at before falling asleep, the first thing they look at in the morning, and the only thing they look at when there's briefly nothing to do.

As convenient as it may be to have a constant, unending flow of information, it generates a need for further stimulus, a craving for that same flow. It seems to keep us alive the same way that sharks need to keep swimming forward to avoid drowning. Its constant presence has consequently generated in us a fear of silence, as if every second not filled with it is a second wasted.

The mere idea of putting the phone away and staring instead at a tree or at the sky, seems alien, weird, and unproductive even though that assessment is incorrect on all three counts. Staring at a tree or at the sky is actually a highly effective technique for solving problems, prioritizing, and centering oneself.[2] The mind actually needs time to reflect in upon itself, to process thoughts and to rebalance the body. But this has been conditioned out of us to the point that silence or stillness simply feels wrong. Having gaps on the calendar also seems wrong. Eating lunch without looking at a screen seems wrong. Pauses in conversation seem wrong.

The fear of silence rushes people into a state of permanent mediocrity by not allowing time for creativity to happen. The mind, for all its brilliance, still needs time to process.

Handwriting a letter, for example, seems archaic and a waste of time. Many of us cannot bear to contemplate life in longhand, cursive script. This is sad, because handwriting has been shown to align more closely

---

[2] This is a topic I cover in much more detail in my second book, entitled *Cool Down: Getting Further by Going Slower* (Wiley, 2008).

CHAPTER 5 THE FEAR OF THE UNKNOWN

with higher-level thinking patterns. This has to do with the way the mind thinks things through, which coincides better with both the timing and the fluid, physical movements of handwriting.

But there's also the fear of lost time. What do you do with handwritten material anyway? Store it in a binder? Or put it in an envelope and mail it old-school? Most people could not stand the thought that a message written four hours ago is still sitting in a bin in the mailroom or in a mailbox on the street corner. Are the days of handwriting over and done with forever?

Certainly not.

There are digital devices that bridge the chasm between the benefits of handwriting (aligning with the mind's preferred mode and speed of processing thoughts and ideas) and the pace of modern business. Devices like the Remarkable and the iPad Pro are digital handwriting pads that replicate the feel and positive mental focus of the handwriting experience, but which then converts that writing into digital text in order to reinsert it into the world of email and messaging.

The fear of silence strips people of the capacity for thought, for reflection and for balance. I would attribute at least some of the vitriol and hatred that has emerged on our streets in recent years to the fact that people do not use time to think things through, or even talk them out, before acting on their impulses and their audience-of-one isolation.

But here's a more simple, back-to-the-office example:

You're attending a meeting. As the meeting draws toward its adjournment, the chairperson asks, "does anyone have any questions?" and then looks quickly to the right and then to the left, and mere seconds later, concludes with, "OK, then we'll move on."

In this scenario, no real time was allowed for questions. The chairperson's fear of silence broke through. Possibly this fear was brought forth out of the fear of losing control of the room if too many questions were asked. It might also be a fear of the questions themselves.

CHAPTER 5   THE FEAR OF THE UNKNOWN

"What if I don't know the answer?" Or perhaps it was simply the fear of silence itself – a sense that the meeting would appear flawed or incomplete if there was a gap. It seemed best to close that hole of uncertainty and move on.

But actually it's best to not do that.

People need time to think, and to formulate a question and then to muster the courage or energy to raise their hand and speak up. Most people are not Type-A personalities. They need time to process and to act, and this is even more the case for video meetings. The chairperson could have added enormous color, depth, and dimension to the meeting simply by pausing long enough to count silently to six after asking the question, "does anyone have any questions?"

Six seconds. It feels like an eternity to the person who must stand there motionless and quiet for that entire time. But this is the amount of time needed to give other participants the opportunity to formulate a question and bring it forward. By doing this, by resorting to silence for six seconds, the chairperson would have brought significantly more value to the entire event.

But how hard it is to remain quiet for six seconds!

The fear of silence is what robs meetings of quality, and it does the same to conversations. It forces people to talk more, just to fill the air with words, out of the fear that the specter of awkward silence falls upon them.

But in an ironic twist, a cardinal rule of making great conversation is to talk less and listen more. In so many incidences, the individual you are talking to will reveal more – more depth, more context, more information, and more value, if they are just given the time to speak up and speak first.

Meetings have been around much longer than digital transformation has. But the pace and speed of the new normal more or less guarantees that the fear of silence will be further magnified. Just imagine, pausing to let your eyes and mind rest for a moment, only to have them make eye contact with the boss, whose silent or verbal question will be, "why aren't you working?" This, once again, is how a simple fear such as that of a brief moment of silence can plunge deep down to where it becomes that ultimate mantra – "If I screw this up, I'm going to lose my job."

CHAPTER 5   THE FEAR OF THE UNKNOWN

Then there's the meeting duration itself. Assuming that a meeting has to happen at all, the single greatest influencer for getting people to (a) attend and (b) participate and remain engaged is to give them that vital known commodity: How long will this meeting last, or in other words, when will it be over? This is the meeting-room equivalent of the 12 laps around the soccer field, and it is the most important part of a meeting procedure. The agenda, which most people would argue is the most important part is already a *fait accompli*. If there's a meeting, then there has to be a reason for that meeting, and that must have already been determined. So it is now spoken for, and the most important success factor remains, removing the unknown element of its duration.

This applies equally to in-person meetings and to online meetings. Simply sending out an automated meeting invite as an ICS or Google Calendar entry, will not guarantee full attendance or engagement unless the meeting end is clearly identified, is as short as possible, and most importantly, adhered to.

Digital transformation means more technologies competing for peoples' attention and seeking to fill every second or even fraction of a second with new stimulations. When you read an article or a blog post online, for example, there is often a small note somewhere at the top that tells the reader how long it will take to read it. This note might even be accompanied by a moving status bar that shows the reader how far along they have come and how little there is left to go. That's how far *we* have come in begging for peoples' attention.

The digital transformation of life carries with it an increasing sense of urgency that has made us conscious of every second. That time display countdown bar at the top of a blog post offers that much-needed known commodity, seeking to eliminate from the reader's mind their fear of how much time this article might take out of their life. Similarly, it is well known that the most successful podcasts and YouTube videos are ones that can be played back at double speed or more. Even if you personally have never felt the need to listen to a podcast at double speed, many of those around you have. This same fear of the unknown, of not knowing how long this article will take to complete, is the same one that will influence people's decision to either accept a meeting invite, or later claim that it "must have gone straight to my spam filter."

In an age where life is measured in seconds, people now turn to book-summarizing apps to deliver a summary of a book so as to not have to read the entire thing. As mentioned above, they will abandon shopping carts if they have to re-enter information such as passwords. Even during the previous digital transformation, when email was first released to the world, a cardinal rule of successful email composition was to ensure that the opening "Dear…" and the writer's closing signature and everything in between were all visible in one screen without the reader having to scroll.

We have been conditioned to doomscroll through life, moving from one message to the next in the hope of finding some sort of satisfaction, reinforcing a gambler's compulsion of endlessly counting on the next bet as the big one. The goal, as always, is to avoid perhaps the greatest fear of all: losing your job.

CHAPTER 6

The Fear of Losing Your Job

In February 2021, a water treatment plant in Florida was vandalized remotely by an individual who attempted to adjust the levels of sodium hydroxide in the water from 100 parts per million to 11,100 parts per million, which means it became potentially extremely dangerous to humans.

The attack was made possible because the plant was chronically underfunded, as is much of the infrastructure in the United States and other countries, and the computers that ran the plant, watched water levels, and maintained its safety, used a well-known remote access application which made it easier for technicians to check on things, diagnose problems, and issue commands within the plant's system, without having to incur the expense in time and money to drive there.

Additionally, to make it easier for whoever was on shift at any given time, the employees all used a shared password on this application.

CHAPTER 6   THE FEAR OF LOSING YOUR JOB

And…the computers were running 32-bit versions of the Windows 7 operating system, which had reached end-of-life (thus no longer supported for security patches) a year earlier.[1,2]

These employees were not bad people. They were just trying to do their jobs. The fact that the plant was using non-secure technology and shared passwords to save time and money was just part of what had to be done, and if someone were to question it, it would likely only have caused problems for that individual.

One of the most profound fears of all, for most people, is the fear of losing their job. This fear has kept millions of people chained to work they dislike, too busy to look around to see, or even contemplate what else might be available. It is a singularly powerful fear. Some people are lucky enough to find jobs that match their goals and aspirations. Others fall into interesting careers by happenstance, while others stay with something that is OK for the time being – a time being that stretches into years and sometimes, decades.

As we work our jobs and we get used to the regular paycheck, it becomes awfully easy to fall into the trap of "continually escalating subsistence living." We tend to match our spending habits against – and then beyond – our take-home pay, thanks to easy credit and a culture of immediate gratification. The more we make, the more we spend, and the more we want: a car, a house, vacations, hobbies, and more. As the job starts to pay more, so our personal style of living starts to cost more.

---

[1] Lakshmanan, Ravie. "Poor Password Security Led to Recent Water Treatment Facility Hack." *The Hacker News* February 11, 2021. Retrieved from https://thehackernews.com/2021/02/poor-password-security-lead-to-recent.html Accessed September 2021 and January 2022.

[2] Hanson, Matt. "Windows 7 End of Life: everything you need to know about the death of Windows 7." *TechRadar.* August 2020. Retrieved from www.techradar.com/news/windows-7-end-of-life-everything-you-need-to-know-about-the-death-of-windows-7 Accessed December 2021.

CHAPTER 6   THE FEAR OF LOSING YOUR JOB

The J-O-B Syndrome

Some cynics suggest that the word *job* is actually an acronym for "Just Over Broke." Most of us are not taught much about financial literacy in school, and even when such classes are offered, the trappings of consumption and the normalization of debt are all incredibly seductive. We are not encouraged to save. We become "house poor." We are encouraged to spend, and then to borrow to spend more, and once we fall into the trap of debt and interest payments, we learn just how difficult it is to get back to a debt free, financially balanced life.

Such a situation makes it exceedingly hard for any one of us to feel truly secure. "I can't afford to lose my job," we will say, "I have bills to pay…a mortgage or rent." The fear of losing a current job, in which most, if not all, of the bi-weekly paycheck is already spoken for, is like a death – the death of livelihood and of living.

This is in large part why we feel obliged to answer those work emails and text messages late into the evening, and why we reluctantly say *yes* to back-to-back meeting invites. We do these things not because we want to, but because we are afraid of what might happen if we say "no." There is an all too real fear of rocking the boat and then getting pushed overboard.

This type of fear makes it difficult for many people to embrace change – such as that brought about by digital transformation – with enthusiasm and commitment. The self-protective instinct will always ask, "how will this hurt me? What do I stand to lose?" For example, a new technology might be difficult to learn. It might open up the possibility of making career-endangering mistakes. Or it might make a person completely redundant. These are not comforting thoughts for employees whose primary mission already is to make it through another day without getting fired.

"That's not me," you might say. But there's an easy way to find out if that statement is true or not, and that's whether you are able to turn your email and messaging completely off at the end of your workday, and not look at it again until the next day starts.

When I give that challenge to people, they will reply with, "yes, but what if there's an emergency?" Fair question. It used to be, in the pre-email era, that if something was truly that urgent, you would get a phone call at home. That same rule can still apply. If something is that urgent, the boss, or whoever is in charge, can call you "at home," that is to say, when you're off the clock and not at work. You can even enter their number into your "Do Not Disturb" exceptions list to ensure it gets through. If you do not want to do this, and are instead willing to receive messages even as your head hits the pillow, ask yourself why.

Most ransomware attacks, for example, are the result of overly busy people who do not have the time to think critically about the validity of each email coming in, and who may fear repercussions if they ponder too long over a message that appears to be a missed delivery from FedEx, an invoice from a supplier, or an important message from the boss. Or they may simply have so much on their plate, all they can feel is the pressure to click on the links and move on. So they click on the link, because getting through the day without getting fired is more important.

Blame Steve

I have taught a great many professional development classes in my time, many of them introducing new skills that result in changes being deployed within the work culture. Some were as simple as how to run meetings more efficiently, or how to deliver feedback. But one of the problems that happens when individuals are sent to learn new skills is that they must then go back to their workplaces and actually use them. They must also tell others about these new skills. Like a fish trying to swim upstream, they must seek to change the culture, the *status quo*, all by themselves, and that's an act that can cause great fear. It's a conundrum: being sent to learn a skill, but being afraid to use it.

I used to conclude my sessions by showing the participants different ways to introduce their new skills to their manager, co-workers, and clients, knowing that this would be their toughest test. Many were afraid to do so. Introducing change, even if they had been sent by their employer to learn that new skill in the first place, posed a direct threat to their job stability. There is that immediate fear that if you show your colleagues or manager a better way to run meetings, or a new approach to password hygiene, for example, the response will be, "who showed you that?" or something similar, which is not an ideal embrace of the change.

To neutralize the potential conflict that might come from such an introduction, I would invite the participants to use the "Blame Steve" approach. This quite simply meant they could blame me, if they wanted, since I was the one who taught them the new habit. This made *me* the agent of change rather than them. If this change in workplace habits appeared too threatening to the norm, then the student could at least eliminate their own culpability by stating that "this Steve guy taught me this." It would allow the change to be presented while neutralizing the threat to others implicit in its introduction. It shouldn't have to be that way, but it very often is. That's the kind of fear people live with.

Improperly managed digital transformation promises to further compound the problem by adding new technologies while not removing the implied threat of job loss or punishment that comes with them. People are simply in a hurry to get their tasks done, and they have little time or mental energy available to deploy skills such as critical thinking about how to best make these technologies work.

CHAPTER 6   THE FEAR OF LOSING YOUR JOB

The Zoom Call Gaffe

Around September 2021, a story ran in *Bloomberg* that helped confirm and reinforce people's digital transformation fears. The headline read, *"Zoom-Call Gaffes Led to Someone Getting Axed, 1 in 4 Bosses Say."* The article discussed information released by a workplace consulting firm that had surveyed 200 managers at large companies and had found that a quarter of them had already fired someone, and most had disciplined employees, for committing any of the following four video chat offenses: joining a call late, having a bad Internet connection, accidentally sharing sensitive information, and not knowing when to go on mute.[3] Some people laughed at this story, others did not. As ridiculous as it was, it is a timeless confirmation of that fundamental fear: "If I screw this up, I'll get fired."

Only one of these four offences actually holds a modicum of discipline-worthy offense, and that is accidentally sharing sensitive information. This will be, in almost all cases, a result of inadequate training, and not conscious sabotage or irresponsibility.

Screen sharing might not appear as an overly difficult task, but as a relatively new digital transformation-related skill, it still requires hands-on training to raise an employee's ability to a level that doesn't occupy their full awareness or cause instant, temporary mental paralysis. It's not that the screen-sharing buttons are the problem – it's being aware of the peripheral elements of screen sharing, such as having other tabs open, tabs that might reveal confidential information – that can be accidentally overlooked during a live video chat conversation, in which people are already dealing with the cognitive overload that it delivers. If a person

---

[3] Boyle, Matthew. "Zoom-Call Gaffes Led to Someone Getting Axed, 1 in 4 Bosses Say." *Bloomberg* August 31, 2021. Retrieved from www.bloomberg.com/news/articles/2021-08-31/zoom-call-gaffes-led-to-someone-getting-axed-1-in-4-bosses-say Accessed October 2021.

working in healthcare activates a screenshare and inadvertently shows a tab containing a specific patient's confidential files, that's a huge transgression, and could indeed cost that person their job.

But most organizations do not hold courses in video chat screen sharing. It's a quirky task that seems to carry no threat, and seems too simple to need a course. It doesn't look like a serious problem, so it is not treated as one. The place most people will learn it is on the job, in front of a live audience, which makes it much easier for the mistake to be made. (This by the way, would be a perfect candidate for a micro course, as would "remote access software password management for water plant technicians." Micro courses are described in more detail in Chapter 15).

One day soon, this simple act of screen sharing will be as easy for most people as sending email currently is. But there will always be the next new technology or technique that people will struggle with, and this, too, will come with the millstone of knowing that it could cause a screw-up that embarrasses the company, and which becomes a cause for dismissal. And if you think this is an overstatement – making big mistakes out of simple technologies – think back to the last time that you, or someone you know, accidentally hit the "Reply All" button in their email. It likely wasn't only during your first few days of using email software, but after many years of daily use.

Fear of Face Time Bias

Long before the pandemic hit, the future-of-work specialists were already talking about the opportunities for remote and hybrid work for knowledge workers, and naturally the focus was primarily on collaboration. Not much was said about the fear people might feel about being possibly considered as second class citizens due to not being physically at the office. Op-eds and articles appeared in places like the *Wall Street Journal* and the *New York Times*, suggesting that opportunities for promotion or for even keeping your job, diminished for those who were no longer visible in the main office.

CHAPTER 6 THE FEAR OF LOSING YOUR JOB

Kimberly Elsbach, professor of management at University of California, Davis, was quoted on CNN Business in January 2019, saying, "offices where some of the employees telecommute and others work in the office are perfect environments for face-time bias.... There is this unconscious perception of people who are seen around the office during regular working hours and outside of regular hours as dedicated, reliable, committed, dependable...[while] people who aren't around as much, who are just not as visible, are scored lower on those kinds of traits."[4]

In 2021, while many companies were contemplating deploying their return-to-work or hybrid policies, Google, Microsoft, Twitter, and Facebook all suggested that employees who choose to work from home should receive proportionally less pay than those who commute, especially if they live in less-expensive neighborhoods.[5] They said this had more to do with the relative costs of rent and travel, but between the lines, it suggested to every employee that the value of a worker is seen not so much in the product that they produce, as in the fact that they should be physically present and accounted for.

These return to work deadlines came and went as 2021 gave way to 2022, but it's difficult to erase the implications of this "less-pay" policy. No matter what the official line became, the message of labeling work-from-home employees as second class citizens, as stated by any company, not just tech giants, still resonated within those words.

Since the first Industrial Revolution, and especially since the development of the factory mindset, the interrelationship between

---

[4] Carpenter, Julia. "The downside of working from home" *CNN Business.* January 24, 2019. Retrieved from www.cnn.com/2019/01/24/success/remote-worker-bias/index.html Accessed September 2021.

[5] No author. "Google may cut pay of staff who work from home." BBC News. Retrieved from www.bbc.com/news/business-58171716 Accessed September 2021.

CHAPTER 6   THE FEAR OF LOSING YOUR JOB

machines, workers, and output has been relentlessly studied, with a bias toward defining it as something that happens in a dedicated space – a factory or an office building – where people must travel to convene, to produce, and to be visible to management.

As productivity expert Jack Skeels writes about this first Industrial Revolution:

To stay competitive and to pay their investors back, manufacturers needed their machines to run at the fastest speed possible. The faster the factory ran, the greater the profits, and ideally, the lower the costs. Likewise, workers who could feed the machines faster added less cost to the product. So, what was needed was a way to manage workers to make them work as quickly as possible, and as fast as the machines. [...] The term managing now meant the supervision of the workers.[6]

Since that time, there has been a gradual disenfranchisement of the artisanal class – the individual who bakes bread, makes shoes, or even works freelance. Throughout the twentieth century, it was replaced by the legitimacy of the institution – working for the big company, *getting a real job*.

Consumers, too, actively participate in the disenfranchisement of the artisanal class as can best be seen in the preference for big box and franchised stores over local small businesses. We flock to the comfortable familiarity of the modern shopping center, anchored by a retail giant such as Walmart or Target and surrounded by franchised businesses of every stripe – pet stores, clothing, hair salons, and fast food – all recognized brand names owned by a handful of multinationals. We feel that we go to them for lower prices and better selection, but there's also the comfort of the familiar, which is the polar opposite of the risk and variability that a small independent store may pose.

---

[6] Skeels, Jack. *The Art (and Heart) of Management*. Publication date scheduled for 2023.

CHAPTER 6   THE FEAR OF LOSING YOUR JOB

As digital transformation continues to move into the workplace, employees will fear becoming second class for all the reasons put forward in this book, such as looking stupid as they struggle with new technologies, not being able to keep pace with a changing work scenario, and having the audacity to choose to work somewhere other than the office.

If you can't trust your employees to work from home, then you have hired the wrong people. If you need to patrol the hallways to make sure your people are working, you have chosen the wrong century. When an employee fails a phishing test, it is not the employee who is at fault, it's the way the security training has been set up – one that places far too much of a burden on the end user. When meetings get boring, or when people feel unmotivated, it is far more likely that there is something wrong with the system – the way that meetings and work are designed – than an actual problem with the employees.

But regardless, the fear of becoming a second class citizen continues to be bolstered by the fact that it gives the sense of being one step closer to unemployment.

Taking Your Keys Away

Let's look at an analogy from outside the digital workplace for some perspective. There is a public service announcement (PSA) that appears on TV regularly in the market where I live, that comes from an organization dedicated to eliminating impaired driving. This is an organization that I am very much a supporter of, which is why this particular PSA gives me some trouble. The TV spot talks directly to serving staff – the people who work in bars and restaurants – telling them it's both OK and correct to take on the responsibility to deny an impaired person another drink and to take away that person's car keys if possible. In fact, in many places, it's the law.

CHAPTER 6   THE FEAR OF LOSING YOUR JOB

This imposes an enormous burden on the least powerful person in that business – the server – the person who moves drinks and meals for minimum wage or less, relying on tips to try and make a living, while often suffering verbal and physical harassment from customers. This employee has absolutely no authority whatsoever when it comes to laying down the law to an inebriated customer.

Although the anti-impaired organization's motivations are correct – stopping drunk people from getting behind the wheel – in my opinion, it places the burden on the wrong group. This PSA should be directed at the managers or corporate owners of establishments, showing that it is their responsibility to take on the task of intervening with an impaired customer. A multinational beer company makes more profit off each glass poured than the server does. Alternatively, the spots could still be directed at the serving staff, telling them instead to call the manager every time there is a confrontation of this sort, and advocating for job protection when they do.

It is unfair to assume that a powerless employee, who lives and works just one complaint away from being fired, would have the incentive to enter into an argument with a customer that is rife with legal liability, to say nothing of the potential for physical reprisal from an aggravated drunk.

In my opinion, this PSA places the impetus for protection in the wrong place, even though I agree with the organization's mission and support it fully. This is an approach that is also sadly typical of many companies' cybersecurity protection strategies. It is well-known that humans are the weak link in cyberdefense, with the most consistently successful techniques like phishing, social engineering, business email compromise, and weak passwords pointing directly back to the human operator. Yet these same people are given the burden of cybersecurity without the power to act upon it. The repeated failings of phishing tests, even by CISOs themselves, show that digital transformation must never be solely about technology; it must also usher in a transformation around thinking, problem solving, time management, and prioritization that are wholly non-traditional.

CHAPTER 6   THE FEAR OF LOSING YOUR JOB

> *I hate the 'blame the user' model of phishing tests. Phishing tests are to inform you about how bad your email infrastructure actually is. The user is just one piece of it.*
>
> —Andy Ellis[7]

The Distributed Team vs. the Remote Team

The removal of the second class citizen status obviously requires a changed mindset and a revised definition of what an employee is, with greater attention given to achievement rather than attendance. This type of mind shift was not really conceivable just ten years ago, when anyone who worked as part of a team had no choice but to physically go and congregate at the workplace. But things are very different now. Even the words we use count, which is why it will become vital to distinguish between *remote* and *distributed* when it comes to understanding the physical, mental, and social spaces that teams occupy.

> *When everyone is remote, no one is remote.*
>
> —Alberto Silveira

In his book, *Building and Managing High-Performance Distributed Teams*, tech sector executive Alberto Silveira states that team members who work in places other than the central office can easily be brought on board as members of a cohesive crew. It all comes down to building a management model that recognizes the value and potential of doing so. A distributed team, in his definition, is one where "everyone is remote" and there is no central office or boardroom to patch into. "When everyone

---

[7] Ellis, Andy. Quoted on the *CISO Vendor Relationship Podcast*, August 17, 2021. Retrieved from https://cisoseries.com/we-shame-others-because-were-so-right-about-everything/ Accessed September 2021.

CHAPTER 6   THE FEAR OF LOSING YOUR JOB

is remote, no one is remote," he says, and this allows for significant improvements in cross-team communication and collaboration.[8]

Typically, when meetings are held in a boardroom, and someone calls in via teleconference or video chat, they remain an outsider. They are unable to fully interact with the participants in the room, especially dealing with all-important body language. They might be unable to see all of the visual aids such as PowerPoint and whiteboards, even with screenshare, and most of all, they are unable to fully embrace the momentum and chemistry of an in-person group meeting. People who dial in to a meeting, for which the rest of the participants are together in one space, is truly *remote*.

In a distributed team, everybody dials in from somewhere else. There is no central group. This is precisely what we all experienced during the pandemic – the infamous video chat call. Yes, as detailed in Chapter 2, it didn't all go swimmingly, and we discovered a great deal about how we as humans process information on screen, including seeing ourselves on camera. But we could label that as "Video Chat 1.0," a first full field trial of a technology using average people as the test group. There was much that was learned that will make subsequent iterations better.

The distributed team model allows for solidarity through a common platform, one that can be enhanced to replicate physical togetherness through shared backgrounds and other immersive techniques that reinforce equality and inclusion along with clear communication and collaboration, while eliminating the alienating feeling of *Zoom Gloom*, a term, it must be said, that applies to video chats of any brand.[9]

This, much like the *Blame Steve* concept, requires full endorsement from management, which, in turn, requires that management becomes comfortable with the idea of allowing employees to work from anywhere,

---

[8] Silveira, Alberto. *Building and Managing High Performance Teams – Navigating the Future of Work*. New York. Apress, 2021.
[9] My favorite virtual meeting spaces currently are toucan.events and KosyOffice. This is not a paid endorsement. I just think they work well.

demonstrating trust in those employees, and recognizing this as yet another new and permanent development in the way business is conducted.

The Great Resignation: When Work Is Not Worth It

What will the fear of losing your job do to the workforce? It is likely most people will return to whatever their job demands. It is a job, after all. But many others may have other, better ideas, as was demonstrated in the Great Resignation that started in 2021.

The Great Resignation is a term coined by Dr. Anthony Klotz of Texas A&M University and refers primarily to the skills shortage in the cybersecurity industry. Throughout 2021, the number of people quitting their jobs in the U.S. reached a peak of 4.3 million in August, after increasing throughout the year. According to Dr. Klotz, "plenty of [these] employees don't really want to resign. If their company would let them keep working from home or do fewer hours, they would stay."[10]

In a study I helped produce for the cloud security certification company (ISC)² in 2021, the overall sentiment from security practitioners worldwide who were interviewed for the paper is that the skills shortage was mostly based on the catch-22 of requiring experience and extensive certification before being considered for even the most entry-level of security positions, paired with a tangible communication gulf between IT and senior management. In fact, in too many IT situations, there is just no

---

[10] Cohen, Arianne. "How to Quit Your Job in the Great Post-Pandemic Resignation Boom." *Bloomberg Businessweek*. May 10, 2021. Retrieved from www.bloomberg.com/news/articles/2021-05-10/quit-your-job-how-to-resign-after-covid-pandemic Accessed September 2021.

CHAPTER 6 THE FEAR OF LOSING YOUR JOB

one to listen to them or even give them a chance to do what is necessary in many types of jobs – get hired first, and *then* learn what needs to be done.[11]

> *Hiring is more than the list of certifications or the list of languages that you can speak or write or program in. We've got to think differently about the job.*
>
> —Tony Sager, SVP, Chief Evangelist, Center for Internet Security[12]

> *This is not a talent problem. This is a hiring problem. And it's really a misunderstanding of how to hire into an industry like this that is under constant rapid change.*
>
> —Geoff Belknap, CISO, LinkedIn[13]

The Great Resignation was not simply about comfort or the prestige of being a digital nomad. For many, the decision was made out of necessity: ranging from the need to escape a toxic workplace through to the need to care for family members (elderly parents or young children) because the cost of care for either had become prohibitive, making the job in its current form simply not worth it. There are many other reasons that could be added to this list of resignations, but the point remains, more people than ever are being driven to confront the fear of losing their job by actually, voluntarily quitting.

Technology has made it more possible than ever to make that leap, but the question remains, what kinds of fears are so large as to override that of losing a job? Given the increasing numbers of people who continue to do

---

[11] (ISC)². *Cloud Adoption and the Skills Shortage*. Retrieved from www.isc2.org/landing/cloud-adoption-and-the-skills-shortage Accessed December 2021.

[12] Sager, Tony. Quoted in the podcast, "Why is Security Recruiting So Broken?" part of the Defense In Depth series from CISOSeries.com Aired on October 21, 2021. Retrieved from https://cisoseries.com/defense-in-depth-why-is-security-recruiting-so-broken/ Accessed January 2022.

[13] Belknap, Geoff. Ibid.

CHAPTER 6   THE FEAR OF LOSING YOUR JOB

this, it is worth repeating observations from earlier in this book. When a meeting fails, it is often the fault of the meeting and the meeting planner, not the participants. When a phishing test fails, it is most often the fault of the training, not the individual. So, too, when a job fails, in that a person is driven out of it in despair, it is most often the job or the manager that has failed, not the employee. Hence the old expression that most people don't actually quit their jobs, they quit their managers. Or to update the expression some, "it's not that people don't want to work, it's just that they don't want to work *here*."

What Can Employees Do to Handle This?

Given that the fear of losing one's job is one of the biggest fears that people live with, and given that the fundamental takeaway from this book is that fear is best handled by bringing up the facts to meet it, then employees deserve to know the facts about themselves and the power that they truly do hold over their own careers. Such a concept demands its own chapter, which you will find as Chapter 15, *Is This the Day I Get Fired?*

What Can Companies Do to Handle This?

It's not called a *new normal* for nothing. Those who expected that they could lift and shift the momentum of office life into the home at the start of the 2020 work-from-home era, soon discovered that, no, that can't be done. Work in-office and work at-home are two very different worlds.

Similarly, those who expected a complete return to the workplace, picking up where we left off, have also discovered that this is impossible. Like the magician's trick of pulling a tablecloth off a set table without disturbing a single glass, plate, or spoon, it's an illusion.

There needs to be a full reassessment of what work is. It is no longer an act of giving someone a job. It's a transaction, in which both sides share power. Inasmuch as a company has the momentum and scale to generate business, employees are quickly learning the value of their individual skills and the fact that other work is out there, even for people who live outside of the traditional commuting belts.

Future-of-work discussions often focus on *white collar* knowledge workers who seem to always have a great deal of skills that can be shifted to other companies. But the same holds true to a skilled profession like welding or nursing. There are far more freelance opportunities that are far more accessible via Internet groups and marketplaces than ever before. There are also many opportunities for employees to switch horses midstream, trading a welding torch for a camera, for example, and starting a new, and more fulfilling second or third career.

Companies must recognize that although the fear of losing a job still exists like an infection within each employee, there is now also a vaccine, in the sense of a full awareness of career mobility. This demands a removal of the mindset that work must be done in a certain place on a certain machine, at a certain time, and that now, the work, and each employee's engagement with that work, revolves around their lives, not the office building.

As a reminder, this book's subtitle is "How human reflex stands in the way of digital transformation." As we are seeing, the fears outlined in these chapters have great potential to drive talent away, thus leaving a digitally transformed company facing a talent drought, and an expensive cycle of recruiting and onboarding.

CHAPTER 7

The Fear of Looking Stupid

Nobody likes to look stupid. But in order to look stupid, there has to be someone else around who can make that judgment or, at the very least, be the person from whom you infer that judgment. For example, if you open a door to leave a room, and you accidentally bump into it rather than leaving the room gracefully, you will feel very different depending on whether there was someone watching you, there was no one watching you, or there was someone in the room who *might have been* watching you. If someone was indeed watching, you will feel a little stupid for being clumsy. If no one was watching, you might curse quietly to yourself, but you will move on. If someone *might* have seen you walk into the door, you either let it go and forget about it, or you let it haunt you like a clumsy version of *The Telltale Heart*.

Within the workplace, the fear of looking stupid is tribal and cultural. It connects to the middle layers of Maslow's Hierarchy since it directly affects esteem and the sense of social belonging.

The tools and processes of digital transformation are largely new and unfamiliar for many people. I have already mentioned how these might strike fear in people by threatening their job and disrupting the status quo, but to this we must add the related fear of losing face in front of others. There's that bumping-into-the-door quotient to consider.

CHAPTER 7   THE FEAR OF LOOKING STUPID

The Fear of Making Mistakes

When it comes to learning a new technology or technique, the fear of getting it wrong and looking stupid can be overwhelming to the point that some will procrastinate or even quit the task completely. Learning a new skill takes effort, and people will naturally do things incorrectly as they learn, because that's what learning is – it's about building a new skill based on developing knowledge and physical actions. It's about crafting a sequence of procedures in a way that will carve them into mental and physical memory, a metamorphosis from awareness to knowledge to experience and finally wisdom. But such explanations do little to alleviate the fear people will feel when they are facing something new.

The Act of Learning

When a person learns a new skill, the actions and mindset needed to progressively master the task move through four steps, in which "not knowing how to do it," or "doing it incorrectly" slowly gets replaced by the abilities and knowledge that lead to "doing it correctly." Some educators and trainers will refer to the *Conscious Competence Model*, a technique credited to Noel Burch of Gordon Training International in the 1970s.[1]

In the context of learning how to play a tune on the guitar, the four steps of the model would be

1. **Unconscious incompetence**: "I have no idea how to play guitar and have never tried."
2. **Conscious incompetence**: "I am trying to learn how to play guitar, and I know what I am supposed to do but I can't make my fingers go where they are meant to."

---

[1] Burch, Noel, and Gordon, Thomas. *T.E.T. Teacher Effectiveness Training.* (New York, 1974, Crown Publishing Group).

3. **Conscious competence**: "I can play a tune on the guitar, but I have to play slowly and really focus."

4. **Unconscious competence**: "I can play this tune effortlessly and I enjoy it. I can even interpret this in my own style."

In essence, to move from unconscious incompetence to unconscious competence, a learner must absorb and develop a skill through physical repetition to the point that the action becomes fluent. For most adults, the most familiar example of unconscious competence would be driving a car, which experienced drivers can do with almost no thought whatsoever. The car becomes an extension of themselves, for better and for worse.

In school, however, where learning is supposed to happen, when a student receives an "x" instead of a check mark, they are made to feel they have done something entirely wrong and bad, rather than feeling they got at least some of it right. Despite the fact that there are many great teachers out there, people who are truly dedicated to helping their students succeed, the system in which they and their students operate is still based on a cookie-cutter approach which will inevitably result in grades matching a traditional bell curve.

The shame that failure brings to a student experiencing a new topic for the first time has driven millions of students away from what could have been their chosen field if only a little more time had been given to their individual learning style. Many of us have memories of that teacher who expressed disappointment over a bad mark, immediately changing students' lives forever.

Sometimes it was a teacher, sometimes it was the system, but either way, our incapacity to develop a skill was not always due to a lack of personal aptitude, but from the way we were made to feel during the learning process. That's something that lasts a lifetime, and which resonates powerfully in adults facing changes and the need to learn new skills in the workplace.

CHAPTER 7   THE FEAR OF LOOKING STUPID

Learning is about developing a skillset, and until those skills are completely learned, they will, obviously, remain incomplete. A good teacher will not make a student feel incompetent for making *mistakes*, but will instead analyze the student's personal learning process to see where the gaps are.

Sometimes the student has an inadvertent role to play in their learning shortfall. In school as well as at work, many learners will simply not speak up. They will sit silently in the class, or attend an online session silently, with their camera off, watching, listening, wondering, but not speaking up for fear of looking stupid. I was one of those. That's our way. But because our way does not fit the system, we lose out. As a result

- We do not receive immediate guidance from the instructor (because none was asked for).

- By not asking, we do not get to discover how much we do actually already know. Sometimes, figuring out a challenge comes from hearing yourself describe it.

- There is always someone else in the room with the same question – and usually many people. When a student asks a question, they are also asking for others.

- When people do not ask, it becomes assumed that they already know. That sets the stage for further confusion and misunderstanding.

None of this should be considered the student's fault. It was the way most everything was taught in the twentieth century. But our current era is that of the audience-of-one. In just the same way that fear can be personalized (see Chapter 2), so can learning.

By contrast, if the learning of new technologies and techniques brought about by digital transformation is to be done *old school*, then the tradition of weakened learning will continue.

CHAPTER 7   THE FEAR OF LOOKING STUPID

A colleague of mine in the UK recently described how his son, studying at university, exited a lecture and realized that neither he nor his fellow students had understood the point that was being made. Rather than going back to the professor for clarification, they simply went online and found a lecture on the same topic from someone at the University of Melbourne, whose presentation was immediately comprehensible.

This is by no means an isolated case. Students and employees are both more likely, and certainly more able, to go online and find the teaching style that matches their learning style. This should make people wonder what the future of schools and of corporate education should be. When a student can find the best online lecturers in the world to choose from, they are demonstrating their own form of digital transformation in terms of how they wish to learn.

Those who feel threatened by the onslaught of change and who have neither the time nor the inclination to learn independently – or who simply fear doing so in case it is "out of line" – will resort to faking it, or getting by on just the basics, at which point the tools themselves become less useful.

In the 1880s, German psychologist Hermann Ebbinghaus devised the "forgetting curve," which is a simple curved line that dips downward like a toboggan hill or the left half of a letter "U". It shows how quickly learners forget what they have been taught, even by the end of the same day the information was delivered. A week after a course, a student will be lucky if they retain ten percent of what was taught.

What sort of investment in employees, and, by immediate extension, in the company, is that? If a stockbroker or investment advisor showed their clients a downward-trending curve as the projected path of their portfolios, that person would be fired on the spot. Yet companies assume that sending employees to a full-day training session on any topic will be enough to stock their minds full of the knowledge that they need, and that any mistakes made from that point on will be the fault of the student.

A better route for companies looking to maximize the learning potential for each employee could revolve around using digital transformation technologies to pair flipped schooling with shadowing. Flipped schooling is a technique that has been applied around the world at all types of educational levels from primary school to post-graduate, and primarily involves students watching lesson-related videos or other support material on their own time and then using instructor time to answer questions or deal with problems the student may have experienced.

The value of this teaching method, in my opinion, lies in its degree of receptivity. When a person is simply given facts with no relevance, their memory has no real place to store it. Storing knowledge in the brain is not like sliding a book onto a library bookshelf or placing a box in a storage locker. Knowledge has to weave itself into the mind. It is not so much *placed* as *absorbed*.

As an example, imagine today's course is on writing formulas in Microsoft Excel. As a subject matter expert, I could talk to you about how Excel uses the equals sign and parentheses to delineate a formula and a dollar sign to lock cell references. I can also talk about the wonders of Boolean logic (if, then, else). Bleah! You can probably feel your eyes glazing over already. What a waste of most people's valuable time.

If, by contrast, we work together on a spreadsheet that focuses on deadlines for projects underway in the office. "The goal," I say, "is to figure out which projects are less than thirty days away from being due, and highlighting these projects in a different color on the spreadsheet." This would be a problem that I could introduce to the student by way of a very short video, which simply describes the problem, but not the solution. I could even supply a sample Boolean logic formula for the student to play with for half an hour of their own time, with the challenge of figuring out how to calculate the number of days between today's date and a project's due date. The student would be allowed – of course – to Google the answer, which will likely be on YouTube.

CHAPTER 7   THE FEAR OF LOOKING STUPID

When we get together for a short, 30-minute class, my description on how to write a date formula and a Boolean logic equation (if today's date subtracted from the due date is less than 30, then color the text red, otherwise leave as is), would be the whole content of that short class. Most importantly, the students, having tried to do this on their own, hopefully with a real project in mind, have tilled their mental soil, which is now ready to receive the knowledge. It has relevance and will be much more successfully integrated into memory.

This is a cry for microlearning, which I feel, and hope will be used much more in the workplaces and schools of the future than tedious multi-hour workshops that, despite the wisdom and presentation skills of the teacher, are just too long. Digital connections have almost completely removed the need for auditorium-style lectures. When learning is individual-focused, it really does not need to be dragged into a hall. These should be reserved for communal experiences – either fully interactive learning, or audience-focused experiential events, such as keynote speeches and entertainment, which need to leverage the contagious emotion of a large group.

A complement to flipped schooling is shadowing, in which a student is allowed to observe other people at work. This is the essence of apprenticeship and of delegation. At first glance, such a pairing seems to be far more random than the nice, tidy, one-day workshop, but such workshops are truly just another holdout from the pre-digital age, when the only way to teach a group of people was to talk to them all at the same time in a big room.

Digital transformation for professional development is far more than just using Zoom for a full-day teaching session. In fact that's the worst way to teach. It's just another lift-and-shift. As one client recently shared with me, "in learning sessions on video chat, we expect undivided attention, but more and more we get divided attention. This has to change." Digital transformation will be about using new technologies to apply a new

CHAPTER 7   THE FEAR OF LOOKING STUPID

method of teaching and professional development which, despite its apparent randomness, is poised to deliver far greater ROI than what we have seen before.

As a final note to these thoughts on education in the age of digital transformation, specifically regarding my Microsoft Excel Boolean logic exercise, I would naturally expect my students to jump onto YouTube or LinkedIn Learning to find out how to do it. But what if one or more of them came back and said, "I didn't complete the assignment." The sausage-factory education system would seek to punish this person for not following through. But if I were to ask why, and the student said, "because there's a whole cloud-based app out there that can do it for us and much easier," well, in that case, ten points for Griffindor! That's what digital transformation should be about.

The Fear of Not Being Able to Keep Up

In 2021, the cloud database company Couchbase conducted a survey to examine how digital transformation priorities had impacted digital architects. A digital architect is an internal person or team that helps their company's people use technology to transform their businesses. In essence, they are the enablers of a company's digital transformation.

The Couchbase report found that

> *The sudden acceleration of initiatives to digitally transform businesses put these architects under tremendous pressure, given that transformation starts with the heavy lift of modernizing data infrastructure and then fixing the application stack above it. As a result, the burden on digital architects more*

than doubled since the outbreak of the covid pandemic, with 48 percent of respondents feeling currently under high or extremely high pressure to deliver digital projects.[2]

Similarly, the *2020/21 State of the Profession* report published by the Chartered Institute of Information Security[3] stated

- Fifty-one percent of cybersecurity professionals are kept up at night by job stress and work challenges.

- More than two-thirds (69 percent) believe that risks to their organization's data have increased due to staff working from home.

- Eighty percent of respondents said that staff have become more anxious or stressed during the pandemic.

- Sixty-five percent of respondents felt that the pandemic made security reviews, audits, and overseeing processes more difficult.

- Sixty-six percent agreed that the forced cancellation of education events and training has widened the skills gap in the sector.

There are, and there will be, many other articles and studies commissioned by other companies, in other industries, discussing their specialists, which come to the same point: even the experts are feeling overloaded by the forces of change that digital transformation is bringing on. They are suffering from the fear of being unable to keep up.

---

[2] No Author. *Couchbase: 61 percent of digital architects report past tech decisions made project completion difficult.* Retrieved from https://venturebeat.com/2021/08/01/couchbase-61-of-digital-architects-report-past-tech-decisions-made-project-completion-difficult/ Accessed December 2021.

[3] CIISEC.org, quoted in *InfoSecurity Magazine* www.infosecurity-magazine.com/news/stress-burnout-cybersecurity/

CHAPTER 7   THE FEAR OF LOOKING STUPID

Technology has a remarkable ability to scale up very quickly, largely because so much of it is seemingly virtual. Even though servers remain physical devices, their dynamic, instantly scalable nature, along with the myriad types of software that run on them make them seem infinitely large and complex. Specialists in database, cloud, cybersecurity, and IT see change happening by the minute, with the scope and scale of work growing constantly.

For regular (non-IT) people, the same expansion of the work surface applies. Messages now travel on numerous channels such as emails, Slack, instant messaging, SMS, and phone apps. These require that people keep all of these channels open, staying ready to receive messages on any of them.

This "always-on" existence doesn't only apply to the channels of communication technology – it affects people physically and physiologically as well. For example, there's the physical issue of processing information from a light source. The human eye and its optical system weren't designed to stare at light sources, which is what computer screens and phone screens are. The human optical system evolved to take in and process signals from reflected light. For most of humanity's existence, the only direct sources of light were the sun, the stars, lightning, and fire. Everything else that we could see was derived from light reflecting off surfaces.

People wonder why these technologies are so hard to master and learn. It's not just because they require new skills. In many ways, we are not designed to operate or integrate with these tools. This is why there are so many people who feel more comfortable printing out their emails rather than reading them on screen, and despite the paper that it uses. They wonder why they prefer doing it this way. In most cases, it's because the printed word on the tangible medium of paper is more readily accepted by the body's visual processing system.

It's easy to argue that we have all learned how to read material on a computer screen, and this is true, but a growing body of medical evidence shows that doing this for too long leads to enhanced eye fatigue and disrupted sleep patterns that in turn contribute to a diminished immune system, all due to the "false daylight" that computer screens impose upon our ancient circadian rhythm. Given that bright computer screens have only been part of our lives since the mid-1990s, it will be a couple more decades before medical science can truly observe their long-term impact.

The research done by Professor Jeremy Bailenson in his 2021 paper, referred to in Chapter 2, looked at video call fatigue, and pointed out the challenges that include excessive amounts of close-up eye contact, seeing yourself during video chats, communicating with reduced physical mobility, and an excessive cognitive load due to a lack of nonverbal cues.

The person who prints out their emails and doesn't know why, or the people who do not like video chats, but don't know why, are struggling to penetrate and modify ancient layers of habit and experience that humans have used for thousands of years. This makes the fear of "not being able to keep up" tangible and largely impenetrable.

The Internal Spotlight Effect

The spotlight effect has long been a topic of discussion in psychology circles, especially with regard to anxiety. In its most straightforward form, it describes the tendency some people have to feel that others are noticing them more than they actually are. A simple example would be the day you get a coffee stain on your clothing, and you feel the whole world can see it.

This spotlight effect will naturally magnify any sense of insecurity that the fear of looking stupid has already introduced. In fact, it can create a *double fear*. First comes the anticipation of the event, which is a fear that may last for weeks or months before the dreaded event happens. Then there is the experience of the event once it happens.

In both cases, as already described in Chapter 3, it is natural for the body and brain to respond with a fight-or-flight reflex in advance of the event, causing the mind to stay distracted by it, in some cases to the point of obsession, numbness, and burnout. Performance insecurity fills the mind in advance of the event, bombarding short-term memory with "what ifs." These can magnify themselves to a point of becoming a self-fulfilling prophecy, genuinely preventing someone from performing their tasks.

On the other hand, very often, when people take on the task that they are fearing, they will find it to not be as scary or as difficult as they had imagined. The discrepancies between these two scenarios is where you will find the useful acronym of the word "fear" itself: false expectations appearing real." But until that happens, a person remains alone, in a spotlight with their thoughts.

Social media has done much to further magnify this problem by focusing people's minds into an audience-of-one mindset. This can be seen in the emergence of the *selfie culture*, in which no event or activity, no matter how humble, is valid until there is a photo posted to social media. It's fun to document one's life in this way, perhaps, but it also confirms and reinforces that spotlight sensation.

Even though the world is not really watching everything we do, the transition to a self-focused cultural presence naturally places us at the center of our own spotlight. This can easily magnify the horror of making a mistake in front of peers, and in turn can push individuals even further away from the challenge of learning.

If the fear and subsequent avoidance of taking a risk and learning a new skill remained solely an individual problem, it could possibly be managed as a treatable personality issue. But it's not an individual problem anymore. The fear of making mistakes and of looking stupid inside the glare of an imaginary personal spotlight leads to people avoiding activities that affect everyone.

Once again, I refer back to the password management issue, which serves as a reminder of the fact that we are all connected, and are subsequently all affected by the actions or non-actions of even a single individual. When a person refuses to update their password out of fear of looking stupid, this opens the entire organization up to ransomware and cybercrime. In a digitally connected world, the individual fear of looking stupid becomes the onramp to a global superhighway of company failure.

The solution to this is, as already described, a better system of teaching. But the lesson here is that thanks to the spotlight effect of the audience-of-one culture, that one person's fear becomes everyone's problem.

The Fear of Failure

Once a person or a team breaks through the barrier that held them inside the traditional definitions of failure and mistakes, then neither seem so daunting. SpaceX, undeniably one of the greatest success stories of this digital era, became that way in part by rejecting many of the cultural rules that had guided the rocketry programs of previous decades, primarily by incorporating the learning process into its brand. This is best exemplified by the YouTube videos of its rockets' post-launch landings, especially those on floating barges, where both the successes and failures are placed on display, with the challenge, sometimes verbal, sometimes implied, that if anyone can do better, they should step forward and possibly join the team.[4]

Using SpaceX as a case study in no way intends to slight the efforts and achievements of those who worked in the world's other space programs. Rocket science is really difficult, and failure is inevitable throughout the numerous mega-projects involved. But SpaceX made great use of social media to enhance its mystique and brand by publicizing its failures and setbacks as much as its achievements. Post-explosion tweets by founder Elon Musk such as "So... how was your evening?" or "Where's that

---

[4] An excellent account of the SpaceX/Elon Musk mindset is available in *Liftoff: Elon Musk and the Desperate Early Days That Launched SpaceX*, by Eric Berger (William Morrow, 2021).

CHAPTER 7   THE FEAR OF LOOKING STUPID

FlexTape when you need it?" display something more than bravado or ego. Like all the space programs that went before it, and which still exist, there is a lot that can go wrong with a rocket, yet Musk and his team have successfully embraced the idea of *failing forward* and of failing publicly as a means to further his brand. The same could also be said about Tesla, the Boring Company, and the Hyperloop, all of which belong to the Musk empire.

Musk is by no means the only high profile entrepreneur to publicly use failing forward as a path to success, nor is this practice solely a product of the twenty-first century social media culture. As a larger-than-life figure, he also comes with his fair share of controversy. The same techniques were used by Henry Ford, Thomas Edison, Albert Einstein, Richard Branson, Sara Blakely, Oprah Winfrey, and Steve Jobs, all iconic innovators with a great flair for publicity.

Fear of failure is the ultimate motivator or demotivator for any activity, and how it is handled makes all the difference. Many individuals and organizations seek to bury their mistakes, hiding them from the media or even modifying records to make the mistakes disappear. The bold innovators forge ahead, but most average individuals allow it to dominate their entire thought process.

The digital transformation era is one in which new approaches to collaboration and creativity can happen much more easily if failure is allowed into the stream. Failure should be embraced for what it is: part of the learning process. Rather than allow the mistakes that we make to indelibly stamp the word "failure" on our skin, every action, successful, partially successful, or not at all successful, should be treated as an opportunity to learn and move forward.

None of us lives along a straight line, nor does any company. The path of our lives is more like a *parkour* route – that crazy obstacle course running style in which competitors use their balance and strength to power over, around, or off obstacles as they appear. Failures are simply hard rebounds off these obstacles, and the occasional tumble. The path itself is never straight and is never perfect.

The fear of failure is largely a socially conditioned one, very different from the instinctive fear of danger described in earlier chapters. Babies learn to walk by simply trying it until they get it. One of the most fascinating actions to observe in life is a baby discovering for the first time that they are capable of independent movement. They just wriggle, then crawl, and then stagger until, eventually, they walk. Thankfully, they cannot and will not listen to anyone telling them, they can't or shouldn't try this yet. Instinct knows there is more to be gained from trying to walk than from shrinking from the challenge. So instead of making us fearful of walking, it provides a reflex to put our arms out if we fall. This is the pragmatic wonder of nature.

The fear of failure is taught by others, often during the formative years, which guarantees that it will remain indelibly stamped on our collective psyche, and will always remain something to be consciously overcome.

CHAPTER 8

The Fear of Losing Control

The Pressing Problem of Bicycle Face

During the late 1800s, the bicycle became a popular form of inexpensive transport. But there was a problem with it. It had the side effect of allowing women greater physical freedom. They were now able to get out of the house, travel distances unaccompanied, meet up with other women, and generally enjoy a little more fun and independence. This was wholly unwelcome among the male patriarchy in America, England, Australia, and many other places, who saw the whole idea of women on bicycles as dangerous and distinctly immoral.

To make bicycling less appealing to the female population, a medical condition called *bicycle face* was suddenly discovered. Actually it was created. This condition was described as "a face usually flushed, but sometimes pale, often with lips more or less drawn, and the beginning of dark shadows under the eyes, and always an expression of weariness."[1] A campaign was launched, mainly through print ads in magazines and newspapers, designed to instill insecurities in women and drive them back inside the house.

---

[1] "The 'Bicycle Face.'" The Literary Digest. 11 (19): 8 (548). September 7, 1895.

CHAPTER 8   THE FEAR OF LOSING CONTROL

A great deal of advertising still uses this device to this day. Advertising for any product and on any medium is often designed to generate feelings of inadequacy, to arouse the fear of being rejected by society, and to feel that life without this product is a life partially unfulfilled. It can be subtle, or it can be obvious, but it is almost always successful.

Most advertisements for cars, for example, show the car racing across beautiful landscapes, or along scenic coastal highways, or through surprisingly empty city streets, with their occupants arriving to do something fun, usually going to a party or camping. Very few, if any, car ads show their new model battling for a parking space at a Walmart on a snowy February day. The imagery of the commercial says, "fun, exotic, freedom – an idealized life," and the subtext – the message that is spoken without words says, "without this car, you're not getting this."

You can substitute "car" for any other consumable product and see the same message in its ads: "If you do not buy the right brand of tooth-whitening toothpaste, you will be thought of as less attractive. If you do not buy the right brand of laundry detergent, you will be thought of as a bad parent. If you do not buy these cosmetics, these clothes, or this brand of phone, you will not find a partner, a safe home, or a happy life." That's what advertising is. It speaks to our most basic instinct – fear – a fear that runs completely up and down Maslow's Hierarchy of Needs, which ensures the message is attended to and remembered.

The bicycle face campaign was designed to play on women's presumed fears around attractiveness, but it actually revealed a far more profound fear felt by the men of the time around their impending loss of control. This, too, still exists, to this day in virtually every area of society. In the case of the bicycle face campaign, nevertheless, the women persisted, and cycling became a popular pastime.

CHAPTER 8   THE FEAR OF LOSING CONTROL

From Bicycle Face to Face Time Bias

We see the bicycle face approach to intimidation as quite present in the age of digital transformation, especially as it applies to the idea of the work-from-home employee and the inconvenient notion of a hybrid workforce. As mentioned earlier in Chapter 6, the media op-eds and studies around "face time bias" run up against the fact that some people already enjoy working from home, and others are seriously reconsidering work-from-home or hybrid work as a new professional life choice after now having experienced it for real during the pandemic.

But for some managers, the idea of a hybrid or at-home workforce gives rise to significant concerns, largely around trust, productivity, team dynamics, and control.

This is a wedge issue for managers, a serious unknown element in their lives. Do managers feel that employees who work from home cannot be trusted? Does this represent a crisis of a manager's faith in the employees or a crisis of self-legitimacy among managers, who, more than anyone else, need people around them to justify their existence?

The argument goes that groups function best when everyone is in the same physical space, where *ad hoc* interactions and structured meetings create the optimum culture for productivity. If only that were the case. Since the 1950s, employees have been largely disappointed by the stultifying atmosphere of the workplace. Typical complaints about the workplace included too many meetings, too much commuting, and out-of-touch management. This was the standard for all of the decades from the 1950s onward (if not longer), and was compounded from the 1990s onward by increasing amounts of time-consuming tasks that came in the form of voice mails, emails, messages, and PowerPoint presentations.

CHAPTER 8   THE FEAR OF LOSING CONTROL

Beyond these standard complaints, there is/was the politics and interpersonnel relationships that, in too many cases, became toxic. Sometimes the manager was a direct cause of this toxicity, sometimes it was the employee, but in many cases, the manager or the company simply avoided trying to rectify the problem.

As always, it's important when stating such things to recognize that there are also many good managers out there who actively seek to support and encourage their teams. I speak solely from my own experience in working with a couple of hundred companies over my career, and in talking with thousands of people, regular employees, managers, senior managers, and executives. My observations still place the ratio of unhappy employee-manager relationships to happier ones as 80 to 20.

The physical, on-premises workplace has had 70 years to prove its viability as both the prime location for productive work and the space where employee-manager relationships can be nurtured, and, with a few exceptions, it has not done a good job. It just so happened that for all of the decades prior to high-bandwidth Internet connectivity, it was the only game in town.

Study of Microsoft Employees Shows Bicycle Face Still Possible

An academic, peer-reviewed study of more than 61,000 Microsoft employees was published in September 2021 in the journal *Nature Human Behavior*.[2] It coincided with Microsoft's announcement that employees would not be returning to the office as soon after the pandemic as had been hoped. It was just too soon.

---

[2] Yang, L., Holtz, D., Jaffe, S. et al. The effects of remote work on collaboration among information workers. Nat Hum Behav (2021). https://doi.org/10.1038/s41562-021-01196-4 also www.nature.com/articles/s41562-021-01196-4#citeas

The study, which was based on "rich data on the emails, calendars, instant messages, video/audio calls and workweek hours of 61,182 US Microsoft employees over the first six months of 2020"[3] suggested that

> *...firm-wide remote work caused the collaboration network of workers to become more static and siloed, with fewer bridges between disparate parts. Furthermore, there was a decrease in synchronous communication and an increase in asynchronous communication. Together, these effects may make it harder for employees to acquire and share new information across the network.*[4]

In other words, they felt that collaborative communication technologies wouldn't work quite so well when workers are distributed across the landscape rather than back in the office, and most ironic of all, that such a setup would result in more silos, something that proactive companies had been struggling to reduce.

This study can and will be replaced by further studies as the months and years go by, and my goal is not to single out Microsoft. It's a study based on what was known about the potential productivity of remote work at that time. But in my opinion, studies like these still reflect a profound fear on the part of those who run companies and departments: how can management happen if there's no one in the office?

These types of warnings resonate with the fear of losing control over the workplace status quo - a place where managers maintain an industrial revolution-era approach to work-versus-time that is wholly unsuited to the more artisanal approach of knowledge work. It is understandable that managers feel threatened by changes to the employee-manager dynamic. It's something that confronts the very skills and ethos that managers were trained for, especially as they watched and learned from the managers they themselves worked for.

---

[3] Ibid.
[4] Ibid., Abstract.

CHAPTER 8   THE FEAR OF LOSING CONTROL

So it is natural for managers, company executives, and board members to resist a change in the management–work dynamic. Giving "bicycles" to employees in this way appears to be rife with fear-inducing unknowns. But when you look back over other innovations that were brought into the workplace throughout the twentieth century – the telephone, the computer, and the Internet, it can be seen that all of these developments were greeted in most cases with resistance until they, too, became the new normal.

You Can't Manage What You Can't See

Most managers do not know how to manage in a virtual space. Of course not. Most have never had to do it, and that's where at least some of the fear comes in. They grew up in a world where a blend of *command-and-control* and *management by walking around* made for a practical and workable combination. The concept of management was a literal one. A manager could place credence in an employee's validity, work ethic, and productivity by being able to see them, on-site, doing what they are supposed to be doing.

A caveat here: leaders and managers come in a variety of styles. Some are highly proactive, compassionate, and open to whatever helps individual employees thrive. They work hard to create productive, inclusive environments, and of these, many have greeted the work-from-home option enthusiastically. Managers, too, are by and large, not bad people. But to paraphrase Shakespeare, some managers were born great, some achieve greatness, and some had management thrust upon them.

The "born great" managers are usually natural leaders – socially aware, keen to help their employees achieve their own personal successes, and often frustrated by the same types of corporate cultural inertia and bureaucracy that stultify their staff. Great management is something that can be taught – it's not exclusively innate, but it needs an environment that embraces and communicates a positive culture throughout. Many companies agree with this concept but, for many reasons, let it slide quite quickly, usually due to budget cuts or the adoption of a more *lean* and competitive workplace.

The latter group of managers, those who have had management thrust upon them, is a group often comprising people who are experts in their own particular field and who were later promoted into management as a matter of seniority. A great subject matter expert does not always make a great manager, quite simply because the two jobs are too different.

This is sometimes referred to as the *specialist to leadership* transition, expanding on the *Peter Principle* described in 1969 by Laurence J. Peter.

> *The Peter Principle is about getting promoted into your level of incompetence. This is a specialist to leadership transition, where the person they call the deep specialist becomes a manager. It turns out teams that promote deep specialists and managers are weaker than teams who promote generalists into managers. And that's because essentially, a deep specialist can be more dominant over the team and suppress more of the team function. Whereas a non-specialist manager might ask the team, "hey, what do you need from me?" the dominant manager tells the team what to do. And the performance of the two teams varies greatly.*[5]

Deep specialist managers are also prone to a fear borne out of imposter syndrome, feeling incompetent because "my people should never have an answer that I don't have."

In just the same way most managers are good people, most employees are good people too. They take pride in doing good work, and most put in more work hours than their job description describes, returning emails in the evening, for example. The problem is many managers end up focusing

---

[5] Skeels, Jack. "The Manager of the Future is Chill." Podcast episode no. 8 from *The Art of Management* podcast. 2022. Retrieved from https://theartof.management/managers-of-future-is-chill/ January 2022.

CHAPTER 8   THE FEAR OF LOSING CONTROL

on managing departments rather than individual people, and when those physical departments vanish, replaced by virtual spaces and invisible, home-based employees, the sense of tangible management vanishes as well.

A Matter of Trust

In Chapter 6, I highlighted a *Bloomberg* story about a survey of managers who had supposedly fired someone for making gaffes while on a video chat meeting. This same survey also revealed another interesting fact. Three quarters of the 200 managers surveyed also admitted they could not trust their employees to work from home.[6] They wanted them back where they could see them. In the most extreme cases, some managers went so far as to install spyware to ensure their employees were actually at their desks, or keyloggers to monitor the amount of typing being done.[7]

In addition to being draconian, invasive, and unethical, possibly even illegal, such attempts at employee oversight reveal a profound lack of awareness about how knowledge workers actually work. Whether the work is being done in a cubicle in an office, or at home in fuzzy slippers, people are not machines. They cannot hum along at a constant rate for hours on end. Even the most dedicated employee who wants nothing more than to sit at their computer for eight hours uninterrupted, will still zone in and out of full focus in line with their own circadian rhythm, blood sugar levels, and other metabolic factors.[8] Humans are built to sprint and then rest. The

---

[6] Refer to the Bloomberg article from Chapter 6.

[7] Ballard, Barclay. "One in five firms admit to illegally spying on employees working from home." *TechRadar*. January 2019, 2021. Retrieved from www.techradar.com/news/one-in-five-firms-admit-to-illegally-spying-on-employees-working-from-home Accessed October 2021.

[8] For more information on the daily circadian and ultradian rhythm in the workplace, check out my book, *Cool-Time: A Hands-On Plan for Managing Work and Balancing Time*.

classic expectation of a full eight hours delivered between 9:00 a.m. and 5:00 p.m. is yet another offshoot of the Industrial Revolution factory-shift approach.

The ideal working environment has always been one in which people work and then rest. In the traditional workplace, those rest periods were woven into the fabric of the day: coffee breaks, water cooler/kitchenette conversations, impromptu hallway meetings, small talk at the beginning of a formalized meeting. The difference was, these breaks occurred largely in full sight of the manager, which made them marginally more acceptable.

When these same breaks are done at the home office, they take on much greater significance and tend to eclipse the work that is actually being done.

Aside from all the distasteful aspects of employee spyware, there's no proof that it has any positive effect. People are on average no more or less productive when they know spyware is watching them than when they don't know, or even when there is no spyware at all. Sometimes, such attempts at close monitoring may create an initial spike in focused work, but soon the novelty of the spyware wears off, and so do the exaggerated work habits that the spyware generates.

It is likely that companies that embrace this type of spying suffer higher than average employee turnover rates. It holds to the notion that employees cannot be trusted to do their work anywhere but at the office where they can be closely supervised. Such an attitude also seems to suggest that employees at the office have never been able to figure out how to "not work" while looking like they're working. And anyone who believes that has much to learn about work in general. While a few employees may be held down by such draconian measures, more of them will simply leave, as the Great Resignation described in Chapter 6 illustrates.

One telling example of the trust problem comes in the form of employee training. Training means delivering new skills to people, but it places two separate fears on the shoulders of those employees, both of which I have already described. The first is the fear of making mistakes and

CHAPTER 8   THE FEAR OF LOSING CONTROL

looking stupid, described in Chapter 7, and the second is the post-training challenge of going back to their departments with their newly-learned skill, and then trying to introduce it to the rest of the group, as described in the *Blame Steve* section of Chapter 6. I am revisiting it here in order to add another layer to the *fear* discussion.

When salmon, and many other types of fish besides, go back to their place of birth to spawn the next generation, they must undergo a titanic battle, fighting river currents and all types of obstacles, from human-built dams to rapids and hungry bears. It literally exhausts them. If they are lucky, they manage to deposit or fertilize the eggs for the next generation of salmon, and then they die. It's pretty dramatic.

Employees face the same upstream battle when they are taught a new soft skill, perhaps a new method of managing time, running meetings, or using critical thinking skills. Upon release from the classroom, they will be expected to make changes within their work environment, not only in terms of using these skills themselves but also becoming an unwilling agent of change as they practice them in front of their colleagues.

Being an inexperienced agent of change can be a frightening experience, since it means being burdened with the task of introducing change to others. This is a great shame, and one of the hidden elements that makes a workplace less desirable to work at, because while learning the skill is the student's responsibility, introducing change should not be. That should be the manager's job, since the change being taught affects the team.

So here's the layer I want to add: In the context of this chapter – the manager's fear of losing control – managers seldom attend these professional development courses, feeling perhaps that they don't need this particular type of training, and would not admit it to their subordinates even if they did. But that's not the point of the need for them to show up. If a manager took just 15 minutes out of their day to sit in on just a small part of a professional development course that one or more of their employees were attending, it would deliver an endorsement of what was being taught, and what the student was expected to learn. It would set a tone of trust and confidence in the students. Seeing their boss paying attention to the lesson – or even just a part of a lesson – would pave the way for a much more confident deployment of the skills, while empowering employees to embrace the change that the skills deliver.

Rather than a fish swimming culturally upstream, there would be a greater sense of communality and solidarity – a sense of comfort rather than fear.

On a similar note, some managers might declare they are unwilling to spend money to train employees, especially new hires, out of the fear that the employees will take that training and then leave to work elsewhere. Sadly this easily becomes a self-fulfilling prophecy. When an employee does not feel trusted and supported by their manager, it simply heightens that desire to leave. Richard Branson, the flamboyant entrepreneur behind the Virgin brand (airline, phones, music, media, and publishing), has long been an advocate for better employee treatment. A quote attributed to him puts it into clear perspective: "Train your employees so they can leave, and treat them well enough so they don't want to."

Trust is the backbone of a successful team, regardless of whether that team works together in the same office, or from home, or in a hybrid setup. It, more than any one singular digital technology, will make a team successful. My friend, author Alberto Silveira, calls this *One Team, One Heart*. "Build a culture of 'people first' using empowerment and trust. This generates productivity, connection, and loyalty from team members. The *One Team One Heart* spirit is the synergy that comes from people feeling good about their place in a highly productive team."[9]

The great news is trust is just as available in a virtual or hybrid workplace as it is in the real world. However, it is a new scenario. Managers

---

[9] Silveira, Alberto, *Managing High-Performance Distributed Teams*, 2021, Apress.

CHAPTER 8   THE FEAR OF LOSING CONTROL

and employees both need to learn how to co-exist in a virtual or hybrid space, recognizing that everything that can be done in the office, both formal and informal, can be done remotely.

There was a time, over a century ago, when people feared the disembodied voice coming from a telephone. They also feared automobiles and trains, believing that travelling faster than a galloping horse would suck the air out of peoples' lungs. As fear gave way to acceptance, new technologies were used initially to carry or deliver old methods of activity. As I alluded to in Chapter 2, early motion pictures were simply stage plays put on in front of a camera, early television shows were Vaudeville acts and radio interviews on camera, and early websites were basically digitized books.

Similarly, the early virtualized working world in which we find ourselves is indeed a *lift-and-shift* of current office practices. Video chat is being used solely to replicate the current in-office meeting experience. It has yet to evolve into its own medium, with its own formal and informal presence. This means the fear people express about these technologies is based on a rearward perspective – assessing yesterday's work in terms of tomorrow's technology, and quite appropriately seeing no benefit.

Fear of Delegation

Looking past the fear of digital transformation, it becomes easy to see how new technologies do actually offer teams and individuals the opportunity to expand their skills and grow, since they do not simply replicate tasks in the *lift-and-shift* method just mentioned, but instead allow us to do new things that were not possible in that earlier pre-pandemic era.

Being able to collaborate simultaneously on a shared electronic version of a document posted to a cloud-based drive is becoming a normal thing for many people now – but it was something that we were not able to do just a few years ago, when email attachments were the standard way of document sharing.

CHAPTER 8   THE FEAR OF LOSING CONTROL

Similarly being able to *coexist* in a virtual workspace, not just for meetings, but for the whole day – but doing so without having to leave your home – well, that's still in the "trains will suck the air out of your lungs" phase for many.

As people embrace new skills, the need (or opportunity) to hand off some lesser valued skills to others becomes more urgent. In fact, this is one of the most fundamental and practical principles of productivity: if there is ever a chance to hand off a task to another person in order to free yourself up to do something of greater value, then you should do this. It's called *delegation*, but it, too, is often held back by fear, and so, with this new wave of opportunity arriving, it is important to recognize the fear of delegation as another fear related to digital transformation.

The most immediate delegation-related fear is one of time. The argument goes, "by the time I show this person how to do this task, I could have done it myself." And that's absolutely true, but only for the single next time that the task needs to be done.

Delegation is an act of education, and just like all education, it takes several steps to complete, to move a learner from an unconscious incompetent to an unconscious competent, in the manner described in Chapter 7. Each step should allow a little more involvement on the part of the learner, with correspondingly more oversight on the part of you, the expert, until the time comes that the learner becomes a master in their own right, in which case the task can be confidently handed over.

Delegation has three major payoffs, but each comes with its own specific fear. See if you can spot what the exact fear is in these next three paragraphs.

First, as already mentioned, it allows the expert to take on other tasks of greater value. A small business owner, for example, may balk at the idea of hiring a bookkeeper, since the act of bookkeeping is not that hard, and bookkeepers cost money and need to be shown the ins-and-outs of the business, and besides there's an app that can do it. That is until someone – perhaps a mentor – shows them how much more money the business

CHAPTER 8   THE FEAR OF LOSING CONTROL

owner could be making if they let go of the time-consuming act of doing the books. They can likely make more money during that time saved than the bookkeeper actually costs.

Secondly, delegating tasks to a junior employee is a great way of keeping good employees on board. As described earlier, most employees want to develop more skills and do good work. By delegating tasks and therefore providing the opportunity to learn new skills, and equally importantly, entrusting them with the outcome, these employees are much more likely to blossom and grow with the company.

Thirdly, this new *owner* of the task, the employee to whom it has been delegated, will likely take that task, and make it their own, doing it in a slightly different way, and maybe even a better way than you, based on their own past experience, education, and comfort with technology.

Do you see the problems here?

The first fear of delegation is the fear of letting go. This is related to the fear of change since it is quite simply all about change – removing a habit or an act with which you, the expert, have grown comfortable. Giving it to someone else, giving it away, is like giving away a part of yourself, an activity that you know and trust – an old normal that now must be changed.

Even if the task that is being delegated away is one that you did not particularly love, the fact that it is now going to be done by someone else can be unsettling, at the very least if there's that worry that you will have to come back and correct what you perceive as mistakes. It's a bit like handing your smartphone over to another person. Your whole life is in there and having it leave your hands and go into someone else's hands, especially if it is unlocked, is nothing short of terrifying.

The second fear involves trusting the employee to do the work to your standards. Trust, as I have already suggested, is a unique item in the collection of human mind-states. It can be described as an emotion, but also as a product of knowledge. To trust someone, you must feel something – a willingness to allow an individual to do something, but based on what? Based on objective observation of their actions. I can feel trust toward another individual after having repeatedly and consistently observed them acting in an honest, trustful way. Similarly, I can trust an employee to do the work I delegate to them after I have repeatedly and consistently observed them doing the task correctly. Trust is a significant polar opposite to fear. It's a hybrid of emotion and knowledge, bridging the gap between left brain and right brain. Not many other internal actions can do that.

The third fear revolves around the fact that the student might be able to do the work better than you, and that's where the fear of looking stupid comes back in. If they can do it better, how does that reflect upon you? There is the first fear that if a new employee can do it in a better way, then might this be the thin end of the wedge that leads to this employee taking your job? Secondly, and related to this, the task that you are handing over to a new person is now being exposed, and any shortcuts or omissions that you may have grown used to are now on full display for the learner to observe, leading to the question, either spoken or unspoken, "that's how you did it?" And then there's the fear of looking stupid once again, if this task gets handed back to you, even temporarily, and you realize you are no longer able to do it, either because its process has changed substantially, or because you're out of practice. Either way, it's way too unsettling.

Let's move this delegation fear fully into a digital transformation scenario. Imagine starting a new project with your team. You want to give a junior member a chance to grow, so you assign this person part ownership of the planning and project management. First, this will require a little bit of time up front to teach the junior member the finer points of project management generally and "how we do projects around here."

The junior member goes off and sets up a planning scenario using a new third-party online app that uses kanban, Gantt charts, and internal whiteboarding and messaging in a way you have never seen before.

CHAPTER 8   THE FEAR OF LOSING CONTROL

The app's demo videos show just how easy it is to click this, drag that, summarize everything on a customizable dashboard, and store the whole thing in the cloud.

That's a lot of new stuff, and it suddenly pulls the ownership of the project completely away from you and puts it in a world you are not familiar with. You, the master, must now seek help on how to use and understand this new and unfamiliar app that has swooped in and digitally transformed your project.

That's where fear comes from. Although the act of delegation has been around for as long as humans have worked together, it now comes with a larger and newer set of risks. Even if you personally do not feel the fears that this new-age delegation scenario presents, there will be many around you who will.

CHAPTER 9

The Fear of the Known

The *End User License Agreement* or EULA is a piece of legalese that most of us have never read, but that most of us are bound by. It often arrives in the form of a tedious contract that stands between us and the enjoyment of a new app or device. By clicking on *I Agree*, each user does things like willfully handing over possession of original content, absolving the provider of liability in the case of loss, granting permission for your data to be handed over to law enforcement, and a host of other permissions for the provider of the service. All the details about what you are going to commit to are there, of course. They are completely visible. But most of us simply click on the *accept* button and think nothing more about it.

Willful Blindness and Overload

Given the powerful instinct for self-preservation that seems to rule so much of our lives, it would seem natural that we would want to take every precaution possible to protect ourselves by scrutinizing what we sign in a contract such as an EULA or updated terms of service. But most of us don't. When we purchase a cool new device like a smart doorbell, we don't want to spend the time reading the legalese that comes with it. When a website tells you it uses cookies, what do you do? Click on *Accept*.

CHAPTER 9   THE FEAR OF THE KNOWN

It's not like we don't know about the potential dangers. We have all heard enough about viruses and data breaches to know they happen daily, but is that enough to generate interest in creating better passwords or scrutinizing the legalese? As Chapter 4 discussed, it does not. We know the dangers, but apparently in spite of all that the limbic system is trying to do for us, we continue blithely on.

But perhaps it's not as contradictory as it may appear. It's not a lack of fear that causes this willful blindness, but the fear of knowing too much. This is a state that can lead to mental overload, sometimes called *analysis paralysis*, in which there are just too many thoughts and signals fighting for the very limited mental space reserved for moment-by-moment conscious thought. This same *analysis paralysis* or mental overload is what we see when people have trouble prioritizing conflicting tasks, or thinking straight during times of crisis.

With each new technology, there comes a time when too much information becomes too much to bear and where we willfully carry on, ignoring the growing awareness of impending danger, and throwing a cloak over it so that it cannot be seen. As contradictory as it seems, it is still a form of self-preservation. Contemplating things that might only have a possibility of happening is generally too much for people to bear, and although this seems like a minor issue when discussing online license agreements (it's not), it is also one of the fundamental causes of security lapses within organizations – contemplating threats that might or might not happen (they will). Security is too often seen as an expense rather than a feature.

A next-level example of this fear of "excessive known" may be seen in the Covid-19 contact tracing app. Many were developed and distributed by various countries and regions, with governments working in league with health authorities and software companies to alert people that they may have been exposed to a person who is a carrier of the coronavirus.

CHAPTER 9   THE FEAR OF THE KNOWN

In theory, this type of application makes great sense, and should appeal to peoples' innate instinct for self-preservation. In practice, however, such awareness becomes just too worrisome. First, there is a constant and justifiable distrust of where the personal data actually goes and how secure it is. But further to this, many people simply did not want their days ruined having to worry about what a contact alert might or might not mean.

We do not have a true coping mechanism for when there are too many inconvenient facts to handle. Denial or shutdown become the automatic go-to spaces.

In the digital world, we see this everywhere, all the time. Companies and organizations continue to use outdated software for which updates and patches are no longer available. This means they are prone to exploitation by cybercriminal elements who look precisely for the presence of such outdated software. Perhaps the companies' decision makers feel that the odds of being detected and exploited by a rogue actor are small, especially if they themselves are a small company, or who work in a seemingly out-of-the-way industry. They may be unaware, or willingly blind to such dangers, despite the fact that organized crime can sniff such weaknesses out with just the same ruthless efficiency that allows them to dig into exposed ports on the back of every computer.

The same willful blindness happens when organizations must deal with software vulnerabilities that exist in the wild, including those that have been identified, announced, and for which patches have been created by their manufacturers or developers. The gulf between the time a vulnerability is announced and the time a company gets around to applying a fix, even if it is just days, remains infinitely large to a threat actor or to an exasperated cybersecurity expert. But being intangible, these types of gaps also remain abstract to the decision makers – just another vague threat.

CHAPTER 9   THE FEAR OF THE KNOWN

These are the types of dangers that, due to willful blindness based on the fear of overload, will persist into the new era of digital transformation. Take, as an additional example, organizations that share identical network access logons among all their staff, or who use a third party remote access tool with a common password, as happened with the water treatment plant mentioned in Chapter 6. Management often knows the risks, but the company might consider itself too small or insignificant to spend time and resources on cybersecurity technology. Or they simply just don't care.

If you arrive home one day and you realize you left your credit card or bank card somewhere behind – maybe on the counter at a store, or still in the card slot of an ATM, you will likely have a pretty rough evening, until you either physically recover the card or spend time on the phone getting the card cancelled. There's a lot of worry there. Yet most people seldom feel the same when they hear about yet another data breach. Perhaps they feel their credit card data simply isn't that important, or that it won't make a difference to them either way. Perhaps they feel protected by their bank's fraud laws, or the fact that the card itself will expire soon, and that the CRV number is probably not included. Or if it's passwords that were stolen, once again the odds of their password being used are just too small.

All of this willful blindness has enormous chances of going wrong for the individual. Cybercriminals have thousands of creative ways to use stolen data to access other data. For them, a piece of stolen personally identifiable information (PII) can be an ingredient, even if it fails as a meal.

Sometimes this willful blindness manifests itself as fatalism – "It's going to happen anyway, so why should I worry?" – or superstition – "If I'm aware of it and I fear it, it's like summoning a demon, it will come true." Sometimes it just comes down to simple apathy or overload – "I have other problems to deal with right now."

CHAPTER 9   THE FEAR OF THE KNOWN

Willful Blindness and MFA

One of the most secure ways of protecting an organization from hacking and unauthorized break-ins is two-factor authentication (2FA) or multifactor authentication (MFA), both of which require, during the login process, a confirmation code sent to a separate device. Currently the most commonly used separate device is a person's smartphone, which is assumed to always be with its owner and securely locked even if it is lost.

Security experts will point out that a smartphone is not the best device for authentication, because SMS, the most common method for sending authentication codes, is itself prone to getting hacked and having those codes re-routed to bad actors. An authenticator app is preferable when using a phone for receiving a 2FA message. But for most people, their phone by itself is their preferred authentication – if they absolutely have to use authentication, that is. It's easy, it's there, and it's up to someone else to make sure it works (there's that fatalism again).

The non-use of MFA or 2FA is just one of many situations in which people opt to be willfully blind, counting on fate to excuse them from appearing in the line of sight of a hacker. They know the risks, but they count on just keeping a low profile.

Getting stopped in the middle of a task to enter a password feels like a lot of effort, and is not at all convenient when there is work to be done. It's no surprise therefore that many people opt not to use 2FA when they set up a login arrangement with a network or application. It's too much effort and too much information that they will have to know about.

As we move to a digitally transformed workspace, there will be numerous opportunities for people to shrug their shoulders and simply carry on with their non-secure actions. Here are just three of many:

CHAPTER 9   THE FEAR OF THE KNOWN

- People who work much of the time outside the office may on occasion need to access a file that is stored internally on a network drive. They don't have the time to go and look up the correct login procedure, so they will contact the system administrator with a request to turn off a security control on a firewall "just for a moment."

- Coffee shops are great places to get free Wi-Fi. If nobody in there looks particularly suspicious, it seems like it shouldn't be a problem to jump on the store's public Wi-Fi. After all, everybody does it, right?

- The router that your cable company installed to give high-speed Internet for everyone in your household – it came with an instruction manual. Perhaps your employer also sent a memo about how to secure your home router or how to set up a VPN before connecting to the office, but somehow you never got round to checking them out.

These are all examples of activities that require end users – the general public – to carry an added burden of awareness and accountability throughout the day, a burden that, frankly, many people are not willing or able to bear.

Willful Blindness: The Watering Hole Concept

If 100 gazelles are drinking at a watering hole on an African savannah and one of the gazelles gets taken out by a lion, the other gazelles will keep on drinking, with only a few even registering that an attack has taken place. It's unlikely they will all run away because there's water available and there's also safety in numbers. It is also unlikely that the herd will turn together to fight the lion and rescue their fallen comrade. It's easier and better for everyone just to keep their heads down and be happy the lion went for someone else.

That is what a great many humans do when it comes to risk and beating the odds. They'll keep their head down and hope they're too insignificant to be singled out.

They do this when they activate a new home security camera, and they do it when they dash into a convenience store leaving their car's engine running and the keys inside. "What's the point," they say? "I'm just one person."

The problem with this attitude is the assumption that anyone is too small to be noticed. It's what security specialists such as Ed Featherston call "security by obscurity." But threat actors are not lions. They are not limited to just being a single lion or even a pair of lions. The ubiquitous connectivity of the entire Internet, multiplied by automated threat technologies and a relentless drive to discover new weaknesses mean that bad actors, from the most sophisticated gangs to the newest copy-and-paste script kiddie better resembles an infinite swarm of locusts than any single lion.

The question becomes, if end users are given greater awareness of this swarm, would that be enough to overcome willful blindness, or is willful blindness an absolute state that exists regardless of any external threats?

The Fear of Delay, and the Power of Defiance

A study released in September 2021 by HP Wolf Security showed that 91 percent of security teams had felt pressure to compromise security during the pandemic in the name of business continuity. This was due in large part to the challenging situation of people working from home. The willingness

CHAPTER 9   THE FEAR OF THE KNOWN

to overlook strict security controls in the name of just getting stuff done led 83 percent of the respondents to admit this created a "ticking time bomb" for corporate security incidents.

The same report showed that there were significant feelings of apathy and frustration toward managing cybersecurity in a remote workplace, with younger workers in particular more likely to circumvent existing security controls in order to manage their workloads. In fact, 48 percent of this group stated that security tools, including website restrictions or VPN requirements, were a hindrance, with 31 percent having at least attempted to bypass them.[1]

These actions are not uncommon, and they reveal a disturbing combination of bad workplace attitudes. The first is the willingness for organizations to place pressure on individuals to look the other way and bypass security measures in the interest of short-term gain. It is a clear example of the watering hole principle at work – the hope or expectation that the security lapse will not be noticed by the *lions* out there.

This is similar to the old-fashioned *five second rule*, in which people believe an item of food that has been dropped on the ground is still safe to eat if it's picked back up within five seconds. It's a defiance of logical fact driven by hope and fear, whether it's the fear of missing out on work opportunities, or in the case of the five second rule, of missing out on a tasty snack.

The fact that, in the HP study, certain employees sought to bypass security tools, considering them to be a hindrance, may not seem to be fear-based at all. In fact, it seems to smack of confidence, arrogance, or even belligerence. Perhaps it could be categorized as in the same type of social resistance that brought about anti-masking and anti-vaccination movements during the pandemic, but at the same time, it still swims in

---

[1] Wolf Security – No Author Given. "HP Wolf Security Rebellions and Rejections Report Uncovers Remote Workforce Security Trends." Retrieved from https://threatresearch.ext.hp.com/blog/

CHAPTER 9   THE FEAR OF THE KNOWN

the same deep waters of fear – the fear of extra effort, of the unknown, of overload, and most of all the fear of not getting work done and its immediate impact on a person's job.

The study points out that younger workers in particular are more likely to circumvent existing security controls. That is not a surprise, biologically speaking. Nature demands that younger people be fearless, or perhaps more accurately, to be less influenced by the fears that surround them. Young people often feel immortal, untouchable, and impulsive, and are willing to take risks that their elders would not. All the military forces of the world rely on the fearlessness of youth. In 2019, for example, just about 50 percent of all active duty United States Armed Forces personnel – 605,942 out of a total 1.3 million, were aged 25 and under, with 280,585 between ages 26 and 30. Just for completeness of this list, 195,000, were between 31 and 35, 140,000 between 36 and 40, and 103,000 aged 41 and over.[2]

It can be argued that in general young people are charged by nature to win the competition for a mate and for procreation. Not every person seeks this, of course, but on a macro level, when looking at the overall population of the world (7.75 billion in 2020, on track to reach 10 billion by 2100), nature and instinct still play a dominant role in all of human activity. Defying danger and fear in order to succeed in the procreation race is an urge that tends to swim in the bloodstream of younger people, undiluted by the worries and gravitas of their elders. This may help explain reckless youth-related activities ranging from street racing to Covid-catching parties.[3]

---

[2] www.statista.com/statistics/232711/number-of-active-duty-us-defense-force-personnel-by-age/

[3] "Alabama students throwing 'COVID parties' to see who gets infected" (September 2021), retrieved from https://abcnews.go.com/US/alabama-students-throwing-covid-parties-infected-officials/story, and "Alberta COVID party sends several people to hospital with virus" (September 2021), retrieved from https://toronto.citynews.ca/2021/09/23/alberta-covid-party-hospital/

CHAPTER 9   THE FEAR OF THE KNOWN

Such actions in younger demographic groups appear to show the opposite of fear. Collectively it appears to be the condition of having no fear. But this does not leave fear out of the picture. The actions of young adults and others who follow this same defiant course is rooted in the need to overcome fear, not the lack of it. From a procreation standpoint, fear makes a person hesitate, and so nature infuses defiance in its place.

But the activity of defying the rules set down by an older generation can also be tied directly back to the drive to leave the nest, a rite of passage that demands the conquest of one of the biggest fears of all – leaving the safety of one's first home and venturing out into the world. Not every young person feels this, and not every childhood home has an ideal situation, but overall, leaving the nest and hoping you can fly is a big, scary leap of faith for everyone.

I Am Not in Denial

Denial is a self-preservation technique that springs directly out of the fear of the known. It is related to willful blindness, but it is not the same. As we have seen, bad news is always a shock to the system, and when it happens, the fight-or-flight instinct kicks into gear as does the struggle between emotion and logic. The effort required to grasp the magnitude of the change often results in denial – an act of lashing out driven by an incapacity to accept and process news that has shaken the normalcy of life.

This is best illustrated by Elisabeth Kubler-Ross's grief-change curve mentioned in Chapter 3, in which the five phases of denial, anger, bargaining, depression, and acceptance follow a pattern in which emotion leads and logic follows up and tries to balance things out. As mentioned earlier, it doesn't always follow an exact schedule, and in some cases, it can even repeat, but the multi-step sequence of grief is by and large an expectable one.

CHAPTER 9   THE FEAR OF THE KNOWN

The first of these responses, denial, represents the incapacity to accept a change that deviates from a comfortable norm. Emotion – feeling the horror of the change – battles with instinctive desires to either flee the change or fight it, while logic tries to make sense of it all.

Denial happens when the known change is considered to be abhorrent or unwelcome. The result, in many cases, is a stubborn unwillingness to accept the facts – a fearful attempt to hold on to the status quo.

Perhaps there can be no more profound and obvious example of this in recent times than the responses from anti-vaxx and anti-mask protesters to science-based plans for eliminating or at least controlling the Covid pandemic through isolation and inoculation. Protests and civil disobedience broke out in countries all around the world, and shared a theme of violent rejection of Covid protocols, in which staunch emotional denial, rather than cogent evidence-based argument, was pre-eminent.

The fact that these protests occurred in so many places around the world is one indicator of the universality of denial within the human psyche. The fact that anti-vaccination movements have existed since the very earliest days of needle-based inoculations – around 1800 – show that this is not simply a modern, social media-fueled phenomenon:

> *English doctor Benjamin Moseley emerged as a prominent early anti-vaxxer...in an 1806 essay, he claimed mixing cow matter into humans was a violation of natural law. He described fictional post-vaccination ailments like "cowpox face" and speculated that British women "might wander in the fields to receive the embraces of the bull."*[4]

Denial is a reflex of the fear impulse – a knee-jerk reaction that tries to keep people on their path of existing momentum by remaining convinced

---

[4] Watling, Eve. "The 200-Year History of the Anti-Vaxxer Movement: From 'Cowpox Face' to Autism Claims" *Newsweek.* March 13, 2019. Retrieved from www.newsweek.com/history-anti-vaxxers-vaccination-1358403 Accessed August 2021.

CHAPTER 9   THE FEAR OF THE KNOWN

of the correctness of their existing belief or of the status quo. This is different from defiance, in which individuals continue to reject a situation after having reviewed the facts, and even agreeing with them. Denial comes earlier. Defiance comes later. Both, as the world has seen, are highly influential.

Part of the reason why denial is so powerful is the very fact that it is emotion based, and therefore closer to the instinctive core of the human being and much easier to relate to than logic. Two expressions come to mind here. The first is this:

A lie can travel halfway around the world before the truth puts on its shoes.

This quote has been attributed to a great many writers and thinkers, from Jonathan Swift to Mark Twain to Mahatma Gandhi, and many others besides. It speaks to the fact that a lie usually has an emotional component to it that will catch fire with the public, who will act upon it without further thought.

The persecution of witches, heretics, and unbelievers in previous centuries, as well as in the present, has much to do with this crowd-based madness. Politicians especially have learned in the last few years just how powerful a provocative, yet inaccurate or untrue, comment or tweet can be to muster an angry crowd. Any corrections or retractions that are subsequently made, whether by the person who first made it, or by others – including major media – are merely words lost on the wind. No one hears them, and the instigators of the original lie are very aware of this and unfailingly use it to their advantage.

The second key expression is this:

Facts never won a street fight.

There are variations on this statement too, but they point once again to the reality that emotion drives people to act, while leaving logic in the dust. During the Covid pandemic, scientists did their absolute best to explain what was happening and what should be done to minimize the spread and the time spent in lockdown. Unfortunately, since scientists seldom ever speak in exaggerated, emotional terms, preferring instead to deliver a logical summary of their findings and projections as per their training, their words often go unheard. It only takes one person on a social media soapbox to shout out a lie suggesting that a scientist is in league with big pharma to allow the madness to take over once again.

It turns out that, in many cases, people just don't want to know. It is too much to bear, too much to worry about, and, in any case, goes against their existing mindset.

Problems with Prioritization and Procrastination

Two other areas in which we have significant problems with known activities have to do with deciding when to do tasks. When it comes to tasks we don't like, we procrastinate. When it comes to tasks that all need to be done at once, we go blank. These too, have their roots in fear and their branches spread across the short-term memory area of the brain. Let's look at prioritization first, and we'll put off the procrastination discussion for later.

Prioritization is the act of placing a collection of tasks in the order they are to be done. There seems to be nothing scary about this, except that it's an activity that many people grow very fearful of, especially when the tasks in question all appear to be equally important and equally urgent. At the point where too many priorities converge simultaneously, fear, confusion, and overload will impede the mind's ability to think clearly, and will become another cause of *analysis paralysis*.

The brain's limited short-term memory space makes it difficult to juggle three or more tasks and figure out which one should be done first. It quickly causes confusion. Each of these tasks has facts, deadlines, and people attached to them, and all of this must be addressed, usually under significant pressure.

CHAPTER 9 THE FEAR OF THE KNOWN

Added to this, a person who is trying to prioritize is also laboring under additional mantles of fear – fear of upsetting or angering the people who are waiting for these tasks to be completed; fear of looking stupid for not being able to do them; fear of looking stupid for not being able to decide which to do; fear of losing their job over this, or over repeated mistakes like this; maybe even the fear of just being in this type of position where there seems to be no way out. No matter which task is chosen, someone is going to be unhappy.

When the active emotional brain is allowed to let loose its fear without facts backing it up, problems ensue.

Procrastination, on the other hand, is the act of putting off a task despite knowing logically that a delay to this act will cause further damage or trouble. But the task itself fills a person with such dread or repulsion that despite the logical awareness of its importance, emotion overrules and says "no." Putting off a visit to the dentist or doctor, not filing taxes on time, delaying a meeting where bad news must be delivered – these are real world examples of actions that can fill a person with dread, and they, too, have a connection to digital transformation.

It's an instinctive response, an act of self-protection, to succumb to this fear and ignore the logical facts of the situation. Fear will give you the power of defiance to continue to delay this activity despite the knowledge of what problems such avoidance may cause. This is another case in which emotion wins and logic loses.

In both cases, though, facts can be used to overcome the fear. In the case of prioritization problems, a tangible computer screen, whiteboard, or, best of all, pen and paper is all that is needed to list the tasks and write out their relative importance, their urgency, and their stakeholders. Writing gives the brain an appropriate amount of time to think. Seeing the words and ideas on paper, screen, or whiteboard allows them to be reviewed and freshly vetted once again by the eyes and the mind. It gives the individual an opportunity to take a birds-eye-view of a problem rather than staying mired in it at ground level.

CHAPTER 9   THE FEAR OF THE KNOWN

Writing these to-be-prioritized tasks out also has the benefit of making it easier to inform each of the stakeholders – the owners of each task – when they can expect their deliverables to arrive. You may be in a situation where you assess tasks A, B, and C and find there is no single task that is truly the most urgent and important. So you choose to do Task A first, just to get one out of the way. Before starting on it, it would be wise to inform each stakeholder of their task's status, since bad news is better than no news. It will always give the stakeholder something to work with.

Conversely, when no news is given, stakeholders will form their own opinions and will likely come back asking for better service. However, delivering the news that the awaited task is in the queue might not seem like the best news, but it nevertheless gives each stakeholder comfort that it will be worked on soon and, frankly, might be all that they need to hear.

Thirdly, having the tasks laid out on paper might also allow other people to help you in the prioritization process, including the stakeholders themselves. It is not always fair or right that an individual, already under pressure, should be forced to make a decision, especially if their mind is inside a fog of fear.

When people procrastinate, it's because they are facing a task that they don't want to do – the emotion of fear is holding them back *despite* the fact that logic is telling them how important the task is.

Think, for example, of a small business owner who delays doing the bookkeeping, or even filing taxes, possibly due to the fear of delegation discussed in the previous chapter. (Although I am using a small business example here, the stages and steps of this problem can be easily extrapolated to other types of situations, for businesses and departments, small and large.) For an entrepreneur who is spending every waking moment pursuing their dream and building a business based on passions and skill, sitting down to do the books presents two significant emotional blockages.

CHAPTER 9   THE FEAR OF THE KNOWN

The first is doing a task that runs counter to the passion of the work. Bookkeeping is tedious and often takes too long. No freelancer or small business owner wants to spend a day or a weekend doing paperwork. There is a fear there – the fear of spending precious hours doing something that has absolutely no appeal and no connection to the spirit of the company.

There may be a second fear here too: the fear of coming face to face with the reality of the business – how much money is actually coming in, how much is going out, how little is left, and what that means for the prospect of the business going forward. Businesses are built on passion and optimism, emotions both. The threat of facing the reality of a less-than-stellar ledger can crush that passion.

There may be a third fear: the cost of hiring a bookkeeper and an accountant. When cash flow is unpredictable, fixed recurring costs become scary.

So here we have three levels of fear. These are all based on emotion – the distaste for the bookkeeping work, its potential for showing the reality of the business as being less than hoped, and the fear of committing to payments when income is not stable. This fear might be enough to stop the entrepreneur from doing the books at all. There will always be an excuse to not do them today, and this may eventually lead to the entrepreneur failing to file on time, which leads to much greater problems.

The point is the small business owner knows this. The reality that paying taxes is not an option is not lost on this person. But the emotion of the situation – the distaste and the fear – is strong enough to overrule the logic of its reality.

An easy way to solve the entrepreneur's fear of bookkeeping would be to demonstrate how much a bookkeeper would charge per month and shift the perspective away from the money going out to the fact that the entrepreneur can use the time saved to generate more money than the bookkeeper costs.

CHAPTER 9 THE FEAR OF THE KNOWN

When fear overtakes logic and prevents people from doing what they logically know to be right, delaying or refusing to do the action will result in further problems. Emotion is just that strong. Fear puts up a wall that is very hard to see over. It grows itself huge in the mind's eye.

At least that's how it is until facts are brought to bear. Facts balance out fear by giving the logical side of the brain something to work with. It doesn't come equipped with substance the way emotion does. Solutions do not come automatically to mind. We can see this in individuals, and we see it in groups and populations. Whether it's a specific habit like procrastination or a general distrust of change, we have to bring out the facts to meet the fear and balance it out.

The Password Manager Example Revisited

To see this in action, let's go back to the example of the password management software described in Chapter 4. If people are avoiding using this technology out of fear and distrust, then they need facts to neutralize their fear.

Let's escalate the scenario to look at proactive internal defense strategies for companies. Breaches, hacks, ransomware, and supply chain incidents are daily occurrences, and no company or organization is immune. In many situations, victim companies get hit directly or indirectly as a result of fear. Here are three of the most common types:

- The employee described above, who resents having to learn how to use a password manager, and instead stays with the old way, using an easy-to-remember, re-used password, hoping no one will notice, or willfully not caring if they do.

CHAPTER 9 THE FEAR OF THE KNOWN

- An employee who is working on the road who needs to get hold of a PowerPoint deck they left back at the office and jumps on a coffee shop Wi-Fi to log in, without going through a VPN. This person's fear of not getting access to the deck, and of consequently not getting their work done on time, forces a conscious decision to just go and get it

- A senior manager who is fearful of going over budget, and who also fears annoying the higher-ups with increasing security costs, paired with *sky-is-falling* hypothetical cybersecurity scenarios, puts off requesting a budget for more resources until the next budget cycle.

These are fears that are rooted in the day-to-day trials and tribulations of work: trying to get things done while not looking stupid or causing a problem with the boss. These are the fears that most working people live with every day. In succumbing to these fears, they turn a blind eye to the reality of the threats around them, hoping that they, as humble individuals – gazelles at the watering hole – will not be noticed. Others will staunchly resist any modifications to their comfortable status quo, and will do so either overtly or, worse, covertly.

When individuals fearfully opt out of participating in digital transformation, it weakens the entire structure, which is precisely what the bad guys are waiting for.

CHAPTER 10

The Fear of Communicating

Of the many notable stories involving social media and video chat technology, especially during the pandemic, there is one that matches the shocking nature of that famous website company's internal phishing fiasco, and occurred almost a year to the day after it, when the CEO of an online mortgage company fired 900 employees via a Zoom call, before allegedly taking some time off to recover. He later apologized for the act, but not before the three-minute call had made worldwide headlines.[1]

This is just one of thousands of examples where people have chosen to have difficult conversations without actually having the conversation, choosing instead to lob the bad news over the wall like a digital hand grenade, while they themselves take cover.

It may be that the group firing happened as a result of the manager's inability to meet people in person due to distance or ongoing pandemic-related isolation. However, that does not excuse the way in which it was done. It is symptomatic of a condition that is becoming all too common in the digitally transformed world, and that is the diminishing ability to communicate face-to-face.

---

[1] "Not great news": US boss fires 900 employees on a Zoom call. The Guardian December 7, 2021. Retrieved from www.theguardian.com/us-news/2021/dec/07/not-great-news-us-boss-fires-900-employees-on-a-zoom-call

CHAPTER 10 THE FEAR OF COMMUNICATING

The Covid pandemic forced most of us to put aside two vital essentials of social intimacy – the handshake and the hug, and the loss of these actions has been one of the most difficult things that we have had to go through collectively.

We are literally born craving communication. From the moment of birth, skin-to-skin contact between mother and infant helps establish a physical and emotional bond and encourages stability borne out of a sense of safety, and a baby's piercing cry ensures a regular supply of attention and food.

Touch is vital to all of us. There are touch receptors in the brain that release oxytocin, a stress- and pain-management hormone. The release occurs when a *wanted* touch occurs, such as a hug, a handshake, or a high five. These are touch experiences that are socially permitted and desired. They play important roles in social bonding rituals, can reduce stress, and can even increase tolerance to pain.

Being deprived of the ability to be physically close to other people in social situations like restaurants and concerts undoubtedly contributed in part to the fervor of the anti-lockdown protests around the world. It wasn't solely about any government's mandate; it was also about not being allowed to be together.

But even before the pandemic, people were starting to self-isolate in other ways. In the years since email and texting became ubiquitous, we have started to prefer electronic messaging as the primary medium of communication, replacing the live dynamic of the phone call, and of face-to-face conversation.

It's ironic that the device that started out as a mobile telephone quickly became more popular as a launchpad for texting, a technique that provides the immediacy of a conversation without the need for the emotional depth, context, and the unpredictability that a phone conversation provides. There is a great deal of uncertainty in a phone conversation: how long is it going to last? What will the caller say or ask? What will I say? How can I end the call and get out of this uncomfortable situation? Why don't I just let it go to voicemail?" In fact, many of us who set out to make a call are relieved when it goes to voicemail, since a voicemail message is essentially an out-loud version of texting.

When people converse, either face-to-face or by phone, they will often fall into a rhythm. The nature of the conversation is based not just on the words themselves, but on tone, cadence, and, in the case of a face-to-face chat, body language, hand movements, eye contact, and eye deflection (looking away from the other person). A good conversation involves two people falling into a pattern of speaking and listening. There is an art to subtle interruption techniques, and to guiding and cueing each other further along the mutual thought pattern through positive gestures. It becomes a type of dance.

Conversation is a skill first learned in childhood and practiced throughout life. Even babies who have not yet learned to form their first word take great delight in mimicking the rhythms of speech that they hear all around them.

In the end, the value of a conversation is not solely in the words spoken but in the emotional connection it makes with others through these additional physical layers. So what happens when we place a pane of glass between people?

Message in a Bubble

Social media has, by creating its own audience-of-one culture, largely removed the need and desire for in-person conversational interaction. It has instead replaced it with various forms of messaging. Text messages need no eye contact and demand no in-person physical context. This is a technology that makes us feel that we can communicate more, when, in fact, it makes us *communicate* less.

The text message breaks the interaction down to packages of words without context. This seems to make messaging easier, but often leads to situations where meanings are misconstrued due to ambiguous word choices or phrasing, which can lead to delay or even insult. These are problems that are easily clarified in the face-to-face world through a wink, smile, or frown.

A good example of this is the word "fine." You send a text request to someone – an employee, customer, manager, or even your partner/spouse – and you end your request with, "Is that OK?" The reply that comes back is

"Fine."

Now what are you going to make of that? How many ways are there to say "fine?" And what happens if you interpret it the wrong way, when it passes through existing filters of guilt, enthusiasm, or cognitive bias?

The medium of text messaging is generally so sterile that we had to invent emojis in order to re-inject that emotion.

With text messaging, each text message carries itself as a complete thought, encapsulated in a bubble. The recipient receives this message and responds to it, either immediately or later. The response is another message in a bubble. It's the preferred way. It's easy, it's fast, it's straightforward, and it's controllable.

Although some people may prefer live, in-person conversation, many, especially those who have grown up in the Internet age, find live conversations too random, and not controllable enough. Thinking about having a face-to-face real-time conversation generates fear over how the other person might act and react, as well as how they themselves will handle it.

A live conversation is often assessed and feared in terms of what it will cost (my time, my sense of control, my dignity). It is less likely to be looked upon in terms of what it stands to gain: creative synergy, greater clarity, overall time saved, a growth in friendship, or personal credibility. Once again, it's about "what do I stand to lose?" rather than "what do I stand to gain?"

Some may argue that text messaging is simply the evolution of human communication, but so long as people still have the physical ability to speak in person or by phone, it's not so much an evolution as an alternative. But the message in a bubble mindset is spreading across into other areas of human interaction, and that's where problems exist.

Leadership Needs Communication

Text messaging as a primary communication form can easily lead to a fear of the type of professional intimacy that is needed when managing or working with others. If it is easier and seemingly quicker to send a message than have a conversation, then it naturally becomes the go-to technique. But in doing this, the skills of social interaction will atrophy.

Communication is a vital component in all leadership and management activities. Specific examples include critical thinking with others, giving and seeking feedback, mediating conflicts, leading teams, solving problems, giving bad news, giving good news, and simply taking care of the people in a team. It's important to know how much or how little involvement is needed for a team to be efficient, and to communicate that policy clearly.

When managers realize they don't actually know how to *really* talk to, and *really* listen to their people, they might procrastinate, recoiling in mild fear at the thought of having a conversation – especially a difficult one. They might resort instead to firing off an email message, a text, or a video chat announcement, which is what happened at the online mortgage company. When this happens, the foundations of a team can start to crumble.

Great leaders know that things don't always go well. But that's what makes them great leaders. Their chief strength is their ability to lead people through the unknown to a place of safety. But the sterile, unidirectional bubbles of messaging that texting and email deliver tend to reduce the capacity for leaders to lead through such tough times.

CHAPTER 10   THE FEAR OF COMMUNICATING

Some leaders might feel a self-imposed obligation to be as perfect and flawless as superheroes in the movies, and anything that smacks of trouble or weakness, such as the inability to predict how a live conversation might turn out, seems to be a step in the wrong direction. This makes it easy to justify staying within the bubble. But to see just how live interaction works to strengthen leadership, go to the gym for a moment.

If you have ever gone to a gym or a health club to tone your muscles or maybe build them up, you will (hopefully) be taught a thing or two about physiology from your instructor. Muscles get toned and then grow and get stronger through the process of repairing the mild damage that comes from a tough workout – one that is slightly tougher than you are used to. A good healthy workout generates microscopic tears in the muscle fiber which must then be repaired. It's also why muscular exercise is so good for weight loss, since the process of muscle recovery helps burn calories for hours after a workout.

The point here is that strength comes from mild breakage; from going into situations of friction, and coming out better for it. The same thing happens in the brain when you learn. Learning something new is mental exercise. During this process, synapses form new connections, which expands mental abilities exponentially.

Leadership and management skills are reinforced by going into areas that may be slightly more challenging than staying behind a desk. This includes having difficult conversations and interacting with others in situations that may have unpredictable outcomes. These can happen in person, of course, but they can happen equally well in face-to-face virtual environments.

Email was never a practical method of communication; it was instead a method of notification. Millions of hours have been wasted over the past three decades as people have resorted to sending excessive numbers of email messages back and forth. It seemed fast, convenient, and free, although, in regard to time spent and resources used, it was none of those things, and still isn't. Its only benefit was that it allowed people to say what they wanted to say without all that inconvenient and uncomfortable interaction with others.

Texting and email continue to provide a convenient isolation booth that itself helps foster a fear of interpersonal communication intimacy. It will continue to grow so long as humans choose to stay entirely within their messaging bubbles.

Why Not Just Pick Up the Phone?

As described in Chapter 2, people who were working from home for the first time suffered through video chats, feeling cognitively overloaded during the call, and then feeling isolated once the call was complete. Frankly, more phone calls might have helped.

But there is another fear involved in using a phone, one that email and text messaging handily resolved long ago. This has to do with how long a call might be. To people who have grown comfortable with the neat controllable packaging of messaging by text, it seems there is no way to control the type of *organic* conversation that comes with a live phone call or video call. This is one of the many reasons people prefer to text in the first place.

But this is where things come full circle in a bad way. It is extremely possible to influence and control the duration of a phone call, primarily by establishing time boundaries in advance of the call, and having cues and exit lines at the ready when it comes time to end it. But these techniques depend largely on having access to those interpersonal skills that have been eroded through life in the speech bubble.

Managers who are not comfortable having live, face-to-face conversations become managers who are less able and less willing to hold face-to-face feedback meetings with their reports. Then, when managers find themselves unable to relate to their employees in person, that's when they find themselves unable to trust them, especially if they ask to work from home more often. So life in a text bubble becomes life in a trust bubble, and the quality of the relationships continues to decline.

What about the argument that emails are more efficient than calling because they take less time and cost nothing? Or that they are less intrusive? Or that they provide a valuable paper trail? These are all good points, but they still do not elevate email to a superior place over live interaction.

For a start, email is not and was not ever *free*. Whereas a postage stamp served to partially cover the cost of paying people for the time spent in moving a physical letter from Point A to Point B, the time and cost of reading and creating multiple emails has simply been absorbed by the workday. This has meant either pushing aside more valuable tasks or using personal, after-work time to catch up. Or both. This by itself has come at a terrible cost to organizations and individuals.

Email is also a perfect example of ergonomic inflation, since an increased number of emails does not actually yield any proportionate progress. There are so many emails (and text messages) because they are easy and emotionally safe to create and send, and, because of this, we create and send more than we need to.

It is also an example of *induced demand*, a term used when discussing the building of new highways with the goal of alleviating gridlock. New highways just invite more vehicles. As Adam Mann writes in *Wired*, "It's the roads themselves that cause traffic."[2] If there was no text messaging available at all, the option would be to use live communication – phone, intercom, video chat, or in-person to talk in real time. "Who would have the time for that?" would be the response. The answer would be that we

---

[2] Mann, Adam. "What's Up with That: Building Bigger Roads Actually Makes Traffic Worse" *Wired*, June 17, 2014. Retrieved from www.wired.com/2014/06/wuwt-traffic-induced-demand/ Accessed December 2021.

would have fewer live chats, but they would be of much higher value – essentially having all your ducks in a row, rather than throwing one duck at a time via email.

In terms of having a paper trail, it has always been possible to record conversations, and this is even more possible now with AI powered real-time transcription apps. Relying on email simply because it keeps a record of itself is a little like putting the cart before the horse.

Ultimately, people fear picking up the phone or appearing live on camera because the muscles of social interaction have atrophied. Many of us simply do not know how to do it anymore, and that is costing us dearly.

The Fear of Appearing Outside the Bubble

In Chapter 2, I mentioned the reluctance many people currently feel about keeping their camera on during a video chat meeting. We talked about how some people might be self-conscious about how they appear on camera, whether it's their background, or their *resting face*, or perhaps confusion over where to actually look. But there's one more camera-related issue to mention, and this has to do with allowing people to see you as part of the conversation relationship, in terms of the benefits to them – your conversation partners.

The general reluctance to be visible on camera shows just how people have forgotten the reason for the *visual* component of video chat: that your face and your facial expressions together form a vital messaging system that helps guide the conversation while boosting emotional connection and trust with the people on the call.

In an increasingly digitally transformed world, human relationships depend on the visual component of having a face to relate to. It's a vital tool for establishing trust in every relationship. (This is assuming you are not visually impaired – something I make mention of in my Apology section at the end of this book).

People want to relate to a face. It doesn't matter what you look like, but it does matter that you are not faceless. A person's face is the start of their personal credit rating – a status of credibility and reliability that is built over time, fed by trust, and which is central to establishing positive and collaborative working relationships. We are comfortable around people who we know to be genuine. By contrast, our fear of the unknown means a person without a face presents a barrier or, at the very least, a possible threat.

It is as important for live video meetings as it is in person to help guide the conversation, to demonstrate comprehension or confusion, empathy, agreement, or disagreement. A face is like a set of traffic signals for the relationship. These signals are processed largely unconsciously by your conversation partner, based on a lifetime of practice. But to put it bluntly, during a video chat, your face doesn't just belong to you, it belongs to the relationship.

The Fear of Saying No

The word "no" is one of the shortest words in the English language, but in many cases, one of the most difficult to pronounce. Saying "no" to a request to join a meeting or accommodate an additional task request might lead to trouble. So to avoid potential repercussions, most people simply say "yes."

The problem here is not just one of semantics or wordplay. It's about emotion. Negative memories last longer and more intensely than do positive ones. This is due, once again, to the priorities that instinct places on self-preservation: it's more important to remember the bad things that happen to you so as to be able to avoid them the next time.

The fear of saying "no" to work-related requests is another of the reasons the workday has extended to well beyond the agreed-upon hours. Long before the pandemic, as email and smartphones became constant

CHAPTER 10 THE FEAR OF COMMUNICATING

companions, the expectation that a person would be available for a meeting at times not wholly convenient, was based in great measure on the impersonal nature of the online meeting request, which flattens the sender's personality to a simple faceless command.

There should be no reason why an employee at any level should be expected to be available to answer messages 24/7. We should be able to organize our time around our own work and life priorities and use our ability to communicate to manage expectations as to when calls can be taken and when emails will be returned. But we don't. And we can't, most of us anyway. And the reason is most often fear – of the unknown, of missing out, of offending, and of possibly losing your job by not being a team player.

What's missing in this situation once again is the ability for people to chat live – to negotiate and to identify times and circumstances that are genuinely, mutually convenient, and to build personal credit ratings at the same time. It helps to remember that the letters in the word "no" also appear in the word "negotiate".

Imagine if, instead of sending a faceless meeting request, your colleague calls you and asks, "can we meet up tomorrow at 10:00?" You reply truthfully, "sorry, I can't. I have a dental appointment." It is unlikely your colleague will say, "no problem. I'll come with you, and I'll sit in the chair next to you. We can meet while you're having your teeth seen to." It's obvious that a dental appointment is a higher priority and is also a socially acceptable excuse that can easily eclipse the importance of most meetings. The meeting can be negotiated to another time, and each person's social credit rating remains undamaged.

In a digitally transformed workplace, the solution is to build a system that balances availability and non-availability in a way that appears genuinely flexible while still defending your time against unreasonable attack. It should be able to identify times when an employee is available to respond and times when they are not. I, as a member of a team, should be able to let people know when I will be able to respond to emails and when I am in the "do not disturb" mode.

CHAPTER 10   THE FEAR OF COMMUNICATING

In addition, the culture of a workplace should be designed and maintained to support that. In the physical office world of old, if you came to see me and you saw that I was clearly not in today – my cubicle is empty, the computer is off and there is no half-full coffee mug to be seen, you would correctly assume I was not in, and that would automatically adjust your expectations for the day.

This concept of adjusting expectations is not new, but it is still rare. People have always struggled with being able to say "no" to requests for their time, out of fear of offending or of getting into trouble. And it turns out that even hiding in your house doesn't make it any easier. But if you have ever been to a restaurant, the solution has been staring you in the face.

The Power of the Restaurant Menu

When you walk into a restaurant and take your seat, you will be presented with a menu. No surprise there. But what does a menu mean to you as a customer? For most of us, it feels like it's a ticket to a world of personal dining freedom. After all, we can select anything we want from this list, and someone will bring it to us. It feels very liberating to have such power of choice. But there's another side to what is going on here. The sense of personal power is an illusion. A menu is actually a powerful tool of influence, with the power belonging to the restaurant.

For any restaurant to survive and thrive, the owner must collaborate with the chef to create and plan meals that they know their customers will want to order. They must then purchase most of the ingredients in advance, and ensure what they have planned will maximize sales and minimize wastage.

To make sure this happens, they will draw up a menu that summarizes what we, the customers, can choose. It's a fixed list. There are no other choices; yet, as customers, we still feel good about this. There is usually

CHAPTER 10   THE FEAR OF COMMUNICATING

enough variety to make it seem that we have been given a choice and that we have chosen of our own free will.

The concept behind the restaurant menu is to make it appear that there is choice, by providing more than one option in terms of meals to choose from. But the options still remain part of a finite and limited set, based on the ingredients that were purchased. It has to be this way if the restaurant owner wishes to stay in business.

The restaurant menu concept is an example of presenting the illusion of choice within a fixed collection of options. It's something that can be applied in the workplace when it comes to appearing available, yet making that availability selective and plannable. Rather than saying "no" to meeting requests, it should be possible to create time choices from which people can choose. By doing this, you can turn your online calendar into a type of restaurant menu.

Let's say you schedule a task from 9:00 to 10:00 and then another between 10:30 and 11:00. Why not simply start working on Task 2 at 10:00? Because, by intentionally leaving a half-hour between 10:00 and 10:30, you create a space for someone to use for a quick call or meeting. Structuring each day with a few of these spaces consciously and carefully scattered throughout will deliver an impression of availability. It will give people choices as to when they can meet with you, but these choices are far more on your terms. This helps eliminate the need to say no, while not sacrificing your valuable time.

This is a great application of the 80/20 rule. By strategically ensuring that 20 percent of your week is left open to *ad hoc* communications and meetings, you can develop a genuine reputation for accessibility.

As digital transformation forges ahead, the danger will always be the expectation and pressure to be available. It is up to us to move beyond the limitations of such technologies by pairing tangible tools of influence such as the restaurant menu-inspired availability calendar, with the skills of human influence that come from well-toned muscles of social interaction.

CHAPTER 10   THE FEAR OF COMMUNICATING

The Fear of Not Knowing Where You Stand

Employees crave feedback. But they also fear it. They also might fear not being able to get feedback if digital transformation changes the manager–employee relationship. That's a conundrum.

In earlier years, and for older employees, feedback on job performance might have been a once-per-quarter or even annual event. But the need for feedback has grown, quite appropriately, with the change in personal media and culture. Gaming, for example, provides feedback pretty much every second on a character's achievement, powers, and wealth. Even for those who are not gamers, we as consumers have grown to expect feedback in the shape of the speed of response to messaging apps, confirmations for online purchases, and delivery. Everything must happen immediately, or it will be in danger of being abandoned.

For employees of any age, performance feedback connects directly to their concerns about their work performance, which, as described already, connects back to everything else about life. Whether they work from home, on-premises, or in a hybrid situation, the fact remains they will expect a personalized experience in terms of how their progress is being rated and what this means to them.

The capacity to deliver feedback as a manager, and to receive it as an employee, must be factored into the technologies of the new workplace, and indeed, it is one of the primary concerns managers have about the work-from-home scenario – there is a perceived lack of intimacy and immediacy that comes from conducting a feedback session by video chat. I disagree. Feedback may be a confidential and somewhat professionally intimate conversation, but it is still that – a conversation. Video chat allows for facial communication and body language, and scheduling time for these events is still a matter of just that – scheduling time.

CHAPTER 10   THE FEAR OF COMMUNICATING

The Fear of Breaking Linear Thought

When we look at communication as an activity, thoughts go immediately to the people involved. But communication also involves ideas, which must then be converted into words. From the time each of us learned how to read and write, we have been imprinted with the need to process information in a linear order. While this seems vital for forming letters into words and words into sentences, both of which are linear strings, it becomes counterproductive when it comes to the type of thought required for working creatively.

Reading is a remarkable activity. To be able to elicit meaning from a series of shapes and squiggles on a page without having to think about it is, in my opinion, one of humankind's greatest achievements. To have become an *unconscious competent* in this activity means that you do not need to spell out every letter and every sound to make words comprehensible in your mind. You can look at a group of letters or a group of words and instantaneously grasp their meaning. You're doing it right now.

The amazing power of literacy is best experienced by taking it away. Looking at a phrase like this

怕什么, 来什么

will mean nothing if you cannot read Chinese. (It's a Chinese expression: "the more you fear it, the worse it gets.") But if your brain is not attuned to the physical construction of the letters and symbols of any foreign language, reading it is a waste of time.

CHAPTER 10   THE FEAR OF COMMUNICATING

For a fully literate person, words, and sequences of words, become images to be ingested whole. Your mind actually reads ahead, and sees what it expects to see. That's why this "Paris in the Spring" graphic works so well to impress upon people the importance of proof-reading, which is another skill that is often lost to the technology-induced pressures of time, despite being easier than ever thanks to those very same technologies.

However, whether you read left-to-right, right-to-left, or up-and-down, it still helps to have all the words laid out in the right order, so this is a case where the linear process still holds.

But that doesn't mean the linear rule should dominate the thinking process. Think, for example, about writer's block. We have all been there. Whether it's an email, a report, or a PowerPoint presentation, you sit and stare at the screen, and struggle to come up with the first words. You may already have many of the key things that you want to say floating around in your short-term memory, where they are forced to stay while you struggle to think of what to write first.

So, why should you write the first thing first? Because that's how you were taught: to start at the beginning, and work through to the end. The problem with this is that some of those brilliant ideas floating in your short-term memory might vanish altogether while they wait their turn, which is a great tragedy.

The better route is to write or type everything that comes to mind in a random, flow-of-consciousness release, without worrying about order. Putting the ideas in order comes later. The most important thing to do at the beginning of a creative process, which includes writing messages of any length, solving problems, thinking creatively or even managing a crisis, is to get the thoughts and ideas on a surface as soon as possible and edit them into the proper order later. This has at least three benefits:

- It gets those ideas out and saved before you forget them.
- It clears space in your short-term memory for more ideas to arrive.
- In a brainstorming scenario, others can see your ideas and build on them.

Much of this has to do with how short-term memory works, and the fact that we only have space for about eight live ideas at a time. There may be lots of room in long-term memory for actual memories, but the memory used in the short term, for in-the-moment processing, is highly limited. As such, trying to get the right sequence of ideas in order inside this tiny space is exceedingly difficult.

So, my advice to anyone starting work on a project, concept, or document is to just write whatever comes to mind, and put it in order later. Just get it out onto something safe: paper, a dry-erase board, or an on-screen document. The same thing should happen with a team – when meeting in person or online – to solve a problem or work on a new creative idea. While brainstorming, use a virtual or physical board or document space to keep the ideas together, and let everyone know there is no need to put anything in order yet. That will come later.

The key here is to overcome writer's block, which is not so much a condition of not knowing what to say, as of not knowing what to say first. The reason it becomes a blockage is based in the same reflex as *analysis paralysis* – too many facts descending into the short-term memory space too quickly.

CHAPTER 10   THE FEAR OF COMMUNICATING

The fear of breaking linear thought is not just about writing memos or brainstorming with a team. It is a concept that can extend into other areas of work and communication. It is also an attitude toward business. It's about recognizing that things can be done in a way other than the traditional a-to-z linear approach. For example, that work can be done in places other than just the office, at times other than just 9-to-5, and by people other than just those who live close enough to commute, and by using tools that best fit our individual way of doing things.

CHAPTER 11

The Fear of Losing the Business

In Chapter 9, I mentioned a study released in September 2021 that showed that 91 percent of security teams had felt pressure to compromise security during the pandemic in the name of business continuity, creating a "ticking time bomb" for corporate security incidents. Compromised security leaves holes in an organization for criminals to walk right through and these holes can remain there for years.

Yet, among certain business leaders, there is a willingness to leave these holes unpatched due to the fear of what it might do to the current flow of business. Interruptions are costly. Upgrades and fixes can cause downtime and delay, as can training and retraining employees. Installing secure endpoints in the houses of every employee who chooses to work from home is seen as *spending money we don't have*. It all appears, in the minds of some, to be an abundance of unrealistic caution that is greater than the possibility of an actual attack.

The key words here are *the current flow of business*. There is a fear of change among senior management that is palpable – these are people who have created long-range plans and who have made significant commitments, financial and otherwise, to their company's viability, only to have it threatened first by digital transformation itself and then by digital transformation magnified by Covid-related issues.

CHAPTER 11   THE FEAR OF LOSING THE BUSINESS

Myles Suer, in his article, *Digital Transformation, Post Covid-19*, in August 2021, quotes a number of experts who highlight these fears. Although this article, like others quoted in this book, will be eclipsed by others as the months and years go by, the attitudes of corporate management described within are timeless.[1] For example, he quotes Rita McGrath in her April 2020 *Harvard Business Review* article:

> *At the time, McGrath wrote, "simply asking CEOs of traditional companies about digital would throw them into a panic. This is because they believe digital technologies and business models pose an existential threat to their way of doing business — and of course they're right."*
>
> *For former CIO Wayne Sadin, "CIOs are doing everything from before, they are just doing it 25 percent faster, from home. If you had a digital transformation strategy pre-Covid, you would have built an organizational culture that reacted faster to changes in markets, products, customer experience (CX), and employee experience (EX). In this case, you would have evolved relatively smoothly. Lacking such digital experience means you're scrambling faster today to get there."*
>
> *CTO Stephen diFilipo noted, "The pandemic surfaced disparities among employees' ability to comprehend and adopt to the requirements of digital business capabilities."* This means leaders can only advance as far as their employees' capabilities allow them to. For this reason, digital maturity level and the quality of digital business initiatives are dependent on employees. Success is less about digital and more about workplace readiness for digital.

---

[1] The following quotes are from: Suer, Myles. "Digital Transformation, Post COVID-19" *CMS Wire* August 10, 2021. Retrieved from www.cmswire.com/information-management/digital-transformation-post-covid-19/ Accessed December 2021.

CHAPTER 11   THE FEAR OF LOSING THE BUSINESS

Former CIO Isaac Sacolick suggested "Most businesses need a top-down review of the markets they want to be in, customer needs, product and service offerings, and technology/data impacts. Many changes need to be made post-Covid, so it is best to start with customers and then consider your supply chain. The threat is that hybrid work will create a new digital divide between the valley's openness and Wall Street's traditional ways of doing business."

CIO Deb Gildersleeve agreed, saying, "Most organizations need to really take a step back. This process should start by prioritizing agility, resiliency, and continuity. It's no longer just about large-scale transformation. The world we operate in makes it impossible to ignore an organization's need to adapt to changing business conditions. From getting employees the physical technology and tools to do their jobs when the pandemic hit to creating digital solutions that drive collaboration and productivity as we're all approaching work differently, it's all completely changing how we think about digital technology."

A central office isn't required to be productive. CIO Jason James said we should acknowledge that as a starting point: "We have proven that productivity isn't tied to offices. This gives more options to protect the workforce in areas that may have been in the past considered higher risk."

To summarize these five experts quoted in this one article:

- CIOs are doing everything from before, they are just doing it 25 percent faster.
- Leaders can only advance as far as their employees' capabilities allow them to.
- Hybrid work will create a new digital divide between the valley's openness and *Wall Street*'s traditional ways of doing business.

169

CHAPTER 11   THE FEAR OF LOSING THE BUSINESS

- It's no longer just about large-scale transformation.
- Productivity isn't tied to offices.

There is a fear among those in management that the business *as it was*, and also *as it was being planned for*, is no more – that things will not return to the normalcy of 2019 and earlier, but will require significant shifts in strategy and financial commitment – a restart. That is a change that few in management want to see happen.

Trying to Grasp the Infinite

Digital transformation is not just about remote teams, of course. It has much more to do with the addition of more technologies into the work cycle, technologies that are simultaneously more intelligent than ever before and more connected.

These technologies are not well understood. Companies have teams of IT specialists and cybersecurity specialists, all of whom work hard to maximize their companies' productivity and profitability while simultaneously trying to protect it from an infinite universe of cybercrime. They know a lot about their craft, but every one of them, if they're being honest with themselves, knows that cybersecurity is a game with no end, but with severe consequences for losing. From viruses on through to ransomware, the invisible nature of cybercrime is difficult to visualize. Perhaps there is no better illustration of this than the image of the stereotype hacker: a young looking person dressed in a hoodie, hands hovering over a keyboard – a misleading caricature of an invisible and incomprehensible enemy.

The problem is that, in the private sector, a company is always free to fail on its own due to an inadequate understanding of their marketplace, or from selling a poor quality product. But when it comes to failures in the digital world, these potentially affect everyone on the planet due to the fact that every company and individual is connected via the Internet.

CHAPTER 11   THE FEAR OF LOSING THE BUSINESS

Breaches, hacking, and ransomware can happen in any one of a million ways, and that fact alone makes it difficult for any person – but especially one whose responsibilities involve leadership and decision-making – to contemplate the enormity of an infinite criminal landscape without losing their senses.

The Fear of Ransomware

Ransomware, for example, is a relatively new form of cybercrime, having been around for about a decade, but it has been continuously escalating in severity and sophistication to the point that stories of ransomware now happen daily. Whereas computer viruses have been wreaking havoc on computers and networks for much longer, ransomware closes the circle of destruction by making it enormously profitable. It's robbery without the hassle of having to show up in person with a gun. It can be applied to companies anywhere in the world with minimal outlay – the cost of a few million emails sent, and you can remain as anonymous as you want to be.

Ransomware payments are often made in cryptocurrency, Bitcoin being the most famous, but other, less traceable currencies like Monero always a favorite. This, too, is an area that leaves most people in the dark. Cryptocurrency and the blockchain system upon which it travels are not well understood and become yet another unknown in a collection of digital unknowns.

Ransomware always seems to happen at the worst time, because, frankly, there is no best time. People are busy. They have files and messages to retrieve, and a great deal of work to do. Most of this work is done in some way by interacting with a networked computer.

When the "locked" screen appears, informing every member of the staff that their files are no longer available, fear explodes in all directions. Employees suddenly have to find out how to access the documents they need. They struggle to remember where the alternatives and backups might be, such as paper records. They panic as they try to remember what they were working on the moment the lockout happened. They call for help from the people who attend the IT helpdesk, who themselves are scrambling to put out a thousand fires and pull out ten thousand cables.

There are fears about what is being stolen, what is being violated, what damage is already mounting to records and data, but also, by the minute, to the company's brand, and reputation. How is the public reacting? What is this doing to the share price? To the company's credibility? How long will it take to restore and repair? Who is going to talk to the media? Who is going to take the fall?

A company under ransomware siege is a company gripped by panic. It requires careful and well-planned steps to work through the crisis without making rash, tunnel-vision-based mistakes. It demands access to people who know what to do and what to say, and who know just what cards the company still holds.

When ransomware strikes an individual company, that company must close ranks and fix itself with minimized damage. When it hits a hospital, the stakes become even higher. Peoples' lives are at risk, as all the electronic machinery freezes. When it hits a part of a country's infrastructure, such as a water purification plant, an oil distribution center, or an agricultural hub, it becomes everyone's problem.

The Fear of the Cost of Prevention

So it seems that the fear of ransomware should be enough to ensure every organization takes sufficient steps to ensure they do not become vulnerable. This includes establishing a solid and efficient backup and recovery process, proactive vulnerability scanning, and appropriate cyberhygiene training for all employees at all levels. In theory, if the data that is being held for ransom has been backed up, then the pirates lose their leverage. Simply restore the data and carry on.

CHAPTER 11   THE FEAR OF LOSING THE BUSINESS

But it's not as easy as that. Restoring data to a full operational state can take days, weeks, or even months, during which time the organization remains hobbled.

At that point of crisis, when turning to a backup is the only option, some companies might then discover that their data has not been backed up for many weeks and is correspondingly out of date. How could this happen? Because backups are costly and time-consuming. They appear to be like money poured down the drain. They impede the fiscal flow of business.

Humans really don't like thinking about the bad things that might happen to them, and they certainly don't like paying for things that might or might not happen.

Y2K was a great example of this. In the 1980s and 1990s it was discovered that hundreds of thousands of computer systems worldwide that were using a two-digit date system would, on the last minute of the last day of 1999, tick over to 00, which would be interpreted and calculated as 1900.

> *There were worries of aircraft falling out of the sky, power grid shutdowns and all manner of destructive events to come. Fortunately, enough skilled programmers, many brought out of retirement, were martialed, and enough money was spent – estimated at $500 billion globally – to thwart most of the problems. The fact that nothing much happened on January 1, 2000, was not hailed as a victory of proactive crisis avoidance, but more like a disappointment that the entire thing had always been a non-event, and perhaps was overstated from the start.[2]*

---

[2] Prentice, Steve. "From Y2K To NYC Parking Meters: Have We Learned Anything About Complacency In Cybersecurity?" Written for (ISC)² and posted at *CloudTweaks*, August 2020. Available at https://cloudtweaks.com/2020/08/cybersecurity-complacency/ Accessed December 2021.

CHAPTER 11   THE FEAR OF LOSING THE BUSINESS

This is a problem that happens with human beings in general. Being wired for reaction and not pro-action, it becomes exceedingly difficult to comprehend threats until they are actually upon us. Endless case studies will be written on this same theme by people observing different countries' responses to the Covid-19 pandemic, climate change, earthquake preparation, and much more. And by the way, the next Y2K events on the horizon are in 2036 and 2038, so we are not safely through those woods yet, either.[3] As a reminder of how pervasive and possible these types of events are, a minor one happened to Microsoft on January 1, 2022, when a bug started blocking email delivery with on-premise servers. This again was due to a date value that maxed out at the end of 2021 and was not able to handle any higher numbers. It was localized and did not cause major carnage, but regardless, it happened.[4]

This amounts to a dilemma: the fear of losing the business crashes headlong into the fear of commitment to an intangible threat. The collective instinct of many decision makers or their directors is to stick with the adage *better the devil you know than the devil you don't*.

Pay the Ransom Already!

The unwillingness to prepare adequately to face intangible dangers is not just a quaint quirk of human nature. It has enormous consequences. Despite having authorities like the FBI and the Cybersecurity and Infrastructure Security Agency (CISA) and others around the world recommending that ransoms not be paid, once the ransomware virus hits,

---

[3] Ibid.

[4] Abrams, Lawrence. "Microsoft Exchange year 2022 bug in FIP-FS breaks email delivery" *Bleeping Computer.* January 1, 2022. Retrieved from www.bleepingcomputer.com/news/microsoft/microsoft-exchange-year-2022-bug-" in-fip-fs-breaks-email-delivery/ Accessed January 2022.

CHAPTER 11   THE FEAR OF LOSING THE BUSINESS

the sudden fear of being sidelined for days or weeks makes it seem like a good idea to simply pay the ransom. It is starting to be seen as simply the cost of doing business.

This, despite the fact that actually paying a ransom is no guarantee that seized data will be released fully or even partially, or that stolen data will be left untouched.

Some companies have started to rely on their insurance companies to reimburse them for the cost of the ransom. In fact, in many documented ransomware cases, the pirates have actually chosen a ransom amount after having analyzed the coverage held by a company's insurers, and then calculating accordingly.

A fascinating example of this happened to British retailer FatFace in early 2021. It made headlines by appearing to ask its customers to keep its cyberattack "strictly private and confidential," while paying a $2 million ransom to the Conti cybercrime gang. According to security analyst Graham Cluley, the gang initially demanded an $8 million ransom based on its assessment of what FatFace's insurance would cover, but the company talked them down after explaining revenues had tumbled due to the Covid lockdown. Furthermore, in accepting the payment, Conti offered tech-support advice to FatFace's IT team about how to harden its defenses against future attacks.[5]

As of 2021, insurers the world over started to refuse to pay out claims relating to ransomware. It's off the table, since it is simply too great a risk to insure.

But even without the insurance companies as a backup, the fear-stricken mind carries on: opening the checkbook to get the business back on track as soon as possible. But what many tend to forget in

---

[5] Cluley, Graham. "FatFace pays out $2 million to Conti ransomware gang." GrahamCluley, March 28, 2021. Available at https://grahamcluley.com/fatface-pays-out-2-million-to-conti-ransomware-gang/ Accessed December 2021.

CHAPTER 11 THE FEAR OF LOSING THE BUSINESS

their panic is that when you're doing business with criminals, you're doing business with *criminals*. They are not always going to play by the Queensbury Rules.[6]

Furthermore, in some cases, companies have paid the ransom, but then have changed nothing on their systems, security-wise. They are then surprised when the ransomware pirates strike again in exactly the same place, and ask for more ransom. Criminals in this business take neither the high road nor the hard road. They seek the easiest and cheapest route, and will often go back and strike a victim again since they know the lay of the land. To expect them to move on after having had their fill is yet another extension of the "watering hole" willful blindness scenario described in Chapter 9: the assumption being that the lion has eaten, is no longer hungry, and will move on.

In an active ransomware situation, fear flies all over the place. Fear of losing the business drives the Executive to authorize a ransom payment. But fear of the cost of prevention then sends them to re-start the company without building new defenses.

Very few executives have ever encountered the type of fiendish brilliance and ruthless minds that drive the top echelons of cybercrime. The vulnerabilities within software, networks, and hardware are discovered and exploited by criminal gangs even before the software manufacturer is aware of them. This is known as a zero-day, since that's how many days advance notice the software makers get before the weaknesses are exploited. Naturally, such brilliant minds are to be feared. Equally naturally, most humans will look the other way and avoid them.

The same goes for newer modes of communication and group coordination that occur quickly and highly effectively through new

---

[6] The Queensbury Rules were originally drafted as a code of conduct for the sport of boxing in the mid-1800s but is also used as an idiom to describe standard rules of polite or acceptable behavior. It would be naïve to expect cybercriminals to follow them.

CHAPTER 11   THE FEAR OF LOSING THE BUSINESS

social media platforms. Hacktivists bent on resolution of climate change, economic inequities, and a range of other causes need not have to resort to injecting malware or writing code of any sort, if they can instead mobilize to sabotage a company's brand. Many who are in senior management today tend to come from a pre-Internet or early-Internet era, where things ran at a different pace and scale. Most are smart enough to educate themselves on such dangers, or at least hire people to take on these roles, but there will always be a mental imprint of behavior and norms that comes from much earlier in their individual lives.

When You Were Ten

What was going on in your world when you were ten years old? Can you remember that far back? The age of ten can be a pivotal moment in life experience, as it is generally a point of relative stability between the activities of infancy – self-awareness, physical movement – and the chaos and changes of the teen years. At this point, at the age of ten or thereabouts, kids start to take a look at the world around them and evaluate their place in it.

This is important when talking about fear, especially the fear of losing control over a business, because the intellectual response to fear – the use of facts to level out emotion – will be based on knowledge and presumptions.

A leader or manager who turned ten years old in the mid-1970s, let's say born in 1965, will have arrived at this point of situational awareness at a time when there was no public Internet, no computers, and no smartphones. The telephone was a rotary dial or early pushbutton type, hardwired to a wall socket, and property of the phone company. News was delivered via newspaper as well as by well-known and trusted TV news anchors at one of the three major networks in the United States, and similarly in other countries. Learning about the world in general came

CHAPTER 11 THE FEAR OF LOSING THE BUSINESS

from reading an encyclopedia, and ordering things from a catalog involved a delivery period of four to six weeks. The closest people came to texting back then was passing notes in class.

The point behind talking about all of this nostalgia is that it fostered a sense of formality and hierarchy. Your parents got their telephone from the one-and-only phone company, not from a choice of retailers at the mall. News came from a recognized source. Observing these types of activities, passively, as a ten-year-old, naturally instills those same senses and indelibly stamps them into long-term memory.

This means that a manager born in 1965 will likely still feel that meetings should be measured in 60-minute blocks, that they should start at the top of the hour, and that work is something you commute to and from five days a week. Even those progressive managers who have learned to overcome these biases still have to actually overcome them. They are still there.

These biases are also responsible for the seemingly slow response time to cybercrime. When it took weeks for a product to be delivered by mail order back in the day, it is difficult to grasp the idea that a newly released brand of software can be hacked and exploited within hours of its release, or that an IoT-connected smart doorbell can be in any way connected to a DDoS attack on an oil pipeline a thousand miles away.

The "ten year old's bias" sabotages progress, and is in part responsible for the fact that even today corporate boards of directors seldom have time for cybersecurity discussions. A PWC survey of corporate directors conducted in 2016 showed that the majority of respondents reported that their boards

> *...had at most one technology-related discussion a year, and almost half claimed that the attention they gave to technology was insufficient. More than half of board members also felt they should hold more discussions of how technology will affect their industries in the coming years, but fewer than 30% actually had these kinds of discussions. Only one-quarter of*

boards report that they review formal reports from the CIO at every meeting, and on average boards claim to spend about 5% of their total hours each year on IT oversight.[7]

Although 2016 was a long time ago, progress has been slow on this front, leading some in the industry to suggest that IT should no longer be a silo unto itself, but should be moved "out from under IT and treated as a business risk rather than a technical problem."[8]

The Challenge of Agility

Frankly, it's a tough time to be agile. Companies have been using this term for a while to help describe themselves as nimble and responsive to changes in the marketplace. Yet they still try to hold on to a *lift-and-shift* mentality which tries to copy real-world office practices such as meetings, and paste them, often reluctantly, into a virtual space.

The word *agile*, whether capitalized or not, refers to a philosophy of software development, in which substantial transformation was introduced to the vast global community of coders, developers, and testers in the form of the *Agile Manifesto*, written by a team of seventeen software developers in 2001. It substantially changed the way software was to be developed, tested, and managed, by essentially following a non-linear design approach.[9]

---

[7] Keller, Don, Berlin, Barbara, and Strott, Elizabeth. Directors and IT: A User-Friendly Board Guide for Effective Information Technology Oversight. p. 18 2016 Published by PWC. Retrieved from www.pwc.se/sv/pdf-reports/directors-and-it.pdf Accessed June 2021.

[8] Jeffery, Eric. "Why CISOs Shouldn't Report to CIOs in the C-Suite." *Security Intelligence.* December 21, 2021. Retrieved from https://securityintelligence.com/posts/why-cisos-shouldnt-report-to-cio-c-suite-conflict/ Accessed December 2021.

[9] Full details and history can be found at the Agile Manifesto website at agilemanifesto.org.

CHAPTER 11   THE FEAR OF LOSING THE BUSINESS

In short, rather than move the software in steps along an assembly line, or as they called it, a waterfall (as in water cascading down successive layers or steps in a landscaped waterfall), the culture of testing had to be radically shifted to earlier in the development timeline in order to maximize the chances that the software – that runs apps, gas pumps, and everything else we depend on – works properly the first time out.

Agile for software development was a new and fear-inducing change for most people in the software development world, and it was not universally well-received. A great book that covers this specifically for the high-tech sector is *The Kitty Hawk Venture*, written by Aruna Ravichandran, Jeffery Scheaffer, and Alex Martens.[10] It highlights the significant degrees of cultural resistance put up by software developers who face the threat of transformations in the world of DevOps. It is surprising to discover such stubbornness and fear within a culture that to outsiders seems dynamic and progressive. But software developers, too, in cloud and mainframe alike, are fearful for their livelihood. They do not wish to be digitally transformed out of a job.

For mainstream companies, being *agile* will always be a challenge. It is not easy to turn a large ship in a tight circle, and that's what agility truly means. All attempts to move companies digitally forward were already facing resistance prior to 2020, but were further substantially stymied by the Covid pandemic, which damaged economies and slowed progress, and also let the genie out of the bottle regarding work-from-home options.

So, in addition to contemplating the introduction of technologies like artificial intelligence and machine learning, and in addition to struggling with the incomprehensible world of cybersecurity, companies found

---

[10] Scheaffer, Jeffrey, Ravidchandran, Aruna, and Martins, Alex. *The Kitty Hawk Venture: A Novel About Continuous Testing in DevOps to Support Continuous Delivery and Business Success*. (New York, Apress, 2018)

themselves having the rug pulled out from under them almost literally as they saw their need for floor space get reduced due to their workforce opting to work from home.

The fear, then, of losing the business is a bit of a *double entendre.* It refers first to a concern that the business itself might fall apart due to the changes described above, but it also reflects back on individual managers and leaders. In addition to losing control over their employees as described in Chapter 8, here they are also, feeling that they, too, are being pushed out of the loop, that they are losing much that they understood business to be about.

CHAPTER 12

The Fear of Missing Out

As I described in Chapter 5, when people find themselves having to stand still for more than thirty seconds, they will invariably pull out their phone and check it. They are not necessarily checking it because a message or email has dinged, beeped, or buzzed. There might not be anything new there at all. There's no actual *unknown* tugging at their instincts. There is instead that fear of silence that forces us to fill the void with more stimulus.

But the fear of silence goes even deeper.

Through the constant influx of information and audiovisual stimulation, we have become conditioned to believe that silence means that we're always missing out on something. Rather than silence being an absence of sound, it is seen as an absence of content, an actual presence, an awareness of deprivation, where the lack of stimulation becomes tangible. There's stuff going on out there in the world, especially the online world. We know it's happening, but we don't know what it is. Whereas the fear of the unknown (Chapter 5) is based on our need to know what is going on, the fear of missing out speaks to our ceaseless need to know what *else* is going on. This is an urge that has found a new and infinite playground on social media.

The fear of missing out, or FOMO for short, has driven people to become social media addicts. We will doomscroll for minutes or hours

CHAPTER 12   THE FEAR OF MISSING OUT

on end, looking to see what the next story, image, or video will be. Even if we start out on a search for something specific, so many of us will end up spending minutes or hours per day scrolling ceaselessly through an infinite collection of media. We will scan our favorite feeds on Twitter, Instagram, YouTube, TikTok, SnapChat, and others, looking for – looking for what exactly? Looking for that *something* that isn't here right now. Something to distract us. Something more interesting than what else is around us.

There was a similar compulsion in the pre-Internet era with channel flipping on the TV, except that this activity was slower and definitely more limited. There is something altogether more stimulating and addictive about social media.

For a start, there's an endorphin thing going on here. A dopamine release. There is a pleasure factor in its endless stimulation that has similarities to sugar addiction. Enough is never enough. Every link takes you down a new path, populated by more links. These claw at the psyche with intriguing come-ons written in clickbait language, and beckoning with tantalizing and often misleading thumbnails. The satisfaction of the stimulus is limited only by the speed you can read and the time you have available.

There are hundreds of studies that have been published on the topic of social media addiction. In my observations, one of the most significant costs of the compulsive behavior triggered by the fear of missing out is measured in loss of depth of critical thought, which is being eroded like sand cliffs on a shoreline. Critical thinking, deep thinking, requires effort. It forces – and allows – people to look at both sides of an argument, to play devil's advocate against their own opinions and to engage in discussion with other people without feeling threatened by them.

In just the same way that I compared social skills to toned muscles in Chapter 10, the same analogy can be used here, too. Using the brain – testing it with new knowledge and abstract thinking is a form of exercise that works in a way that is similar to building muscle strength and greater cardiovascular ability. The more you do it, the more synaptic connections are made, and the smarter you get.

CHAPTER 12   THE FEAR OF MISSING OUT

The opposite, unfortunately, is also true. Those who shy away from critical thinking and the pursuit of knowledge for knowledge's sake tend to fall into the social media-driven traps of becoming influenced rather than independent.

Critical thinking builds ideas and the capacity to rationalize. It is a *soft skill* and is considered one of the most valuable skills to possess for the future of work. Although the most obvious reason it is considered so valuable might seem to be the sheer practicality of being able to think through a problem or a situation, the real reason may be more basic than that. Critical thinking might be – should be – the activity that saves a company from the negative effects of digital transformation:

- It gives people the ability to question every email before clicking on a phishing link – no matter how legitimate the message looks.

- It gives people the power to better detect social engineering scams by thinking about, and then independently researching the validity of the people and messages that enter their space.

- It gives people the opportunity to think about the implications of unsafe cyberhygiene practices, rather than merely reacting to them as undesirable effort.

Because when people inadvertently bring down their companies by allowing malware into their world, or even when they simply fail a phishing test, they will say, by their own admission, that they did it without thinking.

This inability to apply critical thinking is not unique to FOMO, of course, but it is certainly amplified by it, since every opportunity to pause and think gets quickly subsumed by the tantalizing siren of social media.

CHAPTER 12   THE FEAR OF MISSING OUT

Gap It

One of the most insidious outcomes of phishing, vishing, and smishing scams is how easily people fall for them. (Vishing is voice mail-based phishing, and smishing is SMS-based phishing – scam messages sent by text message.)

The fear of missing out, or simply the fear of an unknown danger compels people to follow a text message that warns of a frozen bank account or trouble with outstanding taxes due. These are messages that strike to the very heart of a person's need for safety and causes them to click on the link without thinking. It can be seen as a fear of missing out on a quick solution to a fear inducing problem.

If there is just one technique that I would like people to take away from this book, it would be the following two-word mantra:

GAP IT

I regularly ask everyone I know to practice it, and to teach it to their colleagues – especially to elder family members such as parents and grandparents. These are people who grew up in a world before sophisticated cybercrime was a thing, and who consequently still think every message and every phone call should be answered out of politeness and trust, rather than proven credibility.

GAP IT simply means: if you receive a message on any device that alerts you to a problem such as

- Your bank account is frozen
- You missed a delivery
- You're in trouble with the tax authorities
- Your utilities are about to be cut off

...or any other message that strikes fear into you, whether in your personal life or your work life, it is vital to place a gap between that message and your actions. Do not click on the link in the message to try

CHAPTER 12   THE FEAR OF MISSING OUT

to solve the problem, but instead, go in via a different route – your regular route. If the message is about a frozen bank account, then log in to your bank account through your computer the way you usually do. If the message seems to be from the government tax authority, then call them using their regular number.

Whatever utility or authority is involved, if there is a genuine problem, they will be able to find it through your account number. The point here is to place an "air gap" between this threatening letter and your reaction. Not everyone is aware that this threatening letter links back to a criminal organization staffed with people who are skilled in techniques of further persuasion.

Teach people to GAP IT. If an email-based invoice appears in an employee's email, teach them to follow through by using the connections they already have on file. Call the supplier company directly through the number you always use, not the link on the message.

This technique started out as a critical thinking technique, but it can also be trained into people as a conditioned response. The intent here is to break the habit of unthinking reaction and replace it with the habit of inserting a gap. In other words, "this message says there is trouble with my bank? OK, then I will call the bank directly with the number I already have on file." In other words, put a gap between the fear stimulus and the fear response.

This is another example of where companies can do their part to build this into the culture. Even though the GAP IT technique is a personal activity, it can be made more prevalent through increased cultural endorsement in the workplace – through repeated messaging, permission, encouragement, and reward, in the same way that messages dealing with health and safety, and with respectful and safe workspaces are regularly repeated and practiced.

Companies can also do their part to modify the work culture so that employees do not feel under enormous time pressure, because it is just that type of pressure that allows oversights to happen. This, to me, is an example of what Eric Jeffery suggested in his article that I quoted in

CHAPTER 12 THE FEAR OF MISSING OUT

Chapter 11: "that IT should no longer be a silo unto itself, but should be moved out from under IT and treated as a business risk rather than a technical problem."[1] Phishing, smishing, and similar activities are a risk to a business. By allowing and actively encouraging a GAP IT culture to thrive, companies will be taking one more step to help ensure the safety of the entire organization.

The Fear of Not Fitting In

Another fear related to the fear of missing out is the fear of not fitting in. Humans, as already mentioned, are tribal by nature. Instinctively, we all feel that we want to be part of a group or tribe, and consequently, activities that threaten to pull us out of that tribe will be met with fear.

A seminal moment in life for most of us happened during our formative years, the day we experienced pre-school or kindergarten for the very first time. This was the moment we were moved from the protective cocoon of the family unit to an open environment that brought other humans – other kids – into our world. It was also the moment that we first started to discover that not all of these kids were going to be wonderful, caring friends.

We started to learn about tribe dynamics at this point, something that continues through every age and stage of life. Tribe dynamics, for pre-school-age kids and adults in the workplace alike, introduce social influence dynamics that range from bullying and peer-pressure to cliques, alliances, and friendships. Instinctively we know that we need to be part of this, despite its variety of impacts on our own selves. Therefore, for most people, there is a profound and permanent fear of being ostracized from a group.

---

[1] Jeffery, Eric. "Why CISOs Shouldn't Report to CIOs in the C-Suite." Security Intelligence. December 21, 2021. Retrieved from https://securityintelligence.com/posts/why-cisos-shouldnt-report-to-cio-c-suite-conflict/ Accessed December 2021.

CHAPTER 12 THE FEAR OF MISSING OUT

This can manifest itself in subtle ways. Among adults and kids alike, it is one of the primary causes of reluctance to speak or ask questions in a group setting or an online meeting. The fear of looking stupid (Chapter 7), can lead to feeling ostracized from a group. It will have a huge impact on the decision to work-from-home, especially with regard to the knock-on effects of being perceived as "not a team player" for doing so.

The Fear of Being a Nerd

One of the greatest losses to human progress that will continue to spring in part from the fear of not fitting in is the ongoing cultural disdain for people who pursue the sciences or information technology. Thinking back to my description of my first clients back in the 1990s (Chapter 4), there has always been a disconnect between the tech-support people who fully understood computer technology and those who couldn't. The *computer nerds* as they were often called, couldn't understand how regular people could get so lost, and the lost people couldn't understand what the tech people were saying. This was, and still is, one of the reasons people fear and vilify smart scientific types, not only in tech, but as we have seen most recently, in medicine and climate science as well.

Culturally, scientists have long been branded as nerds. They have been portrayed as socially inept, unattractive, and poor dressers. Bill Nye, the Science guy, exaggerates this in his persona, with his bowtie and white lab coat. My favorite, the character of the Professor on the 1960s TV series *Gilligan's Island*, just stuck to his work, and though he helped his castaway friends on almost every episode, he was never seen as the leading man.

These smart people were feared by the non-scientists as the ones who knew it all, like modern-day witches and for similar reasons. Those scientists who tried to break this convention, like astronomer Carl Sagan, with his stylish (for the time) clothes, was never fully ingratiated into the cool non-science set, and, at the same time, he was accused of selling out to the world of "pop-science" by his colleagues.

Perhaps the ultimate and most successful demonstration of this – and what much of this book is about – can be seen in the TV series *The Big Bang Theory*, which ran from 2007 to 2019. The root of much of its humor came from the human yin/yang battle between logic and emotion. The character of Sheldon Cooper represented unyielding logic, and his foil, Penny, represented emotion and passion. Sheldon was book smart; Penny was street smart. He was fact-based, she was feelings-based, and their clashing ideologies and perceptions formed the basis of every storyline and most of the jokes. For those who have not seen this series, there are thousands of similar examples in film, television, theater, and literature, going back thousands of years in every culture and country that ever developed storytelling and performing – which is to say, every culture.

IT people have long suffered a similar fate, being seen as the smart ones with computers – practicing a mysterious black magic that others are either envious of or dismissive of, or both. There is a fear among many of the less computer savvy that they are missing out on some big secret, such as how computers are supposed to work. This is enhanced by actual mysterious developments like hacking, cryptocurrency, and non-fungible tokens (NFTs), all of which are completely practical constructs, but remain difficult to explain, both how they work, and also, why they exist at all.

How Loss of Critical Thinking Leads to Hate and to the Madness of Crowds

> *We find that whole communities suddenly fix their minds upon one object, and go mad in its pursuit; that millions of people become simultaneously impressed with one delusion,*

CHAPTER 12   THE FEAR OF MISSING OUT

and run after it, till their attention is caught by some new folly more captivating than the first.[2]

This quote is from Charles MacKay, who published *Extraordinary Popular Delusions and the Madness of Crowds*, in 1841. One hundred and eighty years later, his book is as poignant and as relevant as ever. In fact, humanity is currently behaving in a way that would allow a whole set of new chapters to be added.

In the book, MacKay talks about times in history in which people seemed to go mad, collectively, following a trend or a social phenomenon with blind, unquestioning fervency. In MacKay's time, these included events such as Tulipmania in 1636, in which investors had begun to purchase tulips madly, pushing their prices to unprecedented highs. The average price of a single flower eventually exceeded the annual income of a skilled worker and cost more than some houses at the time. As prices drastically collapsed, many tulip holders instantly went bankrupt.

The South Sea Bubble happened between 1711 and 1720 and was another example of speculation mania in which investors got caught up in the hype of the South Sea Company which had been founded in 1711 to trade with Spanish America, on the collective belief that everyone would make a huge profit.

There have been many of these crowd-stimulating events over the centuries, including the Salem witch trials in the 1600s, the Red Scare, and the Blacklist in the United States in the 1950s, and more recent ones include the dotcom bubble, real-estate housing bubbles, cryptocurrency, and NFTs.

When MacKay wrote his book, he was looking at a concept of crowd mania in which biases and fervor take the place of clear thinking. Often these biases can be dormant in peoples' minds, or they can be already active, but either way, they are triggered by a certain event and then

---

[2] Mackay, Charles (1841). Originally published as *Memoirs of Extraordinary Popular Delusions and the Madness of Crowds* in 1841.

CHAPTER 12   THE FEAR OF MISSING OUT

expanded into action through mass communication. For others, the stimulus – the topic of the madness – may be brand new, but it still resonates and magnifies irresistibly out of the fear of missing out. When it grows quickly, there next appears a critical point that reaches an often unstoppable momentum.

Some have since questioned the scope and scale of seventeenth century phenomena like Tulipmania, which is easy to do when viewing historical events with modern eyes. Many pivotal historical events, including decisive battles or interactions with key religious figures, happened on a comparatively small scale and were highly localized. But such was the culture in the centuries before instantaneous global communication. They may not have been as large, or as widespread as social media or cryptocurrency, but they still made a huge cultural impact and represent a type of mania that exists to this day.

The global resistance to masks, social distancing, vaccinations, and even 5G technology shows that the madness of crowds is as prevalent today in the information age as it was in all centuries prior. These crowds consist of people who, steadily, over the past two decades, have slipped into a trance of collective ideology. Beliefs and biases, many exceedingly bizarre, are magnified by the media and social media, which together grant large groups of people permission to give up any last form of critical thinking and get swept up in a vortex of abject belief.

How does this happen? Well, for a start, believing is always easier than learning. Learning requires the willingness and opportunity to comprehend, absorb, process, and recall information. That requires energy. It takes effort to look around and seek out confirmation from other sources. Belief is much easier. There is no effort required to accept the concepts as given.

Once a person has fallen under the spell of abject belief, the proof of the correctness of that belief appears to them everywhere. Like seeing a holy image on a piece of toast, the convert sees only what they wish to see, and will dismiss that which doesn't correlate. The tendency to perceive

CHAPTER 12   THE FEAR OF MISSING OUT

faces in nebulous things is called *pareidolia*, by the way. What they see will become further confirmation of those beliefs, and that is the root of confirmation bias. Stories told by others that align with an existing belief become the only facts required. Any people who hold disparate ideas are seen as a challenger or enemy that must be discounted and eliminated. This is the complete opposite of critical thinking.

It is also, by the way, the reason that so many groups of people bent on an ideological crusade tend to focus their adoration on a person rather than a body of knowledge. They idolize someone who appears strong and perfect – and they use symbols and symbology as their altar, their totem, and their fetish. It's a passion based on the cult of personality and has pervaded religion and politics all over the world for as long as humans have existed.

This, perhaps, is one of humanity's greatest failings, because the madness of crowds gives birth to its own self-justification – a belief that what is being done is right and is good because it supports the belief. This is a form of circular logic that actually lacks logic. Despite the fact that every one of us has access to all the information of the world literally at our fingertips through our Internet-connected phones, many people choose instead to follow abject beliefs to the extreme, whether this is over the dangers of 5G technology or vaccinations, or the benefits of dubious miracle cures, and they then use that same device to locate and align with like-minded people.

The reason for pointing out the dangers of the madness of crowds is to demonstrate how quickly and broadly a crowd mania can set in despite the presence of facts, and how this can easily penetrate the world of digital transformation, creating opportunities for people to reject proactive cyberhygiene behaviors or hybrid work scenarios simply through contagious and toxic resistance.

CHAPTER 12   THE FEAR OF MISSING OUT

How Hate Leads to Bullying

The most profound example of this is – and will continue to be – cyberbullying, an activity that affects adults as much as children. Although bullying easily and regularly occurs in the real world, in the schoolyard and in the office, the ease by which groups of people can gang up on an individual from the safety and anonymity of their keyboards is shocking and knows no bounds.

Race, gender, physical appearance, marital status, being a new hire, being assigned to a team or group, being a seasoned veteran, or being someone deciding whether to move on to a new job – there are thousands of reasons why some people bully other people. It is part of our nature as predators to seek out and destroy potential rivals, and anyone who looks or thinks differently will easily qualify. This observation is, of course, not an endorsement of bullying, but forms part of an attempt to understand it.

Although statistics show[3] that the majority of people bullied are between 18 and 25, there is still a great deal of it happening in every other adult age group. It has been magnified exponentially through the use of digital messaging, primarily on social media, but also through more direct media such as email and texting.

As new technologies enter the workspace, the focus will often be on the good things they are capable of, such as virtual collaboration, meetings, and hybrid work. Most of us do not think about the dark side. But the same can be said of the Internet itself, which was never intended to be used for pornography or cybercrime.

Going back a step further to the history of computers and software – during its initial development, little thought was given to viruses. But they

---

[3] Psychology Today, www.psychologytoday.com/us/blog/shame-nation/201911/adult-cyberbullying-is-more-common-you-think, and Cyberbullying Research Center, https://cyberbullying.org/advice-for-adult-victims-of-cyberbullying

happened anyway. Viruses were created by people. They are different from bugs that are errors in programming. Viruses are, and have always been a form of manually created vandalism designed to damage or destroy computer technology. They are a testament to humankind's baffling desire to destroy rather than build.

In this situation, we see a potential for abuse of these new technologies by legions of maddened crowds seeking to bully or eliminate those who disagree with them.

I Know What You Did

If someone looked at you straight in the eye and said, "I know what you did," in a menacing and accusatory way, how would you feel? Where would your mind go? What terrible secret would your subconscious drag to the surface of your memory?

This phrase, "I know what you did," is enormously powerful, even though most of the time it holds no actual substance at all. People in power, especially political and religious leadership, use variations of it all the time.

"I know what you did" is just one example of a phrase that allows a listener to fill in the blanks with their own thoughts, feelings, and guilt. It's a leading statement. I can look at you and say, "I know what you did," without knowing a thing about you. Maybe I've not even met you before, and I certainly have no way of knowing anything about what you might have done. But if I say it with enough conviction, you will do the rest of the work for me. Your conscience will fly to something you did – something you are not proud of, something you fear being exposed – and will assume that I somehow found out about it. You might even capitulate, allowing me to extend my dominance further, blackmailing you emotionally without ever learning what your terrible secret actually is.

CHAPTER 12   THE FEAR OF MISSING OUT

People who feel guilty about something carry a heavy emotional burden. So heavy, in fact, that unless they are true sociopaths devoid of the capacity to feel, they are likely to give away their own game. Shakespeare summed it up best in *Hamlet*, when he writes, "So full of artless jealousy is guilt, It spills itself in fearing to be spilt."[4]

Guilt forces most people to act differently, to always be watching out for a slip of their own tongue or a glint of recognition from someone else that the jig is up. It's an uncomfortable way to live. Police who investigate crimes in which more than one person is an accomplice often count on the guilt factor, that one of the accomplices will break, and will come forward to spill the beans.

So back to the initial phrase, "I know what you did." This is a term of influence. Not a nice form of influence but influence just the same.

Does guilt influence us from a survival and self-preservation standpoint? Do we seek to eliminate an enemy who knows our guilty secret in order to stay alive? Not really. It is more likely a proof of a moral conscience – that point of interference between fact and emotion guided by an innate sense of right and wrong.

There are many varieties of this type of leading phrase, all of which allow people to fill in the blanks with their own perceptions. The expression, "Many people say," implies a majority consensus on a topic without ever having to justify who these "people" are. Audiences are willing to allow such a statement to neutralize their own curiosity. The remainder of the sentence will already have been legitimized by the concept of these "many people."

Another version of the "I know what you did" leading statement is the loaded question, "what else is going on here?" or " what is this person hiding?" These types of phrases help plant seeds of doubt and suspicion in the minds of listeners without actually coming out with a straight factual statement that runs the risk of being proven wrong.

---

[4] Shakespeare, William. *Hamlet* Act 4 Scene 5.

CHAPTER 12 THE FEAR OF MISSING OUT

Doubt and suspicion are cousins of guilt – emotions that feed on fear. To say, "I don't know, but there's definitely something going on here," infects the listener with fear-based emotions while still allowing a back door of plausible deniability on the part of the instigator.

These types of vague yet accusatory questions go back centuries and were key tools of incrimination during the Inquisitions of Europe and the real, actual witch hunts in the age of the Puritans in America in the 1600s. The mere questioning statement about someone being a witch was all that was needed to convict and execute them. "I'm not saying she's a witch, but..." It doesn't matter what happens after those ellipses. The die has been cast. It is happening still in Ebola-stricken areas of Africa, where outcasts like people with albinism, and even visiting medical personnel are accused of witchcraft or of bringing the disease with them into a village. It has been and continues to be the cause of much suffering and death throughout the centuries up to the present when the word "witch" is replaced by the word "homosexual." Sadly, the mob doesn't need facts. They just need the right collection of vague words to inflame their feelings of fear and translate them into destructive action.

In pre-literate centuries, the primary megaphone for knowledge and social awareness in Europe and the New World was the church, which never missed an opportunity to impose this same guilt-inducing tactic when considering the many sins a person was capable of. They literally wrote the book on it. Virtually every memorable passage in the bible, like turning water into wine, mutated from colloquial to miraculous as people interpreted from that what they wanted to hear.

Now we live in a post-literate age, where most people are able to read, but what they read merely supports their existing beliefs and fears. People choose news or pseudo news outlets because they know the stories they hear on this network will match their existing state of mind. They don't go there to learn facts, they go there to reinforce feelings. We seek out a safe haven of a shared mindset rather than pursue independent knowledge through critical thinking.

Therefore, populist political leaders around the world have flown like vultures into a perfect feeding ground where a receptive audience laps up vague statements and swaddles them in the context of their own fears. Those who choose to actively question the vagueness are dismissed as enemies of the state and hence enemies of that audience. This is the ultimate success of a phrase like "I know what you did." It doesn't need to say anything, it just needs to convey the spark that touches upon the tinderbox of fear and guilt that we all privately hold.

The examples in this chapter seem to stray somewhat from the workplace in which digital transformation is taking shape. But in reality, they are not so far removed. The preceding chapters have outlined how fear will keep people from wanting to learn new technologies, and from wanting to talk face-to-face with others, from wanting to communicate in live dialog, and from wanting to think critically. Unfortunately, these are the skills that allow humans to stay human and to strengthen the social support fibers of the global tribe.

To assume that what happens in the workplace has no bearing on the world outside is as incorrect for these human activities as it is for computer viruses. We are all connected, which means we will all be infected. A process that inhibits critical thinking and social interaction in the workplace leads to dissolution of tribal support in public, and we are observing, in many countries around the world, a dangerous slide backward toward extreme social polarization.

CHAPTER 13

The Fear of Keeping Your Job

I have now put forward that the most obvious and predominant fear of digital transformation revolves around losing one's job. But there will also be a larger set of employees, much larger even than the gig-economy-minded lone wolves and freelancers, who will continue to choose the perceived security of their current jobs, but will fear what they are losing by doing so. They will look at their current position not so much in terms of what they are gaining, but instead, in terms of what they are losing.

The terminology of work and life are changing. What was once known as work–life balance is now being referred to as life–work balance, and it is not mere wordplay to reverse these two terms – it reflects a change in priorities. Some observers suggest that both terms are outdated because work has already dissolved itself into life, leaving nothing to actually balance out. They instead call the whole thing work–life integration.

Long gone are the days when a person could leave work behind at 5:00, like Fred Flintstone sliding down his dinosaur's tail. (In the interest of accuracy, it must be stated here that Fred was a "bronto-crane" operator at Slate Rock and Gravel Company.)[1] Work has always had a tendency of following us home, and we have allowed it.

---

[1] No author given. Flintstones Fandom website. Retrieved from https://flintstones.fandom.com/wiki/Fred_Flintstone Accessed January 2021.

CHAPTER 13   THE FEAR OF KEEPING YOUR JOB

Before the age of email, people at least had to manually put papers into their briefcase at the end of the workday and carry them. For some, this mere act of putting them into that briefcase and bringing them back to the office the next day, untouched, was enough to alleviate the guilt of not doing enough work. I called this "taking your work for a walk." But for most people, the evening was chronically reserved, at least in part, to catching up on the emails – labor that was essentially given away for free to the employer, at the expense of one's personal time and health – specifically the impact of work on a healthy sleep cycle and consequently one's immune system.[2]

We were conditioned in part to accept homework as a fact of life from the earliest days of primary school, and this obligation magnified itself exponentially as soon as email and texting took hold. We grew accustomed to the messages coming in, uninvited, and with them the unspoken expectation for an immediate response. There is a predominant fear that to not do this work will ultimately reflect badly on one's career prospects, as discussed in Chapter 6, and basically throughout this book.

What Is the Cost of Your Money?

But there is a change happening. People are questioning the true cost of the money they make. Some of this was growing in the years prior to the pandemic, as people started to notice the wider selection of work options available especially in the gig-economy area. But this has been enhanced through increasing cases of burnout, a genuine desire for physical safety against Covid infection and harassment in the workplace, and a growing sense that the work is just not worth it anymore.

---

[2] For more information on the impact of evening work on the sleep cycle, check out my book, *Cool-Time: A Hands-On Plan for Managing Work and Balancing Time.*

CHAPTER 13   THE FEAR OF KEEPING YOUR JOB

All money costs something to accumulate and keep. For most people the cost comes in the form of labor, which itself comes only after years of practice and education, which also comes at a cost. But the pressures and uncertainties brought about by the pandemic, combined with the need to care for younger and older family members as well as the cost of commuting and owning a home have led to the realization that the activity of earning a salary is far too great to justify the return. In other words it's just not worth it.

The Great Resignation discussed in Chapter 6 started in 2021 and continued into 2022. It was not a one-off event. Many working people in a wide variety of professions are leaving their jobs without looking back.

A report conducted by Future Forum, a future-of-work consortium led by Slack Technologies, in November 2021, showed that 95 percent of people surveyed want flexible hours, and 78 percent of workers want location flexibility.[3] Although one could argue that Slack might have a vested interest in seeing numbers that favor remote work, the dynamic flow of a well-curated Slack is emblematic of the interactive mid-ground or missing link between the static nature of video chat calls and the obligation to be in the physical workplace in order to collaborate. In this regard, I find Slack to be on par with KosyOffice and Toucan that I mentioned in Chapters 2 and 6.

A more neutrally based assessment in support of this came from Brian Kropp, who leads human resources research at Gartner, who stated, "many workers have found their productivity surged while working from home and they achieved the work-life balance they had been seeking, [which is] one reason so many people see hybrid work as the future."[4]

---

[3] Bindley, Katherine, and Cutter, Chip. "Workers Care More About Flexible Hours Than Remote Work," *The Wall Street Journal.* January 25, 2022. Retrieved from www.wsj.com/articles/workers-care-more-about-flexible-hours-than-remote-work-11643112004. Accessed February 2022.
[4] Ibid.

CHAPTER 13   THE FEAR OF KEEPING YOUR JOB

A generation or more ago, it had seemed possible for young professionals to picture themselves buying a house and eventually paying off the mortgage. A partnership or marriage between two people meant that it might have been possible to save for future needs on top of making the payments, and overall, prosper from hard work. That was the "middle class dream" in most prosperous countries through the twentieth century.

Today, many working couples need to work simply to keep up with the bills, and far too many individuals are finding themselves no longer believing that a better life is possible. When this is paired with the ongoing physical and emotional effects of the Covid pandemic and an increasingly polarized and hostile society, it is no wonder that workers in their thousands are saying, "no more! This just isn't worth it." They essentially fear the prospect of keeping their existing job.

It's not that these individuals don't want to work, which is the immediate assumption of others who see this activity as a slacker mentality; it's just that they simply can't work under the terms and conditions of the current market. Their reluctance is not because it's hard work, but because there is simply no ROI. This is an easy concept for people in management to recognize: it's Economics 101 – the Law of Diminishing Returns.

This should be of great significance to employers who are still using the term "new normal" to describe the future-of-work. Employees are seeing some of the wealthiest companies in the country insisting on salary cuts to those who choose to work from home. They are essentially being told, your value is in your presence, not your product.

Business technology expert Mariya Breyter, PhD, shows how this reprioritization being shown by employees – the fact that work must be meaningful rather than solely a means to stay alive – represents an inversion of Maslow's hierarchy, in which self-actualization becomes the primary motivator for staying with a particular employer:

CHAPTER 13   THE FEAR OF KEEPING YOUR JOB

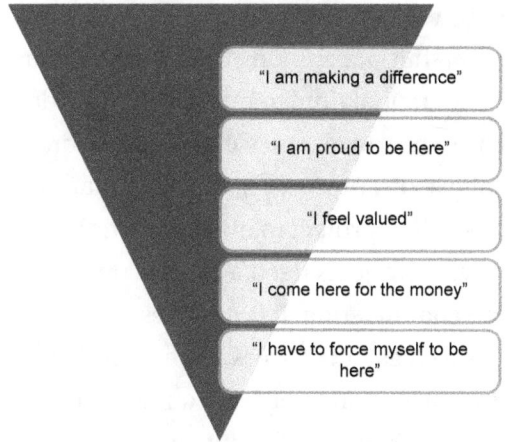

We realized that life is short and developed an increased desire for it to be meaningful. Money and job security are no longer seen as the foundation of the hierarchy of needs. Young employees leave prestigious, high-paying jobs in bulk and take time to travel around the world or contribute their effort to a meaningful cause that helps them feel that they make a difference. This has been a deeply reflective experience for many people.

… People are not willing to stay in their jobs for money. They are intentional in their lives and their careers.[5]

This, she warns, should be taken seriously, especially among organizations that purport to follow the Agile methodology described in Chapter 11.

The new normal should focus less on physical spaces and more on temporal ones. The worlds of work and life can coexist, kept in check with each other not by location, but by mindset and personal commitment of both employee and manager. There are times for work and there are times

---

[5] Breyter, Mariya, PhD, "Turning Maslow's Pyramid Upside Down." *LinkedIn Pulse*. October 5, 2021. Retrieved from www.linkedin.com/pulse/turning-maslows-pyramid-upside-down-mariya-breyter-ph-d-/ Accessed January 2022.

for life, and some of each may occur within the same hour. For example, no person should feel they are shirking their duties by simply wanting to have five minutes of personal time to refocus after a video chat meeting. These five minutes are not an expensive perk; they constitute "closure," the essential fifth phase of a project – something that would be familiar to anyone who has studied project management or lean methods. In just the same way multiyear projects need a closure phase, so too do micro-projects like a video chat meeting. It is an investment in the quality of the meeting just held as well as future work to be done. This, to me, is what digital literacy has always been about: the ability to handle the information of work – not just handle it physically, but also mentally and emotionally.

Let's Play Around with Closure

For people who have problems understanding the value of a closure phase of a micro-project, and by extension, the value of life–work balance in a hybrid workday, there is an easy analogy that comes from the world of golf. Many people who golf, and who can afford to do so comfortably, will announce that golf is not only essential decompression time, but is also good for business, due to the networking opportunities that the game provides.

But aside from that, there is the issue of the follow-through. Every serious golfer[6] will learn that a follow-through is vital to a successful shot, whether teeing off or on the fairway. The question to ask, then, is why a follow-through – the part of the golf swing that happens after the ball has been hit – is important at all. If the ball has already been hit and is on its way, what possible input can the follow-through have?

---

[6] For what it's worth, I am not a golfer, nor do I even like golf. I did, however, work as a caddy in my youth and can attest to the accuracy of much of the movie *Caddyshack*. It really was like that.

The answer is that the follow-through is shaped at the start of the swing, and the entire arc is what makes the shot successful. This to me is what closure is in a project of any size. Closure is built into the project at the very start, and its presence, as part of the arc of the project, helps make the project a success, even when the deliverable, just like a golf ball, has already been sent forward.

In the new normal, teams that recognize this type of arc, the collective effect of the phases of a project and the actions inside these phases (including rest and life activities) will be the ones who will discover the secret to attracting, keeping, and engaging great employees at a time when so many are thinking of leaving. And it costs so little to achieve – far less than recruiting and onboarding.

The Artisan's Curse

Work is transactional. It is an act of trade: my skills for your money. The better my skills are, the more money you should give me. That's how it's supposed to work, but as we all know, most of us put in more time and effort than the job really pays. Unless you have a seasoned professional agent negotiating the terms for you, like celebrities and pro athletes have, or unless you are the owner of a company where people do the work for you, or unless you are the owner of some form of property that generates its own income, like real estate or the royalty rights to intellectual property, then you are unlikely to experience a fully equalized transaction. Even if you are on salary, you are essentially selling your skills for money *at that moment*: a day's pay for a day's work.

This is a classic artisan's curse. An artisan is someone who creates something and then sells it. Although we might picture a traditional *artisanal* profession as being like a shoemaker, working alone in a small shop somewhere back in the mists of time, most of us are artisans anyway, even if our craft is accounting, IT, reception, driving a truck, or flying a plane. We make the money for what we do. Some might get paid a salary by the year, but it still comes in small payments every two weeks.

As my colleague Jack Skeels says in his book, *The Art (and Heart) of Management*, about the creative people in advertising agencies – they struggle to compete against large consulting firms because creative people are too close to their own work. It is a part of them, which makes it very difficult to negotiate, especially around price.

To illustrate this, Jack points out how an artisan (in any profession) will worry about telling their customer how much the campaign will *cost*, whereas a competing corporate consulting firm will tell their clients how much the campaign will *make*. That's a big difference in attitude for artisan and client alike.[7] As such, the millions of artisans who go to work each day in offices, factories, hospitals, and elsewhere will remain grateful for their job and fearful of losing it. They will forget about how much money their work makes for their employer. They just get to work. But part of them will still fear what they stand to lose by staying there.

Let's Not Bring Scurvy into This

As already mentioned, the world is moving forward, and digital transformation is paving the way. It is creating opportunities for work that couldn't have existed in the pre-Internet era, and the pandemic simply sealed the deal by demonstrating that work-from-home was possible, and that it was also possible to work for a company located outside the traditional commuting belt, simply by not needing to commute at all.

The fact that some people might actually be able to work like this will make others envious and fearful of what they will be missing by not catching on to this trend.

---

[7] Jack's book is as yet unpublished as of January 2022.

CHAPTER 13 THE FEAR OF KEEPING YOUR JOB

Though the debate around hybrid work scenarios will rage for some time, there will inevitably be a sense of injustice on either side, with work-from-home employees feeling second class, as described earlier, and on-premises employees feeling they are missing out on the conveniences and freedoms of a home-based, commute-free work-life.

This *grass is greener* problem is an important one for managers to proactively manage and ideally nip in the bud. Not only is there great potential for both groups to feel second class to each other, but this can also start to elicit bad feelings.

A fundamental rule in the world of traditional conflict management – one that every manager should be aware of – is to never ignore the germination of bad feeling within a team, whether this is a conflict of personalities or a specific slight or grievance. Bad feelings borne from experiences, including a tangible sense of injustice around the inequity of working conditions, will fester and grow. They will never go away on their own, nor will they heal fully. Just like scurvy.

Scurvy is a disease brought on by a lack of Vitamin C that causes the body to disintegrate and can be fatal if not treated. The nickname "limeys" which is often applied to British people, came from the fact that British sailors in the 1600s were among the first to accidentally discover a cure for scurvy by eating citrus fruits, including limes. One of the most intriguing features of the disease is that it causes old wounds, including scars and even bone fractures, to reappear – to un-knit the repair that may have happened years ago. This is due to the inability for the body to produce collagen, which is our cellular-level glue.[8]

---

[8] Worral, Simon. "A Nightmare Disease Haunted Ships During Age of Discovery" Retrieved from National Geographic Online. Published January 15, 2017. Retrieved from www.nationalgeographic.com/science/article/scurvy-disease-discovery-jonathan-lamb Accessed December 2021.

CHAPTER 13   THE FEAR OF KEEPING YOUR JOB

I think of this every time I look at conflict management scenarios in the workplace, especially among managers who fear face-to-face communication and who procrastinate or simply hope the conflict will work itself out. It won't. The slights and insults that people sometimes experience in the course of day-to-day work with others will all reappear once a full-blown conflict arises.

A conflict becomes a capital-C Conflict when a disagreement between two people starts to affect business processes, such as refusing to attend the same meeting, or sabotaging or delaying projects. It is, unfortunately, an expectable situation when people are brought together to collaborate. The problem amplifies itself when those in charge of defusing the situation avoid doing so out of fear of communicating within that bad situation.

I mention it here in terms of the specific slights or injustices that employees may feel as they perceive a different level of treatment being meted out between the on-premise workers and those who work from home. It goes well beyond the simple logistics of day-to-day operations. Both groups, the on-premises people, and the work-from-home people, will quietly take note of how management is treating both sides and what will be next. For example, those who choose to stay on-premises might not agree with management's assessment that a work-from-home employee should be paid less, but in the back of their minds somewhere there will be the inkling of an idea: "If management is willing to do *that*, what else might they be capable of, and how will that next decision affect *me*?"

Boosting the Quality of Work Life

The best way to keeping skilled, valuable employees during a period of digital transformation is to create an environment where they want to stay. Whether they choose to return to the office, work from home, or establish a hybrid lifestyle, the mortar that will hold the team together will be the quality of life that the company and its managers offer. The digital technology itself will not be enough.

CHAPTER 13   THE FEAR OF KEEPING YOUR JOB

When you scan the listings of the best places to work, published by employment-related organizations like Glassdoor, you will notice two things. First you will notice that many of the top-ranked companies on any of these lists are not exclusive to any one industry or age. For every high tech company on the list, there may be a bank or insurance company. Some may be very young, not burdened by the trappings of middle management and shareholders, while others may be long in the tooth, but who have put together the leadership that helps the company simply "get it."

What is it that these companies get? When you read the testimonials and comments from the employees whose votes helped put these companies high on any *best places* list, these comments will invariably mention life-related features: a supportive environment, an atmosphere of trust, a diverse and inclusive environment, life–work balance options, great relationships with supportive managers, opportunities to stretch and expand. These are all life and culture issues; they are not money issues. They are cultural developments that energize employees, revitalize the work side of work–life, and make staying an easier decision.

In the world of retail, consumers who abandon a brand will most often do so out of a feeling of being neglected, especially in the area of customer service. Similarly, most employees who quit a job aren't quitting the job so much as quitting the relationship with their manager.

It can be argued that some people will go to a job that offers more money, but as mentioned earlier, more money does not always mean greater happiness. Many employees will actually choose to stay at companies where the culture and the quality of life make up for differences in compensation. But for those who do leave, it's because the cost of working there – the cost of the money they make is just too much to bear.

The act of creating a post-pandemic new normal offers companies the opportunity to double down on building and maintaining a positive environment if they have not done so already. The first draft of the work-from-home experiment, which occurred during the pandemic was not perfect, but it proved that employers in a wide range of industries can offer a variety of work-from-home and hybrid work scenarios alongside opportunities for lifelong learning.

The most astute of these companies also recognize another relatively new and still unorthodox practice, which involves hiring to fit the culture rather than hiring for exact skills only. Given the fast pace of change and innovation, employees at all levels will need to spend more time learning on the job than completing all of their learning in school prior to getting hired.

These types of hiring and employment approaches not only increase the quality of life for employees, they also open the net even further in terms of sourcing quality talent that might live many hundreds of miles from the office, or who may have mobility issues or life situations that preclude them from a commuting lifestyle, but whose talents are clear and demonstrable all the same.

Jellyvision's Graceful Goodbye

Jellyvision is a 400-person Chicago-based company that develops software and communications programs for employees. Among the benefits of working there, in addition to pension and vacations, is their graceful exit program.

Think about what is traditionally involved in trying to locate a new job while still working at your current one. It is exceedingly difficult to do job searches, send pitch letters, and coordinate interviews discreetly, while still trying to get day-to-day work done. It is also quite a challenge to chat with your current manager or colleagues about upcoming projects that you're not sure you will be around for.

CHAPTER 13   THE FEAR OF KEEPING YOUR JOB

Jellyvision is a company that took a new tack on this, and this was outlined in an article in *Fast Company*.[9] As much as they would not want to see an employee leave, and as much as they would seek to find out how they can improve the work situation to get the employee to stay, there are times and situations where leaving is still the best option. And so Jellyvision made it easy and pleasant.

"Those who inform their supervisors at the start of their search will still get their raises, end-of-year bonuses, time off to interview, and other benefits without the awkwardness of trying to hide their actions," says Kelly Dean, Jellyvision's vice president of people. She adds, "Fundamentally, what drives retention here more than anything, and it's a very unconventional thing, is that we trust people and we treat them like adults. And we expect them to behave in the same way."[10]

See that? It's about trust. Even when the work relationship between employee and employer is seemingly coming to an end, there is still trust.

By engaging in this graceful exit, Jellyvision's management helps reduce overall employee turnover by assisting the departure process in a way that demonstrates trust and empathy to the departing employee. As a direct result, trust is equally shown to the rest of the team as well. They actively listen to the departing employees in order to learn their reasons for wanting to leave and how they might better the situation.

A key factor to remember in a story like this is that this graceful exit policy has more than one benefit. Firstly, it makes the process far less traumatic and uncomfortable for the departing employee. If this employee truly was not a fit, then it may be best to part ways. But in doing so gently, it provides a learning opportunity to find out exactly where the relationship

---

[9] Moran, Gwen (2018) *These Are the Three Things to Invest in to Build Employee Loyalty*. Fast Company, May 2018. Retrieved from www.fastcompany.com/40571881/these-are-the-three-things-to-invest-in-to-build-employee-loyalty
[10] Ibid.

went wrong and what the cause of the desire to leave was. It might also be instrumental in finding a position for that employee within the company that is a better fit.

This also makes space to hire someone better suited, without burning bridges with the departing employee, who may turn out to be a great collaborator, referrer of business, and general good contact to keep in touch with. All business is about good networks, after all.

But beyond the individual departing employee, think what this graceful exit does for the employees who stay behind. These people see management walk the walk of respect, empathy, and leadership. It shows just how much the company cares for all of its employees, and that is a powerful and highly valuable message to broadcast.

This too, brings the point of this chapter full circle. The employees who choose to stay will be fearful of what they are missing when the tools of digital transformation allow others to roam free, working from home. They will watch and they will learn how their employer seeks to treat them. The actions that management chooses in eliminating the sense of injustice or unevenness will be key to retaining great people, no matter where they work from.

CHAPTER 14

Turning Things Around

Fear Fatigue

The cybersecurity firm *Malwarebytes* published a report in December 2021 on the topic of fear fatigue. The report stated that nearly 80 percent of survey respondents reported some level of fear fatigue within their organization. The report defines fear fatigue as "the demotivation to follow recommended protective behaviors, emerging gradually over time and affected by a number of emotions, experiences, and perceptions. Fear fatigue can often lead to employees' negligent behavior, such as opening an email attachment without properly scrutinizing the sender or neglecting to turn on a VPN while using public Wi-Fi."[1]

---

[1] No authors listed. "Still Enduring From Home: As the cybersecurity marathon continues, could fear fatigue be the next threat? Retrieved from www.malwarebytes.com/resources/still-enduring-from-home/index.html December 15, 2021. Accessed December 2021.

CHAPTER 14   TURNING THINGS AROUND

In other words, as a suitable bookend to how this book started, digital transformation is not only being threatened by peoples' fear of the technologies and their implications, but after two years of dealing with an unpredictable and uncontrollable pandemic, they have become exhausted – simply tired of fear itself, and no longer willing to cooperate.

In a bitterly ironic twist, this report came out just as the Omicron Covid variant was being discovered in alarming numbers all around the world, leading to yet another holiday season filled with isolation, confusion, and gloom.

Fear fatigue sounds a lot like the psychological term *learned helplessness*.

> *Learned helplessness occurs when an individual continuously faces a negative, uncontrollable situation and stops trying to change their circumstances, even when they have the ability to do so. For example, a smoker may repeatedly try and fail to quit, [growing] frustrated and coming to believe that nothing will help... The perception that one cannot control the situation essentially elicits a passive response to the harm that is occurring.*[2]

The body and mind can only take so much fear, after which it shuts down. With too much energy being given over to the fight, instinct calls back its troops to focus on more basic survival.

Imposter Syndrome and FUD

In the world of cybersecurity, where the professionals responsible for successfully implementing digital transformation work, fear is everywhere.

---

[2] Psychology Today. "Learned helplessness." Retrieved from www.psychologytoday.com/us/basics/learned-helplessness. Edited into gender neutral language. Accessed December 2021.

CHAPTER 14 TURNING THINGS AROUND

Many of these professionals suffer from *imposter syndrome*, in which they truly feel they know no more about cyber-related threats and problems than any lay person, and that their calm bedside manner is just a fraudulent mask. This feeling is common among specialists in many industries, including medicine. It is a trust-based concern, specifically in not being able to have trust in oneself as competent. Paired with budget restrictions and the added layer of complexity that work-from-home presents, it is no surprise that burnout and career change are common among InfoSec types.

Bicycle Face, described in Chapter 8, was a form of emotional blackmail originally intended to force women back inside their homes, but which, as mentioned, can also be seen as the underpinnings of most advertising campaigns for consumer goods of any type. This concept had its own bookend, in the form of fear, uncertainty, and doubt, a tech sector marketing strategy often shortened to the acronym FUD. It's a cocktail of negative emotions deployed to sell software solutions to IT departments, and it serves as a great way to compensate for a product's lack of clear, incontrovertible superiority. Rather than demonstrate how much better a product is, it becomes easier to instill a nagging doubt that if you do not buy this product, your company will fail, or that you, the cybersecurity specialist, will fail personally.

People in any business can be preyed on using the FUD technique. It is simply a matter of abusing a trust relationship by delivering those three sentiments: fear, uncertainty, and doubt about their situation. As the preceding chapters have already shown, we are predisposed to give negative feelings greater attention. So from the following two phrases

a) If you buy this product, you will be happy

b) If you don't buy this product, things could go wrong for you

...it is easy to see that the second one will command more of your mind's attention. Make no mistake, when you see that commercial on TV or online, showing off a new model of car or laundry detergent, the tone of the commercial may say you will be happy with this product, but the underlying message is always that you will be unhappy without it.

When does fear become so overwhelming that we shrug our shoulders and ignore it? Does that not contradict all of the instincts and reactions we have seen thus far?

We observed this pattern emerge during the Covid pandemic. At first, many communities rallied, cheering the first responders, and most doing their part to stay home and support the cause. But with each successive resurgence of the virus, people's fortitude and faith began to fail. There was fatigue, but there was also fear fatigue – getting tired not only of the disease, but of the fear of the disease. Fatalism and defiance took over. Experts became scapegoats, and were reviled and threatened. People started to assert their individual rights over the common tribal good, and the warnings of the scientists fell on deaf and hostile ears.

Can Anything Be Done?

There is much that can be done, and, as I have mentioned, the best antidote to fear is facts. The best cure for the unknown is the known. The best way to eliminate a fear is to fix what is causing it.

As we have seen, fear is not passive. Someone who feels fear on any level is unlikely to ignore it and carry on. Without a strong countermeasure, the fear will amplify, resonating internally against other thoughts and emotions, while resonating externally through the natural frequencies of human society.

Those who are in charge of leading people through a digital transformation must be careful to establish a drip feed of reinforcement, delivering vision and facts in advance, focusing on small wins, and supplying appropriate amounts of emotional support, primarily through two-way communication (listening and talking). For projects that involve change, we cannot keep everyone in a state of blind compliance up until the moment of the "big reveal." Humans need vision. They need victories, celebrations, and sustenance regularly throughout the transition.

Listen and Talk

Worried people need to be heard. People undergoing a transformation in their lives arrive at ideas and thoughts along the way. If those thoughts are left alone to brood internally, they can turn negative and even more fearful. But when they are allowed to be spoken, especially in live dialog, a remarkable catharsis occurs. As people hear themselves speak their worries, they get to relax their hold on these worries, knowing they are now in the safe care of another person. By relaxing this hold, our minds find more processing space to work through the problem even further. It's like a self-cure. This is the essence of good counselling, as you would expect from a therapist, counselor, or psychologist. There is great power in letting someone talk out their problems. Allowing people to feed back their thoughts and ideas, and to work through what they *currently* have in their mind not only can provide additional solutions sooner, it might also alter the trajectory of the change process for the better.

The Five-Why Analysis

Sometimes people are not fully aware of where their fear really comes from. For example, the connection between not wanting to use a password manager and the ultimate fear of losing one's job and livelihood might not be an obvious one. It may be much further down in deeper, colder water.

CHAPTER 14   TURNING THINGS AROUND

Here, we can take a page from the history of quality management in manufacturing. When something goes wrong with a process, it's important to fix it, but just fixing a surface level problem does not make it go away. It's like painting over a rusted support beam. It doesn't make the beam any stronger, in fact it makes the problem worse by covering it up.

One of the best ways to determine a root cause of a problem is to perform a *root cause analysis*, and one of the most effective techniques for digging down to a root cause is to ask the question "why?" five or more times. This, unsurprisingly, is called a *five-why* analysis. It is extremely helpful in ensuring people don't get hung up on Band-Aid solutions when a deeper cure is needed.

This is a technique developed by Taiichi Ohno, one of the founders of the Toyota Production System in the 1950s, which is still used in management and production today – it's a philosophy of manufacturing, quality control, people management, and continuous improvement (*kaizen*) that still stands as one of the best collections of "doing things well" that has ever been catalogued in the past one hundred years.[3] The textbook example of a five-why analysis reads like this:

Q1. Why did the robot stop?
A1. The circuit has overloaded, causing a fuse to blow.
Q2. Why is the circuit overloaded?
A2. There was insufficient lubrication on the bearings, so they locked up.
Q3. Why was there insufficient lubrication on the bearings?
A3. The oil pump on the robot is not circulating sufficient oil.
Q4. Why is the pump not circulating sufficient oil?
A4. The pump intake is clogged with metal shavings.
Q5. Why is the intake clogged with metal shavings?
A5. Because there is no filter on the pump.

---

[3] Retrieved from www.lucidchart.com/blog/5-whys-analysis.

This example shows that the problem with the industrial robot was not a blown fuse. That was merely a symptom. To keep replacing the fuse would simply guarantee more breakdowns.

A psychologist, social worker, therapist, or even an astute vendor might respond to a statement by a patient or client with a similar type of question. Asking "how did that make you feel?" or "why do you think this happened?" can lead to another question and still another, which becomes a technique for digging down to the true source of the problem.

There are detractors of the five-why process of course, but much of the pushback is based on the idea that exactly *five* questions is not enough. They suggest that formalizing the process into five questions tempts people to think the solution is always exactly five steps away. They challenge the validity of the leading question, suggesting that it immediately obfuscates other lines of inquiry by leading investigators down a single path of inquiry while leaving others behind.[4]

These are valid objections. The five-why analysis is a tool and, like all tools, it depends on how it is used. The goal behind the five-why technique is to find *a* root cause and, in some cases, that means it is not *the* sole root cause. It might also indicate that more than five questions are needed.

But the goal of the process has greater benefit in getting people to know that they need to dig deeper, and not rely on a surface level judgment based on the first problem they see. It is not helpful to stop at the first answer because that by itself won't solve the problem. With Ohno's robot example above, you can replace fuses for as long as you want, but the problem will persist.

With every issue, there is always something deeper circling around, and it almost always comes back to fear.

---

[4] Card, Alan J. "The Problem with 5 whys." *BMJ Quality & Safety.* (*British Medical Journal*) Vol 26, Issue 8. Retrieved from https://qualitysafety.bmj.com/content/26/8/671. Accessed December 2021.

CHAPTER 14   TURNING THINGS AROUND

So let's take a second look at the website company's internal phishing story from Chapter 1 by using some of these *whys*. Why did people react so badly to the email? On the surface, they may have objected to having been caught red-handed in a sting. Why? It made them look foolish – they got duped. But that's not far enough. Go deeper. Ask more. Why would that cause such outrage? Making a dumb mistake makes a person appear incompetent or bad at their job, especially if they work in cybersecurity – and yes, security specialists do fall for phishing scams. That's true, but go deeper.

Being bad at your job can get you fired or at least held back from promotion. Why would that be a concern? Go deeper. Fear about your job is connected, as straight as a laser beam, back to where you live. It hits your mortgage or rent, and the bills you have to pay. It's what keeps you awake at night. Your livelihood and your life depend on this job, and any mistakes you make, any time the boss thinks you're not working hard enough, these become ideas that point toward the ultimate fear: a fear of death. If not immediate biological death, then the death of that livelihood.

According to a 2019 study by Charles Schwab, 59 percent of Americans live paycheck to paycheck.[5] Beyond this brutal reality lies homelessness and ruin. That's almost three out of every five people. If your team is 50 people strong, then 30 of those people, in a candid moment, are likely to have that look in their eyes that Quint did, back on the *Orca*.

---

[5] No author given. *Modern Wealth Survey*. May 2019. A PDF report published by Charles Schwab & Co., Inc. Based on an online survey conducted by Logica Research from February 8 to February 14, 2019, among a national sample of Americans aged 21 to 75 and an augment sample of 200 older Gen Zers aged 18–22 for generational comparisons. The national sample was balanced to be demographically representative. The margin of error for the national sample is three percentage points. Retrieved from https://content.schwab.com/web/retail/public/about-schwab/Charles-Schwab-2019-Modern-Wealth-Survey-findings-0519-9JBP.pdf Accessed January 2021.

CHAPTER 14   TURNING THINGS AROUND

The people who criticized the website company's IT security team for sending the phishing email thought it was a cruel thing to do. But the intensity of the anger was likely not aimed at the training exercise *per se*, but at what the repercussions of failing this test could lead to for any of them and any one of us.

Like the fast replicating brooms that quickly overwhelmed Goethe's Sorcerer's Apprentice, the phishing test, intended to solve a problem, can easily lead to multitudes of further problems, such as genuine messages going unread and sliding under the blanket excuse "I thought it was a phishing test."

But by shifting the blame from the end users who get duped to the people who designed, maintained, and approved the email infrastructure, or even the email culture, the same fear factor exists, and can be potentially unearthed as a possible root cause of the problem:

Q1. Why are people failing phishing tests?

A1. They click on email links too fast.

Q2. Why do they click on email links too fast?

A2. They have too many emails to deal with and other work to do as well.

Q3. Why do they have too many emails to deal with?

A3. Most communication is still done by email.

Q4. Why is most communication still being done by email?

A4. Because that's how we've always done it.

Q5. Why is this still how we've always done it?

The answer to question 5 could go a number of ways. It could reveal a reluctance amongst staff or management to change to a new system. Or maybe it's budget issues. Or time issues. Or leadership issues. Or the consensus that there's no time available for retraining. Or maybe there's no interest from senior management about making such a seemingly costly change. Whichever one (or more) of these points emerges as the reason for adhering to an overloaded email culture, at the base of it is fear: the fear of making the change, of initiating the change, or even understanding the change.

Make It Tangible

Whereas fight-or-flight fear is of a high-energy, adrenaline-based variety, much of the fear we live with is like mold. Fear and mold both like dark, damp places. Your brain is, in terms of its physical structure, a dark and damp place. The five-why analysis works so well because it is an exercise in making ideas and contributing facts tangible. Tangibility is a powerful antidote to fear. It is bleach, dryness, and light. Not everything needs to be framed in just five "why?" questions, but every problem needs to be brought out into the open and placed on a dry, tangible surface like a whiteboard, easel paper, or computer screen.

When thoughts and ideas are placed on a physical surface, (including braille and voice-to-text for the visually impaired), your mind gets a chance to vet them once again – to take them in afresh, and this allows for further processing and creative thought to happen.

Any time there is a worry or crisis that is creating fear, it helps to lay out all of the items, facts, and potential actions on a surface. Don't worry about what order they are in. Dispense with that fear of linear thinking described in Chapter 10. Get the issues and the what-ifs up there on a tangible surface to dissolve *analysis paralysis* and replace it with actionable items.

If other people need to be brought in, involve them in this brainstorming action too, whether they are in the same room or virtual, the positive effect is the same.

When trying to explain difficult concepts to people who may not be subject matter experts in your field, consider presenting issues in more visual formats. Most people will relate to a line chart or pie chart much more readily than a table of numbers. They will be more receptive when they feel they are neither being talked down to, nor over their heads, and everyone relates better to stories and case studies than theory.

Making problems, facts, and possible solutions tangible on a writing surface gives people something to hold on to intellectually and emotionally. The restaurant menu calendar technique described in Chapter 10 is an example of a tangible tool that helps others understand and even appreciate your availability and non-availability, especially when they can perceive it visually.

Mountains Have More Than One Face

When people fear something, they will seek to avoid encountering it, which leads to procrastination, direct avoidance, pushback, even sabotage. I have mentioned numerous times throughout this book that the best antidote to fear is facts – giving people the knowledge to balance out and then exceed the weight of fear.

But fear can make people blind to everything except the situation immediately in front of them. This, too, might be as a result of the fight-or-flight-based need to escape immediate danger, but it can also substantially delay or threaten its resolution.

Part of successful change management, and therefore of fear management, is to re-instill a sense of continuity that in turn delivers better perspective. This can be done by giving people an awareness that there is another side to this mountain and there is a road beyond. It may require that you set out the steps, the plan, or simply the perspective – to help them move toward this future, but giving them the factual awareness of other, better events that exist beyond the immediate threat helps put that threat into perspective, ideally bringing it down to a manageable size.

As an example, a manager who is dreading having a difficult conversation with an employee may procrastinate on the appointment because the fear of an uncontrollable or unpredictable situation is overwhelming. It looms like a dark shadow for days or even weeks, affecting mood, focus, and productivity along the way. In addition to the techniques described in this book already about the conversation itself, it will be helpful for the manager and the employee to remember that this meeting is finite. It will be over in thirty minutes or maybe an hour. There are other things to get done that day. There is more "day" to follow. There needs to be a higher-level perspective over the difficult task itself and its place in the day, in order to free the mind of its paralysis.

A simple and relatively mild example of this that I like to share with anyone who needs to hear it is the parable of the person who sought out advice from a mentor on whether to return to school to complete a degree that had been put on hold for family obligations. "It's three more years of study to complete this degree," the person says, "and I'm already 47. What should I do?" to which the mentor asked in reply, "well, how old will you be in three years if you *don't* take this degree?"

I like that story because the fear, though mild, threatens the person's opportunities for advancement due to a self-imposed stigma of age. The mentor's perspective, from the other side of the mountain, provides the necessary facts that neutralize the fear and deliver a balanced perspective.

The Job Insecurity Paradox

A real estate agent and a travel agent are standing in the "12 items or less" line at a supermarket. Next to them, where the other express line used to be, there is now a large scanning machine, resembling the ones you

CHAPTER 14   TURNING THINGS AROUND

send your carry-on luggage, shoes, and laptops through at the airport: a conveyor belt on the bottom, and a tunnel through which all items must pass before emerging on the other side. [6]

This supermarket scanner does not use x-rays. It uses lasers, weigh scales, and photo-recognition technology to identify every item placed on its belt, removing the need to scan barcodes, and speeding up the checkout process.

The estate agent and the pharmacist regard this new machine with scorn, sharing a few words about how it's just more jobs being taken away. The supermarket employee who oversees the machine, helping customers with their questions, and occasionally unjamming the conveyor, just smiles.

As an employee of the supermarket, the cashier is taking microcourses in coding and diagnostics to work as the conveyor's "mechanic," and is also taking free courses online after work to be able to seek out better work in the software field.

Some may see this scenario as looking through rose colored glasses, assuming that coding and other high-tech jobs are only available to those who can spare the time and the money to take full-time education. But that's where digital transformation comes full circle, in that the courses required to learn these skills are now much more available online, often for free, to be taken as and when possible. Plus the relevance of these courses to the immediate situation ("how do I help code a grocery scanner?") make the learning actually stick. Furthermore, the company that provides the scanners to the supermarket, embracing the as-a-service philosophy would likely also be open to training and maintaining supermarket staff as part of the vendor–customer relationship.

---

[6] Prentice, Steve. *Automating Job Insecurity*. Originally written for a business course delivered at a university in Luxembourg, this article now appears elsewhere on the Internet, including `https://zerwaste.com/automation-and-job-insecurity/` Accessed January 2022.

CHAPTER 14 TURNING THINGS AROUND

The threats and opportunities posed by advancing digital technologies apply to a wide spectrum of the workforce, as the authors of a recent *MIT Sloan Management Review* article[7] point out. They observed the type of value jobholders delivered to end customers (either retail or internal) and the skills they used to deliver it, and then identified four paths of evolution for jobs: *disruption, displacement, deconstruction,* and *durability.*

Certain manual professions like plumbing and electrical work seem somewhat less endangered by digital transformation since the value of the work is based both in motor skills, abstract thinking (problem assessment and solving), and a good amount of experience. These are classified as *durable*. However, these jobs too benefit from a range of digital transformation innovations, including online invoicing and AR- or VR-enhanced visualizations of their designs or fixes.

Real estate agents and travel agents, among others, are seeing much of their current work being moved into the same bracket as telephone operators and toll takers. They indeed have become *displaced*, requiring modifications and upgrades to their skillsets. These skillsets will involve becoming more of a trusted advisor – assisting clients in their house-buying or travel plans, through knowledge and wisdom gained from experience.

The cashier in the supermarket who now oversees the scanner is an example of someone whose first job was a victim of *disruption*, in that the skill delivered to the customer (cashing out the groceries) still exists but has been disrupted by technology. But this job can also be seen as an example of *deconstruction*, in which "the core skill set remains safe, even while the current form of its delivery is threatened." The cashier still exists to assist shoppers in paying for their groceries, but this is now done by

---

[7] All quotes in this segment retrieved from: Latham, Scott, Humberd, Beth. "Four Ways Jobs Will Respond to Automation" (Fall 2018) *MIT Sloan Management Review*. Vol. 60, No. 1 Reprint #60119 https://mitsmr.com/2oemNed Accessed June 2020.

overseeing and maintaining the scanner. The machine requires at least two employees to oversee it – one to watch the machine, and the other to watch for shoplifters and to help customers who may be having trouble with the machine. And added to these two is an area manager who oversees this entire checkout process. So, in sum, three jobs where there used to be one.

The authors of the MIT study point out that not only are all jobs destined to be placed in one of these four quadrants (disruption, displacement, deconstruction, and durability), but the type of education and retraining needed to move through any one of these four (including durability) is also changing.

> *[Workers] should focus on quickly acquiring the most relevant skills in an area with a relatively stable value form. In a volatile job market, lengthy programs that require years to complete (such as extra bachelor's degrees) are likely not the best approach. Micro-credentialing programs – competency-based certifications, mini-degrees, and digital badges – deliver qualifications more quickly and offer more options on the path to a degree along with a sense of accomplishment as individuals obtain marketable skills fast.*[8]

These types of studies, along with the examples delivered throughout this book, show how much of the danger to an individual's long-term career prospects has its roots in simple change resistance. Many will turn their backs on change and the opportunities it brings, out of fear and resentment.

Stubbornly holding on to the past tends to alienate the professional even further from employment opportunities. I am reminded of the vocal and extremely counterproductive reactions that were displayed the world over by professional taxicab drivers, who took to the streets and slowed traffic in urban centers all over the world to protest the existence of decentralized ridesharing programs like Uber and Lyft.

---

[8] Ibid.

CHAPTER 14 TURNING THINGS AROUND

It is easy to understand the fear they feel about seeing their jobs taken away by new technology, but the knee-jerk reaction to flood the streets with their cars, further snarling traffic and annoying their customer base, is an example of the *sabotage* end of the change resistance continuum. It would have been better for a taxicab company to seek to outdo Uber and Lyft with its own cloud-based form of customer-responsive travel, or for the cab drivers themselves to consider joining a crowd-sourced transportation company.

The authors of the Sloan-MIT study leave us with a final message that suggests that "understanding core skills and value form as the key units of analysis will help jobholders of all types respond to workforce changes."[9]

Not only will jobs change, but the way they are delivered will change too. Understanding this key fact is a vital survival skill for individuals and companies alike.

---

[9] Ibid.

CHAPTER 15

Is This the Day I Get Fired?

Fear Fatigue

Given that the core of this book is based on a person's fear of job loss, let's now tackle this question head-on. After all, for all of us who are not independently wealthy, our daily transaction – trading skills and experience for money – is what keeps us alive. But what seems like our key strength can also be our single point of failure.

This chapter is not just for employees. It speaks to the same fear business owners and department managers would feel about their own careers, businesses, or simply maintaining a status quo.

So, what if you were to start each day with the question, "Is this the day I get fired?" you might reply, "How depressing! Why would I ever want to start my day like that?" I would respond that it's only depressing if you know you don't have the right answer.

If you answer this question with, "I don't know. My life would be over," or something similar, then you will be living with a particularly powerful brand of fear that will plague you every day of your life. By contrast, when you can answer the question, "Is this the day I get fired?" with the answer, "so what if it is?" you will have created a pathway away from many of the fears that dominate us. From a digital transformation perspective, this is a concept that applies not only to every employee, but to their managers as well. It's about knowing where people stand, especially when it comes to facing change.

The fear of job loss starts to grow the moment a person lands a job. It gets even stronger when we take on a significant career-type position, and grows with every increased financial and family burden that is taken on. It becomes a millstone around everyone's neck. Most of us have no choice but to work for a living, but that does not mean we must give up all choice in the bargain. To illustrate this, let's step into the shoes of an entrepreneur for a moment.

The 80/20 Rule and Firing Your Weakest Customer

Entrepreneurs, which means anyone who runs a business, rather than being salaried employees of a larger company, must hunt down their livelihood one customer at a time. One of the greatest feelings in the world for an entrepreneur, then, is that of being able to walk away from the table in a negotiation. I learned this long ago when negotiating my prices with potential customers.

As I mentioned in Chapter 13, the curse of being an artisan is that you fear how much your work will cost your client, rather than how much it will make for them. That fear, which is based on whether you think they will pay, heavily influences your attitude to winning the contract and keeping the contract, and immediately gives the client the upper hand. The client can insist on adding more to the project or they may threaten to refuse to pay, in which case you are left powerless. This is the entrepreneurs' equivalent to the just-over-broke millstone that salaried employees face.

Being able to walk away from the table when negotiating a price gives the entrepreneur far greater leverage over the entire job, and will also raise the client's perception of the entrepreneur as a valued supplier.

CHAPTER 15   IS THIS THE DAY I GET FIRED?

Compare this to the "third ring" principle that many employers continue to apply. A company president might say, "we will always answer your call before the third ring," referring to a time when all business was done over phone. They maintain that same mindset today by insisting that employees respond to all emails immediately, and that they remain available 24/7 to answer texts and messages. This, they believe, represents excellent customer service.

I don't agree. As I have already described in this book, excellent customer service comes from engaged employees managing expectations in a way that allows customers to feel cared for, while allowing employees to do good work. Old-school entrepreneurs fear losing every customer, regardless of how much they actually cost to keep and care for. It's often called "being penny-wise and pound foolish," an old English term that refers to being overly obsessed with small details and not seeing the big picture.

A counterbalance to this mindset is to apply the 80/20 rule in terms of regularly firing your weakest, most costly customers. These are the high-maintenance customers that not only eat up a disproportionate amount of your time, but also take that time away from serving the low-maintenance, high reward customers. Costly customers can destroy a business. But a business owner's fear of losing *any* customer, paired with the fear that they might not find another to replace them, becomes insurmountable. It's the equivalent of an employee being scared by the question, "is this the day I get fired?"

A better approach, which sometimes takes an entire career for some to learn, is that of being able to walk away from the negotiating table, and of being able to prune the deadwood from the business by firing the weakest 20 percent of customers – these are actions that further the business, not threaten it. It opens up time and resources to better serve the high-return, low maintenance customers and to attract more like them.

CHAPTER 15 IS THIS THE DAY I GET FIRED?

Fear does not have to dominate anyone's work, whether as an entrepreneur or an employee. But so long as either person does not feel that they have a solid response to the idea of losing a customer or losing a job, they will remain in powerless darkness.

You As-A-Service

The same approach, then, should be applied to every person's career. It's always great to land a great job that matches your personality and aspirations, but it's still a serving that can be laced with fear of loss. Counteracting this fear with a dose of career mobility awareness not only makes your days better, it helps you sleep better, too, which helps boost your immune system and keeps things in balance. It may not be necessary to leave your current job, but it is really nice to have options. Options give you leverage and a genuine sense of personal empowerment.

Anyone already involved in digital transformation will be familiar with the as-a-service model. This is one in which companies deliver more of their value as-a-service, rather than just being a manufacturer of product.

By way of illustration, in the past, a manufacturer of photocopiers might have sold or leased a copy machine to a customer, leaving follow-up activities such as buying paper and toner refills and even performing maintenance to third parties. This meant the copier company missed out on a great deal of after-sale revenue. What is more likely today is that the same copier company will make the machine available, possibly even at a lower price, and will take care of all the other service requirements, including diagnostics, and pro-active service, which is to say performing service before something breaks.

Above and beyond the support service is the approach to quality and continuous improvement. This is the true hallmark of an as-a-service organization: it's about keeping up with new trends, technologies, opportunities, and threats, and making sure their customers immediately benefit from this awareness.

This is why, for example, so many organizations contract with managed cloud and cybersecurity specialists and factor them into their network of trusted suppliers. These as-a-service companies make it their stock-in-trade to know what needs to be known, to provide sage advice, and to deliver tailored services to match. One of the reasons this is so valuable to a company is that internal IT staff have enough to deal with and do not have the time to learn everything they need to know about the ever-changing threat landscape or about innovations in the industry. The same could be said about every other department, too. There has never been enough time for people to look up from their keyboards and see what's developing in their world. An as-a-service provider delivers this type of knowledge and wisdom alongside their more practical services.

How can individual people do this? And how does it affect career independence? Whether as a freelancer or a salaried employee, it means embracing the as-a-service philosophy of staying connected, up to date, and aware of the market. This means investing a small amount of each day in networking and microlearning.

Networking: The Little Black Book

In the pre-Internet era, well-connected people had a little black book, which was usually a well-worn collection of names and phone numbers. Part of its value was its size. It was small. There was not a lot of space inside a little black book, so the contacts in there had to be valuable in order to qualify.

At the same time, business cards were stored on Rolodexes, which were just a collection of small pages attached to a central spindle, each one holding a single business card. People in sales used to pride themselves on having huge Rolodexes full of cards, but they often still wondered why they had to spend so much time cold-calling or begging for appointments, when the person with their little black book simply made a single call and made things happen. The difference, of course, is one of quality over quantity.

CHAPTER 15   IS THIS THE DAY I GET FIRED?

A digital address book like Google Contacts, iCloud, Outlook, or even an Excel spreadsheet will hold thousands of names and contact details. But there is no way that any of us can truly *know and trust* thousands of people, no matter how much storage space we have.

A well-maintained personal network remains every person's safety net and the predominant antidote against fear. Opportunities for careers, jobs, and sales have a much better chance of materializing through word of mouth referral than from cold calling or advertising. The people that you *know and trust* will help you find opportunities, and the fact that you *know and trust them* will also allow you to help them.

The best place for maintaining a network of quality people in my opinion is LinkedIn. Many people have only a lukewarm opinion of LinkedIn, saying it has done nothing for them. But like any great tool or device or even a human relationship, it depends on how much effort you put into it. LinkedIn comes with a lot of extra features that are not really needed, but it still has features that make it work as a highly versatile *little black book*.

When deployed properly, your network will get you connected to mentors, experts, colleagues, and sources of referral. Active networking seems like a waste of time to people whose schedules are already packed with emails and meetings, but that's where the root of career fear truly thrives. Staying trapped inside an unmanageable workload that offers no space for growth is like trying to beat back the advancing tide rather than building a boat.

LinkedIn is not an address book. You might have a separate list of contacts elsewhere that includes everyone at your company, your suppliers, your car mechanic, and your doctor. These are people in your functioning day-to-day world, but few of them are really worthy of being in your little black book.

Your LinkedIn contacts should be your special people. These are people that you know, trust, and respect, and who feel the same about you. Your reputation is at stake with every person you connect with, so it is important to ask yourself, "would I confidently recommend this person's services to a friend?" If yes, that's someone with whom you should connect. This is very different from politely saying *yes* to every connection request that comes your way.

In the interest of conquering career fear and being more confident about your independence from any employer or workplace, my suggestions for the optimum use of LinkedIn have always been

- Keep your own profile up to date with a photo, testimonials, and work history.

- Take a few minutes each day to check LinkedIn's notifications, and acknowledge the achievements of your contacts. Send a short note congratulating them on a work anniversary, or if they have posted an article, read it and comment on it. These might seem like time-consuming activities, but in the long run, they will do better for you than applying that same time to just returning another email. These types of genuine human connections are the true currency of career success.

- Accept a few out-of-the-blue connection requests, but go and meet them first. Via phone, video chat, or in person, get to know them before adding them to your network. Ask them how you could help them. If they really want to be part of your network, they should willingly give the time for this meeting.

Networking on Twitter

Another often-overlooked networking opportunity is Twitter. Twitter has been much maligned over the years for being an open and unfiltered forum for all types of opinions, and there's no question, there's a lot of angry and offensive material there. But there's also a good deal of good people – people with intelligent ideas and conversations.

Often these people will meet up for real time events, ranging from scheduled webinars to live group conversations, held together simply with a hashtag. Participating in these groups exposes you to quality contacts, and also allows you to participate in conversations. These are excellent opportunities to make the valuable connections that can become part of your network of quality contacts.

Lifelong Learning

Another career-security opportunity that is often given up due to the pressure of meetings and emails is lifelong learning. Many employees are already used to taking scheduled professional development courses at work, but these are seldom as effective as they could be, since they are often scheduled far apart, and because too much information is delivered in too short a period of time.

A better alternative is to take a few minutes a day to learn something new about your current industry, or maybe your next one. Social media sources like LinkedIn, Twitter, and reddit provide knowledge in small amounts, from good people with smart things to say. Yes, you have to find them, but they exist.

Much of the value of being an in-demand professional is simply knowing a little more about a topic than your client or employer does. There is no better place to obtain up-to-date knowledge than your social media circles. This, once again, is what as-a-service organizations do. They make it their mission to know what needs to be known, and they deliver that as part of the service. So can you.

CHAPTER 15   IS THIS THE DAY I GET FIRED?

Career Fear As the Ultimate Trap

The fear of losing a job is real and legitimate. As I have already mentioned, your job is directly connected to your lifestyle and your overall personal safety. For most of us, that has always been the case.

But sadly, we live in a system that not only reinforces career fear, but banks on it. Few people are taught about financial literacy in schools. They are taught instead about getting a "good job." A good job ensures that people slide into a position where taxes are deducted at source and guarantees that banks and insurance companies all have a steady stream of income from employees who suddenly find themselves terrified to leave.

Fear has become the ultimate trap, and being artisans of our own lives, we feel powerless to do anything about it. The solution to career fear – the fear of getting fired, lies in everyone's hands, and it all comes down to balancing and then exceeding that fear with facts and knowledge about career-independence. There has never been a time in history where career self-determination has been as strong and as realistic as it is now. This has remained hidden from view due to the overload of emails and meetings that dominate the day but the fact is, other jobs are out there, and increasingly, your location is becoming less of a barrier. Bottom line: if you fear losing your current job, then start learning how to find your next one. Even if you don't take that next job just knowing you can, simply by curating your network and keeping up to date on your as-a-service abilities, substantially levels the playing field and also feels great.

Don't Forget Your Humanness

I used to run a 5:30 p.m. in-person networking group for working professionals who recognized the value of meeting people and learning something new. This was in the days before video chats and virtual anything. No matter. The same lesson would apply equally in an online get-together.

CHAPTER 15   IS THIS THE DAY I GET FIRED?

Every attendee was given 30 seconds to deliver their elevator speech – their encapsulated self-description. After all the attendees were done – there were usually about 50 of them, so this took about half an hour – a vote was held on which elevator speech was the most memorable.

Here's an example of a winning presentation:

"Hello, I am a chartered accountant, but I also own a couple of ponies. On weekends, I'm part of a group that brings kids with disabilities up to meet and feed the ponies and to just have a great time."

This type of self-introduction made this chartered accountant the star of the event, not because of any accountancy skills, but because the story touched people emotionally. It let them remember that there was life outside of their work bubble and it created a deep emotional memory that survived the onslaught of purely factual information from the other 49 participants.

This technique can be used in digital environments too. Whether attending a meeting on video chat or in virtual spaces, or when meeting people in person or even by email, think about how to establish a connection with each person on an emotional level – a shared interest that goes beyond work.

The technologies that we have at our disposal allow us to connect, but the messages we deliver are what will allow us to truly *reach each other*.

CHAPTER 16

The Digital Transformation of People

I cannot count the number of times I have received a contract or a document to sign that comes in the form of a Microsoft Word file sent as an email attachment. In most cases, the form is a mess. It is clear that whoever created it never learned about tables, tabs, and leaders. Leaders are those solid lines that show you where to sign. Leaders can also be a line of dots in a table of contents between the chapter title and the page that the chapter starts on. The creators of these documents also don't seem to understand proportional fonts, which are fonts other than the monospaced `courier`, and which need tabs, and not the space bar, to align properly.

These might be very small complaints amid a world of much larger troubles, but garbled forms symbolize what can go wrong in any digital transformation effort. Microsoft Word has had a sophisticated tab feature for almost all of its four-decade existence.[1] The fact that it is significantly underused means that the recipient of such a document must either

---

[1] The first version of Microsoft Word was released on October 25, 1983, under the name Multi-Tool Word for Xenix systems.

print it out, sign it, scan it, and email it back, or carefully try to type over the underscore characters in order to insert their name, date, and other details.

The technique for setting up right-aligned tabs with line leaders for forms and documents can be taught in less than fifteen minutes. It's easy once you know how. But few people have ever been given that chance. Even if they had been sent on a Microsoft Word training course at some time, the odds are that the course will have covered aligned tabs and leaders as one of a hundred other features, all of which got lost in the fog of overload, to never be touched again.

Of course, contracts and forms can – and should – be created and sent as a signable PDF or as an online signable smart document, complete with special digital signatures to ensure a greater degree of safety and immutability. But using these markedly superior ways of creating contracts also needs a brief amount of teaching or self-guided learning to become the new normal.

When change of any sort is introduced to an organization, it is unlikely that the transformation will be instantaneous. It takes weeks or months of modification, practice, stumbles, and reinforcement before existing habits are replaced by new ones.

It takes even longer when fear is involved. For the person preparing a document for signing, the priority is to get it out as quickly as possible, in order to get to the next task in the queue, so that the manager doesn't start questioning productivity levels, so that a bad performance review does not lead to being let go.

Digital transformation technology is at best just a couple of decades old. But the human beings that interact with it have not changed their body design much in the last 10,000 years. In terms of fight-or-flight response, the body treats emails and Grizzly bears the same way. They both pose significant threats to our safety, and are responded to in the same chemical and hormonal ways. In terms of processing information, we still cannot think straight when holding on to more than one key idea

CHAPTER 16 THE DIGITAL TRANSFORMATION OF PEOPLE

at a time. Our ancient brains cannot yet distinguish the blue light coming from a computer screen from an actual sunrise. In terms of our circadian rhythm and sleep cycle, we are still suffering from the processes imposed during the age of steam-powered industrial revolution, in which alignment with production shifts divided the day into the very same sectors we deal with today.

You might think that in writing a book about all the ways that fear can stand in the way of digital transformation that I myself am opposed to technological change and that I wish for a simpler time. But this is not true for two reasons. Firstly, there never was a simpler time. Whichever era a person gets nostalgic for, there was always danger and change afoot. Wars, disease, political unrest, social inequality, persecution – these things have been part of human society everywhere and always. The pace of change has certainly accelerated, but the threat of change has remained a constant, just like change itself.

Secondly, I am a great fan of technology and the ways it makes life better overall. Take the ironic history of the Internet for example: a secret military device created during the Cold War as a centerless network of communication cables that would have no single point of failure during a nuclear strike eventually turned into a publicly available device that changed the world on a scale similar to that of the printing press and the internal combustion engine. Once humans got their hands on Internet technology, it then spread across the entire spectrum of the human personality, becoming a tool for communication and learning and simultaneously a platform for anger, bullying, misinformation, and self-obsession.

Mostly I am in awe of the way in which the Internet has broken down barriers, allowing individuals of any age to be able to invent, communicate, and interact without being stymied by traditional barriers of entry. I am similarly in awe of the exponential power of connected intelligence,

CHAPTER 16   THE DIGITAL TRANSFORMATION OF PEOPLE

essentially an offshoot of Moore's Law, which has allowed computing power and human innovation to bounce off each other, achieving breakthroughs on a daily basis.

Digital Transformation Is Not Just Digital

The real digital transformation must happen inside each of us. We are the users and beneficiaries of the technologies after all. For example, in Chapter 6, I talked about *Zoom Gloom* and how virtual offices stand a good chance of being the centerpiece of the new normal. Those who think that it's not possible to be together virtually have good reason for doubting it. They haven't seen anything that replaces what they perceive as the reality of the office space. That's an outlook that is very typical of human beings: we judge everything by what we have known in the past, not what is potential in the future.

In Chapter 7, I talked about changing the learning system around, using flipped schooling techniques to deliver relevant information to receptive minds rather than overloaded ones. This, again, is a hard pill to swallow, especially given that virtually every person with the power over such a decision is a product of the stand-and-deliver classroom lecture style and a sausage factory school system.

Despite all the fear responses described in this book, human beings are remarkably resilient. We are capable of evolving, and are basically driven by nature to do so. When we look back at great technological advances like electricity, the internal combustion engine, airplanes, and the Internet, it is easy to think, "what would have happened if these had not been invented?" But they all would have been invented, if not by person A, then by person B. Because the same instincts that drive us to protect ourselves by prioritizing fear also seek – for the same reasons – to ensure that we use tools around us to further our existence, and invent new ones to help in this process.

Today's digital transformation is just one in a long line of transformations that started with cave painting as the first method of communicating ideas, and with agriculture, which allowed humans to generate more food than was needed for immediate survival, thus ensuring sufficient time and energy for every innovation that was to follow.

But underpinning all the actions we take, circling in the dark waters like the great, beautiful sharks that predate humans by millions of years, is fear. The drive to innovate is fueled by the fear of death, but so, too, is resistance to change. Understanding this very human duality will be vital for the full and complete success of every digital transformation yet to come.

Suggestions

What can you do as an employee or as an employer to help offset the fear that will stand in the way of your company's digital transformation efforts? The most important and immediate action would be to review the title of this chapter: it's about the digital transformation *of people*. It's people who need to be the highest priority, as every achievement that your transformation seeks to glean from the technology must come through them.

Recognize that fear exists. People will feel fear. They will fear for their lives and their livelihood. They will grieve over change, seeing it as a threat and a loss. It is easy for companies to overlook such human attributes that might be considered "frail" and not part of the go-go culture. For example, humans have had a long history of sending soldiers out to war and then forgetting to care for them once they come back. There's something about achievement without adequate follow-up support that is sadly a common thread with leaders, not only in war but in business too. But when it comes to technological change, addressing peoples' fear isn't just the nice thing to do, even though that should be enough. It also represents the critical juncture between success and failure of the transformation. It should never be simply expected that people will just "be on board" with change.

As we have seen, fear can be dissolved and even eradicated through facts, which include added information, and time and resources given over to skills development.

Recognize that surface level fears may have much deeper causes. Experts agree that one of the critical soft skills required for the future-of-work is empathy, especially among leaders. This means investing the time to understand employees who are increasingly adhering to an audience-of-one mindset and who require individualized attention and understanding. Breaking through layers of fear, using tools like simple active listening or a five-why analysis may help solve a long-standing fear of change, while simultaneously reinforcing a bond between employee and employer.

Change the way skills are taught. Our education system, for kids and adults alike, is based on a model that was the only one in town prior to the information age. Whether a junior school classroom, a university lecture hall, or a corporate meeting room, the mindset was to have an expert speak to as many sets of ears as possible. The idea that an avalanche of facts can be crammed into a brain inside of an hour was never viable. The option for flipped schooling, self-directed learning, lifelong learning, microlearning, from anywhere and at any time, should be seen as a remarkable boon to education, rather than a threat to a status quo. Rather than placing the blame of not retaining information on an overloaded student, we have the opportunity to engage and retain employees by nurturing skills development, which turns out to have a far more positive ROI than the high employee turnover numbers generated from fear.

Redefine work according to output and input rather than face time. Similar to the classroom example, the idea that employees can only be productive and social in a physical office is one that has had its time.

Although real human face-to-face interaction is definitely something we crave, we don't all crave it all the time, especially when there is work to do. The idea that work can only be done in the office and that employees cannot be trusted to work independently is another fallacy based on a dated, hierarchical mindset. It is easy for work to be defined instead by output, as in needing this report by Friday at 2:00, and leaving the how, where, and when this is done to the individual. In addition, employees are fully capable of contributing to a company's success and innovation culture. Greater dialog and brainstorming with engaged employees is another significant dividend of this redefinition.

Understand that trust is a self-fulfilling concept. Demonstrating trust is one of the best ways of earning trust. In the words of Maya Angelou, "people will forget what you said, people will forget what you did, but people will never forget how you made them feel." Negative experiences last longer and stay stronger than positive ones do. Therefore the act of earning trust from an employee is one that must be done with great care and focus.

Give people more time to do things. The majority of mistakes that are made happen because people try to do too many things too fast. Following the 80/20 rule, it is a demonstrable fact that every one of us can get more done in 80 percent of our time than we can in 100 percent of our time. The hamster wheel mindset gets us nowhere, and the email mindset simply adds more zero value tasks to the pile, as a form of ergonomic inflation. Taking the time for proactive management of peoples' expectations, nurturing relationships so as to allow more live phone chats and fewer messages, and simply taking the time to plan and reflect inevitably leads to better quality output. (This is what my first two books: *Cool Time* and *Cool Down* are all about.)

Recognize that people are more career mobile than ever. The good ones will leave unless you make it worth their while to stay. And that doesn't mean more money, necessarily. It's a quality of life and a life-work balance thing. As the Great Resignation shows, people are willing to go elsewhere once it seems no longer worth sticking around. Career mobility not only means the willingness to go, by the way. It can also refer to the fact that great employees need not only exist within a defined commuting radius around the head office building. There are great people in other states, provinces, and countries who can be available to work, and there are others who, for life or health reasons, have been barred from delivering their talents solely because of the commute.

Yes, But

To the ideas in this book, there will always be a "yes, but" argument. In full, it goes something like, "yes, these are interesting ideas, but they won't work for us." The qualifications that follow include, "we are too different, our industry is not predictable enough, we are too small, we are too big, our people are not ready, it's not the right time," and more like this. The problem is, for companies and individuals alike, if you wait until you are ready, you will never be ready. And you don't even need to be "ready" to embrace change. To stand behind "yes, but" arguments is perfectly natural. It's an instinctive protection response. The "yes, but" arguments can actually represent that first step toward change – the act of thawing the ice of complacency, described in Chapter 3. The act of taking those first tentative steps toward an unknown, like fingers feeling along a wall in the dark.

The ideas in this book are starting points. They are explanations for why people behave the way they do, and how they might behave when digital transformation is thrust upon them. They might equally explain how you might react when it is thrust upon you.

CHAPTER 16   THE DIGITAL TRANSFORMATION OF PEOPLE

The Fear of Being Wrong

One of my most interesting stand-and-deliver moments came a decade or more ago, when I was called in to teach time management and project management skills to a team of construction workers. This was a group of people who installed HVAC (heating, ventilation, and air conditioning) systems into office buildings. Their territory was the construction site. Their uniform was overalls, steel-toed boots, and hard hats. They worked outside and often at great heights.

In meeting them in a classroom office usually reserved for union meetings or to lay out blueprints, they stared at me, arms folded and with that defiant pose that questioned what a pencil-necked guy in a suit could possibly tell them about managing time on a construction site.

I didn't get very far into my presentation when I was interrupted by one of the team, who, as politely as he could, suggested I was wasting my time and theirs. "This isn't a place where you can schedule time on a calendar and expect people to respect it," he said. "We have trucks coming in and out of the site all day. They're not gonna wait around. We can't stop for anything."

To be fair to this person and his team, it was not them who had called me in. It was management who had hired me because mistakes were being made, and projects were falling behind. Clearly something was not working right. And they were right in the fact that I had never worked in construction even with project management in my background (I was more of an IT type).

But I had an ace up my sleeve. Even though I had no direct experience in construction, I brought in someone who had. One of their own, a site foreman who was in his late fifties and had spent all of his career out on the site. He was not "Management"; he was one of them. I will never forget what he said to his people as part of that course.

CHAPTER 16 THE DIGITAL TRANSFORMATION OF PEOPLE

He said, "you all think you have no time to step away from the site and from those trucks, but you do. That's why we have radios and site trailers and deputies. When you need to step away, you can hand over the work to your deputy. They can take care of the trucks while you check the plans or eat your lunch. The question is whether you really don't have any choice, or whether you do, and that you just don't want to own up to it."

There was silence in the room, and I thought he was done. But he continued.

"You're holding onto your job like that because you feel if you let go, just for a second, then maybe you're not that valuable. Like a dog pulling on a rope. If you let go, just for a second, you lose the rope and whatever's on the end of it. And then, after you do that for a few years, and you start to think that maybe that was a wrong idea, then you start to get scared about being wrong. Because if you're wrong about that, what else might you be wrong about?"

The desire to feel important and invaluable strikes at the very heart of the key principle in this book: "If I screw this up, I'll lose my job." At least if you appear invaluable, it seems like an insurance policy.

The fear of being wrong, though, is even more profound. To discover that you were wrong, in an action that you did, or in holding onto the past or to outdated work practices – to have held on so doggedly to that rope, means confronting a reality that no one ever wants to do: "what if I'm wrong?" This is like standing barefoot on a beach at the place where the waves come in and roll lightly over your feet. As the wave withdraws, it pulls all the sand out from under your toes and the soles of your feet, and you feel like you're standing on nothing.

How many times have people stuck to a course of self-destruction out of the fear of being wrong? Especially in these pandemic years, how many lives have been lost or ruined out of the fear that the beliefs they held close were actually wrong?

CHAPTER 16   THE DIGITAL TRANSFORMATION OF PEOPLE

To transform people digitally, we must recognize that not only is change seldom welcomed but that the realization that who you are and what you know are somehow wrong might represent a fear that actually goes beyond a fear of death and becomes a fear of life wrongly lived.

This is the challenge. The facts are available to help light the path. But the job of showing your human companions that light is up to you.

POSTSCRIPT

Two Apologies

In concluding this book, I have four summary points and two apologies to make. The four points are: 1: Fear rules all people, because it is the strongest emotion of all. 2: Despite all the great advances that digital transformation offers, its adoption may be blocked by this same human fear. 3. Most of these fears, in workers and managers alike, points to that of losing one's livelihood. 4. Fear can be matched and often beaten by facts.

Now, two apologies: First, to humans. In many of the examples that I use in this book, it seems that I make the assumption that all people are capable of physical senses like sight. When discussing the importance of being able to establish trust by seeing peoples' faces, this is never intended to be a slight to those who are visually impaired. Similarly, when describing babies' self-discovery of independent motion, I am aware that not all readers are parents, either by choice or circumstance, and also that some readers may have lost their children prematurely along life's path. I am one of those.

When talking about access to high-bandwidth technologies such as video chats and virtual spaces from home, it is easy to make the assumption that everyone has access to reliable high speed Internet, as well as to their own computer.

In discussing people who work for a living, including myself, it might also appear that I make the assumption that everyone has a clearly defined job as a "knowledge worker" (a term I dislike), and are not trying to hold down two or three jobs, only to collapse into exhausted sleep at the end of every day. Or in the case of health workers – nurses, doctors, and support

POSTSCRIPT   TWO APOLOGIES

staff who have been battling overloaded units, a relentless plague, and even harassment – my heart goes out to them – they are working in crisis mode and have other priorities to contend with right now.

Yes, I make those assumptions, but not out of ignorance. The ideas that I put forward in this book are intended to be malleable, and applicable to all types of life situations just like the technologies themselves. My belief is that people in any sort of situation, including those who have alternate forms of vision, hearing, motion, and intellectual abilities, will stand to gain from the personalization and accessibility of these technologies and techniques. I feel the same about anyone who is stuck with one or more lousy jobs – or no job – for the time being. There are now more career options out there than there ever have been. Being able to manage a career path, one that is more in alignment with one's own skills, potential, and desired life story, is at the center of life in the "new normal" and more than ever, is directly under our own individual control.

Secondly, I want to apologize to sharks, and to the people who work to save them from horrendous slaughter, either as a food delicacy, or out of a wholly disproportionate fear of them as mass killers of humans. The movie *Jaws* that I use at the start of this book is an excellent dramatization of primordial fear, but it had the unfortunate by-product of raising people's fear of sharks to ridiculous heights, and to this day, after news hits of a shark attack, legions of shark hunters will happily venture out in boats equipped with fish-finding radar and high-powered rifles to indiscriminately seek vengeance on any sharks that they can find.

Certainly, if you are clinging to the wreckage of a lifeboat in shark-infested waters, as the character Quint was, then you have a right to be afraid of sharks. But for the rest of us, we should reserve that fear for the most dangerous creature of all, one that, as this book has attempted to show, tends to rely too much on instinct and emotion and not quite enough on logic and critical thought, which, of course, is us.

Index

A

Act of learning
    Boolean logic formula, 104
    digital connections, 105
    digital transformation, 102, 105
    education, 106
    employees, 103
    flipped schooling, 104, 105
    forgetting curve, 103
    guitar, 100, 101
    learner, 101
    microlearning, 105
    Microsoft Excel, 104
    school, 101
    skillset, 102
    storing knowledge, 104
    students, 101, 102
    style, 103
    teachers, 101
    teaching method, 104
    university, 103
Agile
    companies, 179, 180
    software developers, 180
    software development, 179, 180
    technologies, 180
Agile Manifesto, 179
Air gap, 187
Amygdala, 7, 8, 31
Analysis paralysis, 132, 143, 222
Artificial intelligence, 14, 48, 180
Artisanal class, 89
Artisanal profession, 205
As-a-service model, 18, 232
As-a-service
        philosophy, 232–233

B

Bicycle face
    advertisements, 116
    campaign, 115, 116
    definition, 115
    face time bias, 117, 118
    Microsoft employees, 118, 119
Big fish, to a Big fear
    brain, 8
    cerebral cortex, 7
    cultures, 9
    humans, 6
    wetware, 8, 9
Big Fish, to a Big Phish
    hacking group, 5
    phishing failure, 5
    social media, 4
Blame Steve approach, 84, 85
Blockchain system, 171

INDEX

Bookkeeper, 127, 128, 146
Bookkeeping, 127, 145, 146
Business leaders, 167

C

Capital-C Conflict, 208
Career mobility, 97, 232, 246
Cloud-based drive, 126
Cloud database company, 106
Communications
    conversation, 155
    emails, 150, 156
    face-to-face, 151
    induced demand, 156
    leadership, 153, 154
    managers, 155
    mobile, 150, 151
    paper trail, 157
    text messages, 150–152
    touch, 150
Computer nerds, 189
Computer savvy, 48, 190
Computer screens, 19, 108, 109
Conflict management, 207, 208
Conscious Competence
    Model, 100
Consumers, 26, 28, 54, 59, 89
Conversation, 21–23, 151, 155–157
Cost of prevention, 172–174, 176
Cost of the money, 200, 209
Couchbase report, 106
Covid-19 pandemic, 4, 9, 15, 18, 35, 150, 174

Critical thinking, 85, 124, 153, 184, 185, 190–193
Crowd-stimulating events, 191–193
Cryptocurrency, 171, 190–192
Customer service, 14, 72, 209, 231
Cyberbullying, 194
Cybercrime, 17, 51, 57, 170, 194
Cybercriminals, 50, 51, 134
Cybersecurity, 5, 6, 14, 50, 133, 170, 220
Cybersecurity and Infrastructure
    Security Agency (CISA), 174

D

Dead of night, 36
Deconstruction, 226, 227
Delegation
    definition, 127
    digital transformation, 129
    education, 127
    fear of letting go, 128
    payoffs, 127
    time, 127
    trust, 128
    work, 129
Denial technique, 140, 142
Designers and marketers, 47
Digital architect, 106
Digital media, 74
Digital transformation, 78, 90, 105, 167, 170, 185, 206, 208, 216, 240, 241, 243
    career mobility, 246

definition, 13, 14
fear, 13, 243, 244
global ecosystem, 17
output/input, 245
personalization, 26–28
self-fulfilling, 245
skills, 244
technological innovation, 12
technologies, 15
video chat fatigue, 18–22
VMware, 14
WiFi or cellular
   connectivity, 15, 16
work, 12
zoom gloom, 22–25
Displaced, 226
Disruption, 226, 227
Distributed team *vs.* remote
   team, 92–94
Durable, 226

E

80/20 rule, 161, 230–232
Elevator, 34, 35, 74, 237
Emails, 5, 22, 68, 83, 109, 117, 156, 200, 240
Emotion, 10, 41, 146, 147, 197, 215
Emotional and practical
   logjams, 47
Employees, 16, 96, 118–120, 162, 202
End User License Agreement
   (EULA), 131
Entrepreneurs, 230, 231
Expectation management, 72, 73

F

Face time bias, 117–118
Face-to-face communication, 208
Failures
   digital transformation, 112
   Elon Musk, 112
   failing forward, 112
   fear, 112, 113
   SpaceX, 111
Fatalism, 134, 135, 216
Fear, 10, 11
   breaking linear
      thought, 163–166
   child, 45
   closing gate, 43, 44
   companies, 96, 97
   contagious, 34
   dead of night, 36
   defiance, 137, 138, 140
   definition, 31, 32
   delay, 137, 138, 140
   dilated pupils, 33
   experts, 168, 169
   fight-or-flight response, 32–34
   forming/storming/norming/
      performing, 42
   job loss, 229, 230
   Kubler-Ross Grief/change
      model, 41
   losing job, 82, 96

INDEX

Fear (*cont.*)
    losing the business, 181
    Maslow's hierarchy, 37–40
    safety features, 34
    saying no, 158–160
Fear factor, 221
Fear fatigue, 213, 214, 216, 229–230
Fear management, 223
Fear of being a nerd, 189–190
Fear of being wrong, 247–249
Fear of missing out (FOMO), 183
    behavior, 184
    critical thinking, 185
    crowd-stimulating events, 191–193
    cyberbullying, 194
    fear of being a nerd, 189–190
    fear of not fitting in, 188, 189
    social skills, 184
Fear of not fitting in, 188–189
Feedback, 153, 155, 162
Fight-or-flight fear, 222
Fight-or-flight response, 7, 32, 67, 69, 240
5G technology, 192, 193
Five second rule, 138
Five-why analysis, 217–222, 244
Flipped schooling, 104, 105, 242, 244
Follow-through, 204, 205
FUD technique, 215
Future-of-work, 87, 97, 201, 202, 244

G

GAP IT, 186–188
Gym class
    commands, 65
    limbic system, 65, 67
    meeting, 66, 67
    self-preservation system, 65
    12-lap assignment, 66
    unknown fear, 66

H

Heating, ventilation, and air conditioning (HVAC), 247
Human innovation, 242
Human limbic system, 53
Humanness, 237–238
Human optical system, 108
Human physiology, 31

I

I know what you did, 195–198
Imposter syndrome, 214–216
Individualized attention, 244
Industrial revolution, 12, 88, 89, 119, 123

J, K

Jaws, 1, 252
Jellyvision, 210–212
Just Over Broke (JOB) syndrome, 83–84

L

Law of Diminishing Returns, 202
Learned helplessness, 214
Lifelong learning, 210, 236, 244
Life-related features, 209
Life–work balance, 199, 204, 209
Lift-and-shift method, 126
Light source, 108
Little black book, 233–235

M

Management, 120, 121, 134, 206, 247
Managers, 40, 62, 120, 121, 125, 155
Medulla oblongata, 7
Messages, 108
    changes, 68
    digital transformation, 70
    email, 68, 69
    employees, 72
    energy, 70
    expectation management, 72, 73
    fear, 73
    fight-or-flight reflex, 69
    human being, 70
    hyper-prioritize, 70
    interruptions, 70, 72
    limbic squabble, 68
    media, 71
    Pavlovian happiness, 70
    radio messages, 71
    recipient, 71
    response, 71, 73
    senders, 71
    SMS, 68
    starters, 69
    sub-par mental performance, 69
    time, 70, 72
Mistakes, 100
Multifactor authentication (MFA), 28, 135

N

Networking
    little black book, 233–235
    Twitter, 235
New normal, 203, 205
Non-fungible tokens (NFTs), 190, 191
Non-secure technology, 82
Non-verbal communication, 25

O

Orca, 3, 4, 220

P

Pareidolia, 193
Password management software app, 54
Password manager, 54–57, 147–148
Passwords
    comfort, 52

Passwords (*cont.*)
    forgot your password, 49
    free credit monitoring, 51
    history, 49
    hot desk, 57–61
    losing identity, 61–63
    My1Login report, 50
    password management
        software app, 54, 55
    password manager, 56
    poor password hygiene, 51
    security, 53
Personally identifiable information (PII), 134
Peter Principle, 121
Photo-recognition technology, 225
Pornography, 194
Post-pandemic new normal, 209
Prioritization, 91, 143–145, 202
Procrastination, 143–145, 147
Public service announcement (PSA), 90, 91
PWC survey, 178

Q

Quality management, 218
Quality of life, 208–210, 247
Quint, 3, 220, 252

R

Ransom, 5, 174–177
Ransomware, 5, 51, 171–172, 174–176
Ransomware attacks, 84
Restaurant menu, 160–161
Rocket science, 111
Roomba, 15, 16, 61
Root cause analysis, 218

S

Scurvy, 206–208
Self-cure, 217
Silence
    books, 79
    conversation, 77
    devices, 76
    digital transformation, 77–79
    fear, 74
    handwriting, 75
    mediocrity, 75
    meetings, 76–78
    messages, 75
    technique, 75
    thought, 76
    Type-A personalities, 77
Skillsets, 226
Smishing, 186, 188

Social media, 4, 110, 149, 151, 236
Social media addiction, 184
Social media-fueled phenomenon, 141
Social skills, 184
SpaceX, 111
Specialists, 55, 87, 107, 108, 170, 220
Spotlight effect, 109–111
State of the Profession report, 107

T, U

Technology, 95, 108
Ten year old's bias, 177, 178
The Big Bang Theory, 190
The current flow of business, 167
The Great Resignation, 94–96, 123, 246
Third ring principle, 231
Trust
    attitude, 123
    employees, 122, 124
    environment, 123
    fish besides, 124
    frightening experience, 124
    managers, 122, 124
    spyware, 123
    successful team, 125
    technologies, 126
    training, 123, 125
    video chat, 126
    virtual/hybrid space, 126

Twitter, 75, 184, 235–236
Two-factor authentication (2FA), 135
Two-note signature theme music, 2

V

Vendor–customer relationship, 225
Video call, 21, 109, 155
Video chat meeting, 22, 23, 157, 158, 204
Video chat technology, 18, 19, 22, 23, 149
Virtual Human Interaction Lab (VHIL), 21
Vishing, 186

W, X

The watering hole concept, 136–137
Water treatment plant, 81, 134
Wetware, 8
Willful blindness
    MFA, 135, 136
    overload, 131
        contemplating things, 132
        credit/bank card, 134
        cybercriminals, 134
        digital world, 133
        excessive known, 132
        fatalism, 134
        network access, 134
        potential dangers, 132

INDEX

Willful blindness (*cont.*)
    self-preservation, 133
    software vulnerabilities, 133
    watering hole concept, 136–137
Work-from-home employees, 72, 88, 117, 207, 208
Work-life balance, 40, 199, 201
Work-life integration, 199

Y

Y2K, 173, 174

Z

Zealots, 28
Zero-day, 176
Zoom Call Gaffe, 86–87

GPSR Compliance
The European Union's (EU) General Product Safety Regulation (GPSR) is a set of rules that requires consumer products to be safe and our obligations to ensure this.

If you have any concerns about our products, you can contact us on

ProductSafety@springernature.com

In case Publisher is established outside the EU, the EU authorized representative is:

Springer Nature Customer Service Center GmbH
Europaplatz 3
69115 Heidelberg, Germany

www.ingramcontent.com/pod-product-compliance
Lightning Source LLC
LaVergne TN
LVHW010338260326
834688LV00036B/772